IMAGES
of America

HANOVER

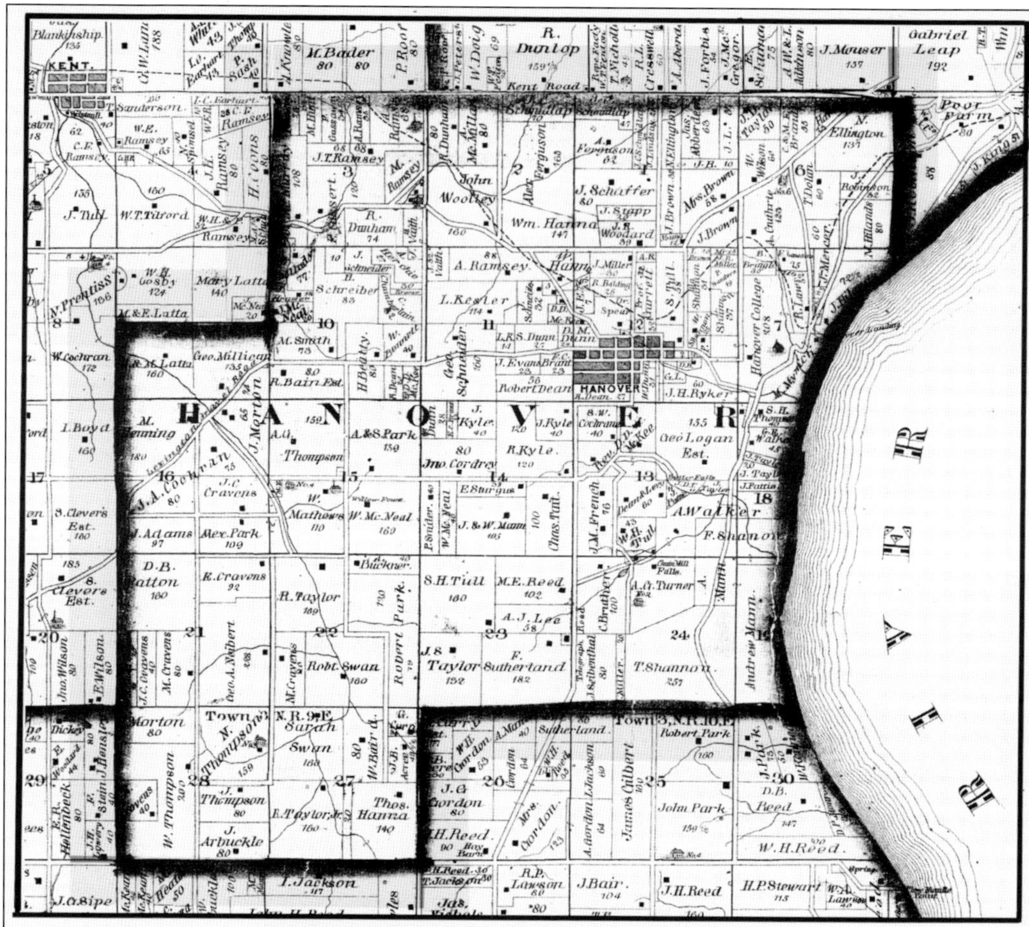

Hanover Township

from 1878 Jefferson County Plat Map

MAP SHOWS HANOVER, 1878. Hanover is located on the western bluffs of the Ohio River where the river forms the southeastern border of Indiana across from Trimble County, Kentucky. At Hanover, the river changes direction from east-west to north-south. This enormous bend has deeply influenced the history of the area. Before modern times, sediment, logs, and other debris were deposited at intervals making sandbars and shallow waters. It was easier during these times for animals and people to make crossings back and forth between modern-day Kentucky and modern-day Indiana. (Courtesy of JC.)

ON THE COVER: FAMILY GATHERS FOR 1902 REUNION. The Duke, Binger, and Means families pose for a family photograph. Pictured are, from left to right, (first row) Raymond Lee Duke, unidentified, Beula Binger, ? Binger (seated), ? Binger (baby), Irma Bridle, Riley Bridle, Tina Bridle, and Carl Robinson; (second row) Cutter Robinson, Clifford Duke, Pearl Means Duke, Rose Burkhardt, Georgia Binger Means, Clare Burkhardt McClellan, unidentified, and Mildred Richardson; (third row) Andrew Jackson Means, unidentified, Charles Burkhardt, William "Bill" Binger, and grandmother Bottort Binger. (Courtesy D/M.)

IMAGES
of America

HANOVER

Marty Lenzini Murray

ARCADIA
PUBLISHING

ISBN 978-0-7385-8335-8

Published by Arcadia Publishing
Charleston, South Carolina

Printed in the United States of America

Library of Congress Control Number: 2010932742

For all general information, please contact Arcadia Publishing:
Telephone 843-853-2070
Fax 843-853-0044
E-mail sales@arcadiapublishing.com
For customer service and orders:
Toll-Free 1-888-313-2665

Visit us on the Internet at www.arcadiapublishing.com

To Janet Catherine Craig Cowen, my cousin, who introduced me to family history. Also, to my husband, James Dennis Murray, who performed as coauthor. To both of you, my love and heartfelt thanks!

Contents

ACKNOWLEDGMENTS

Thank you to the hundreds of people who have helped with this book. I kept a list until it topped 300, and then I knew the book was not mine, but the collective work of others. Thanks to Doris Bloodsworth, an extraordinary friend, who knew this would be a worthy project before I did. Thank you to the Hanover Community Historical Association, the Town of Hanover, the Duggen Library archives of Hanover College, the Jefferson County Public Library, the Jefferson County Historical Society Research Library, and to Hanover Health and Rehabilitation. Catherine Cowen, my cousin, is a remarkable 91-year-old woman who shared her expertise generously. She is a top-notch genealogy researcher and taught me things one cannot learn from a book. Special thanks to the following: Janice Barnes, Fran Carver, Kim Darin, Doug Denné, Gary DuVall, Paulette DuVall, Fred Fedler, Marlyn Duke Finnegan, Ron Grimes, Kristi Harms, Bob Ireland, LJ Jordon, Kim Kreuzburg, Karen Kruger, Rebecca Lathrem, Patricia Lawrence, Kathy Maiorano, Fred Marsh, Stephen Makar, Robert Moore, Thelma Mullett, Phyllis Murray, Robb Osborn, Vickie Perkins, Ken Schneider, Stan Totten, Mary Ann Trout, and Betty Wagner. The Lenzini family has infused my life with joy and showed me what hard work is all about. The Adams connections demonstrated how to hold up as well as rejoice when life brings surprises. Family members Collie Clark, Mary Beth Clark Masi, Mary Clark, Dr. Tom Masi, and Stephen Clark have provided much-needed support. Dennis Murray, my husband, has patiently scanned more than 800 images with never a complaint. He has conducted research and gently reminded me of deadlines as well. He would not consent to being coauthor of this book, but in reality he certainly is! Thank you also to Arcadia acquisitions editor Anna Wilson, publisher John Pearson, and the production and marketing staff.

Deep gratitude is also due to Hanover College faculty member Frank Baker who died in 2005. His work as a photographer and writer was extremely valuable in putting this collection of images together.

Dennis and I examined close to 7,000 images to choose 206 for this book. I apologize in advance to those who furnished images we could not use. We had to leave out some of our favorite images as well as most of the ones we had selected for the "Hanover's Neighbors" chapter. I hope you will accept this book as a gift of love from Dennis and Marty Murray to Hanover. If I have made mistakes, please forgive me and let me know what they are so I can correct them.

INTRODUCTION

Why Hanover? Hanover was called Dunn's Settlement in the early 1800s after its European founder Williamson Dunn who crossed the Ohio River from Kentucky. The name Hanover came from the village's first church.

That first church was organized in 1820. The Reverend Thomas C. Searle was called as its first minister. His wife, Annette Woodward, was held in high esteem by the settlers so they named the Presbyterian church after her hometown of Hanover, New Hampshire. When people first tried to call their village Hanover in 1830, the name was being used by another Indiana community. So they settled on South Hanover. When the other town called Hanover folded, South Hanover switched its name to Hanover.

In the beginning, oceans covered all of Indiana and the surrounding places. After a time, small sea animals lived in the water. When they died, their remains were deposited on the sea bottom. The seas were also inhabited by fish and sharks. After the sea went away, the land that emerged was filled with layers of rocks. Geologists find evidence that the seas came and went numerous times, so distinct layers of ocean bottoms, rich in limestone and distinct coral layers, can be seen today at waterfalls and in cuts through passes for roads.

After seas no longer covered the land, a long period of erosion came about and dinosaurs dominated. Later large sheets of ice covered nearly all of present-day Indiana and blocked northward flowing drainage. This blockage created large lakes next to the ice sheets. The largest lake of all overflowed and carved out a deep channel, which became the Ohio River.

Indiana's first animals were followed by different animals more suited to the climate. Large animals during those later times included dire wolves, saber-toothed tigers, Jefferson's mammoths, American mastodonts, Jefferson's ground sloths, Pleistocene jaguars, Pleistocene horses, giant beavers, stag-moose, caribou, ancient bison, giant short-faced bears, Pleistocene black bears, and giant land tortoises. Smaller animals came later and included skunks, moles, porcupines, otters, deer, opossums, shrews, bats, mice, and rats. Passenger pigeons, wild turkeys, prairie chickens, and ring-necked pheasants were also found in what would become Indiana.

Native Americans lived in Hanover for thousands of years before any Europeans. However historians and scientists find it hard to pinpoint which tribes lived in the area and when for several reasons.

One of those reasons is that the boundaries of Indiana are arbitrary. Native Americans lived in broader areas. Also, in the early 1800s, tribes from as far away as the East Coast of America were being driven from their traditional lands into or through Indiana.

Another difficulty in saying exactly which Native Americans used to live in Hanover involves artifact collection. Funding for archaeological digs has been scarce in Indiana. Very few artifacts found by farmers and collectors are catalogued by precise collection sites, depth in soil, orientation, or location near bones.

From the 1600s, Native Americans were given blankets, trinkets, animals, whiskey, and weapons. Europeans hoped to ensure their own safe passage through Native American lands and to get from them items they could sell. Expansion of influence and the desire to own more land also drove Europeans to become friends with Native Americans. These relationships changed Native American cultures.

In addition to the gifts, Europeans brought deadly diseases to North America. Native Americans did not have weaker immune systems than Europeans, they just had not been exposed to the plagues that had earlier killed millions of Europeans. When the diseases were introduced into Native American populations, they ravaged through entire tribes, often killing almost every person just as they had in Europe.

Some Native Americans were manipulated by various groups to fight their battles for them. French traders and explorers tried to incite Native Americans against the English. The English tried the same with the Native Americans against the French. During the American Revolution with England, Native Americans were encouraged by the English to side with them against the colonists. Also some tribes did not have peaceful relations with other tribes so they fought battles with Native American against Native American.

In the end, it can be certainly said of the Native American presence in Hanover, "It's complicated." Without crucial information, which has been permanently lost, archaeologists cannot pinpoint exactly which tribes lived in Indiana, let alone Hanover.

However it is possible to read proceedings from meetings as well as treaties and capture a glimpse of Native American and European relations. From these records a pattern of disregard for Native Americans, plans for their relocation, and even elimination of Native Americans emerges.

A series of treaties, which addressed land shared by multiple tribes, led to what is called "Indian removal." The way the removal worked was something like this: a treaty was made with "Indians" to buy their land. Other tribes that shared that land were not consulted about the terms of the treaty. Additionally most Native Americans did not consider themselves owners of plots of land. They shared the land. Most felt the land was owned by the land's creator. Misunderstandings and war came from the confusing dealings. In the end, Native Americans said the Europeans did not understand. Europeans said the Native Americans did not understand. Both were correct.

The land that became Hanover was acquired by a deal called the Treaty of Grouseland in 1805. By 1840, almost all of the Native Americans had left or were driven out of Indiana.

While there may not be many Indians left in the state named for them, some Native American villages, towns, and burial sites have been identified in the area. A mound on the farm of W. W. Walker in what was called Hanover Bottoms was excavated in about 1884. Around 1904, a dig was conducted in Graham Township on the farm of Hiram Foster. Graham Township also was the site of a fortification, which was described in detail by Hanover professor Glenn Culberson who taught at the college from 1893 until 1927.

Elaborate funeral rites and deep appreciation of a creator are evident from artifacts left behind. Highly developed, exquisite art pieces and the use of stones and metals also shine through the ages.

According to Lynne Brunelle, who wrote *Indiana, the Hoosier State*, the following tribes lived at one time or another in Indiana: Algonquian, Atchakangoen, Delaware, Iroquois, Kilatika, Mengkonia, Miami, Ojibwa (Chippewa), Ottawa, Pepikonkia, Piankashaw, Potawatomi, Shawnee, and Wea. One or more of these tribes most surely had a presence in Hanover.

A log cabin used to stand at the corner of Main and Main Cross Streets in Hanover. It was built in the early 1800s and functioned as a Native American trading post. It was torn down in the early 2000s and replaced with a parking lot.

People in present-day Hanover say their grandparents and great-grandparents told them about Native Americans they saw walking to and from the trading post when they were children. Also more than one family in Hanover can trace its roots back to Native Americans—often a great- or great-great-grandmother.

Hanover's story continues with Williamson Dunn, who set out in 1809 from Lexington, Kentucky, with his wife, Miriam Wilson Dunn, toward what was then called the Northwest Territory. When they began their journey they had two children under the age of three. According to family oral history, they were accompanied by three slaves named Ike Laurenc, Cloe, and Harkess. After arriving at the Ohio River, there was the business of figuring out how to get across!

How they forded the river remains a mystery today. The group may have waded across where the river grew shallow from debris, such as driftwood logs and sandbars. All types of materials were deposited where the river makes a 90-degree turn from east-west to north-south. Boats or barges offer other possibilities for fording the river.

When the group got on the other side of the river to breathe—as they called it—"the free air," Dunn freed the slaves.

Even though Dunn is thought to be the first European to settle and stay in Hanover, other European pioneers had come before him. Names remembered in local lore include the following: George Logan, George Smock, Archibald Dinwiddie, Halsey Tibbals, John Paul, George Shannon, and Christopher Harrison.

Logan is remembered for landing two flatboats lashed together on the bank of the Ohio River near the present Hanover Beach during a violent storm in 1801. He stayed for three days and loved the view from atop a bluff of the river so much he returned to live in 1816. Like Williamson Dunn, Logan was from the Lexington, Kentucky, area.

Smock came to the area in 1805 and settled with his family about 3 miles west of Hanover in an area first called Big Springs and later Smockville. Dinwiddie came in 1807 and lived about a mile northwest of Hanover. Local historians say he had problems with Native Americans and moved back to his home in Kentucky. He did return to Indiana later, perhaps in 1809.

Tibbals and Paul did not stay in Hanover but invested in property and were known as land speculators. Shannon also bought land and left the area. Like Logan and Dinwiddie, Shannon returned at a later time to live. Harrison began living in the Hanover area perhaps even before the Dunn family arrived. However he lived alone and far away from other people. According to locals, he had been crushed in his love life. Harrison went west to heal his broken heart. At first he lived a solitary life overlooking the Ohio River with a dog for companionship. He wearied of a hermit's life and grew more sociable. He became a local judge and left the area to become a shopkeeper in Salem, Indiana. Later he became lieutenant governor of the new state of Indiana. He never married.

Written records and stories passed along through families give hints of what life was like for the pioneers. One thing for certain: life was tough and Hanover's early settlers worked hard to survive. Diaries and written copies of speeches given by settlers describe the grinding toil.

Excellent health blessed those fortunate enough to have it. Diseases ravaged the population during several epidemics. Malaria hit in rampant proportions in 1821 and 1822. Cholera struck in 1848.

Work to survive consumed those early pioneers. A sound mentioned in several accounts of Hanover's earliest days includes the repetitive noise made by numerous axes chopping through wood at the same time as people cut down trees to use as building material, to cook with, and for a heat source. The chop, chop, chopping of the axes was said to echo through the forest from sun up until sun down.

In addition to constructing buildings, settlers had to get food and water. Squirrels, rabbits, and various birds made up a major part of the settlers' diets. Passenger pigeons were said to be so abundant that when they flew overhead in flocks they blocked out the sun. Smells of campfires and simmering food filled the air. Gardens were planted and cultivated, with corn being a major crop. Water was collected from clear streams, waterfalls, cisterns, and springs.

Domesticated animals were kept and cared for. Animal skins were tanned. Fabric was woven from yarn, which was spun from natural plant fibers or wool shorn from local sheep. Clothing was hand stitched. Quilts were pieced together from scraps of fabric. Soap was made. Knives were sharpened, and long guns were cleaned. Nothing was wasted.

The early pioneers reportedly worked all day and fell exhausted into their beds at night to awaken the next morning to go through the same grinding schedule all over again. The rhythm of work was broken only by the Sabbath. Being pious Presbyterians, the earliest settlers worshipped first at a church in Charlestown, which was about 25 miles away. Methodist circuit riders came to the area shortly after the Presbyterians settled in. A Methodist named Amos Chitwood preached near Kent in about 1810. A Presbyterian church was built in Hanover in 1821. Another Methodist circuit rider named Gabriel Woodfill preached in "The Dunn Barn" according to family records.

War caused enormous hardships from the very beginning. Most of the men in the settlement were gone for months during the War of 1812. The women and children were collected into one or more stockades for safety while the men rode in a company called Dunn's Rangers.

Indiana became a state in 1816. Hanover men met with other settlers in Corydon, the territory capital, to hammer out the details of a state constitution and keep the new state free from slavery.

The people who live in Hanover today in many ways reflect the traits of their pioneer founders. Hanover people know each other and help each other. The college and the town are still intertwined. People have gone out from the area to take the ideas of hard work and Midwestern reasonableness far beyond Hanover's boundaries. Its earliest settlers stood firmly against slavery and demonstrated it by freeing slaves. A U.S. vice president came from Hanover. Ditto army generals and thousands of citizen soldiers. The first food and drug act in America was mostly written by a local man. Hundreds of citizens have served abroad. Teachers, ministers, technology workers, skilled crafts people, and health care professionals grew up in this small town. Colonel Sanders of Kentucky chicken fame had a Hanover connection. Hanover may be small in population but its influence has helped shape the world.

The images in this book appear courtesy of the Hanover Community Historical Association (HCHA), the Archives of Hanover College (HC), the Jefferson County Historical Society Research Library (JC), the Lemen Collection of the Jefferson County Public Library (LC), the Duke/Means family albums (D/M), and dozens of other private collections.

One

BEGINNINGS

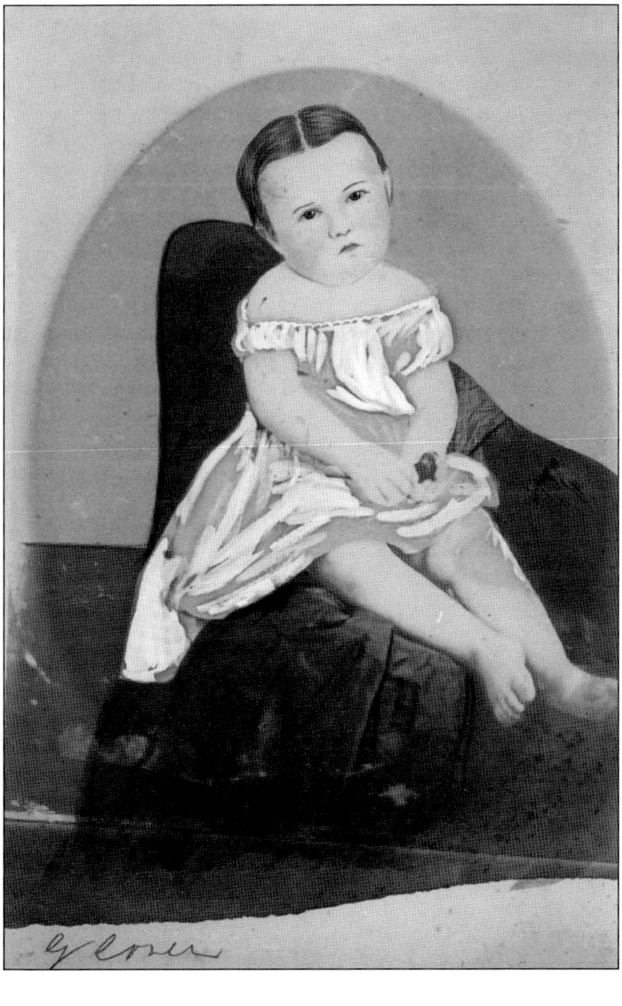

BABY REPRESENTS HANOVER'S 1800S BEGINNING. This rare image is thought to date from the middle to late 1800s. The artist began with a photograph and laid paint down in the style of a naïve painting. The baby may be Mary Elizabeth Dunn Young, born in 1853. She was called "Molly" and was Williamson Dunn's granddaughter. In this chapter, what happened in those early years is chronicled. (Courtesy Janet C. Cowen.)

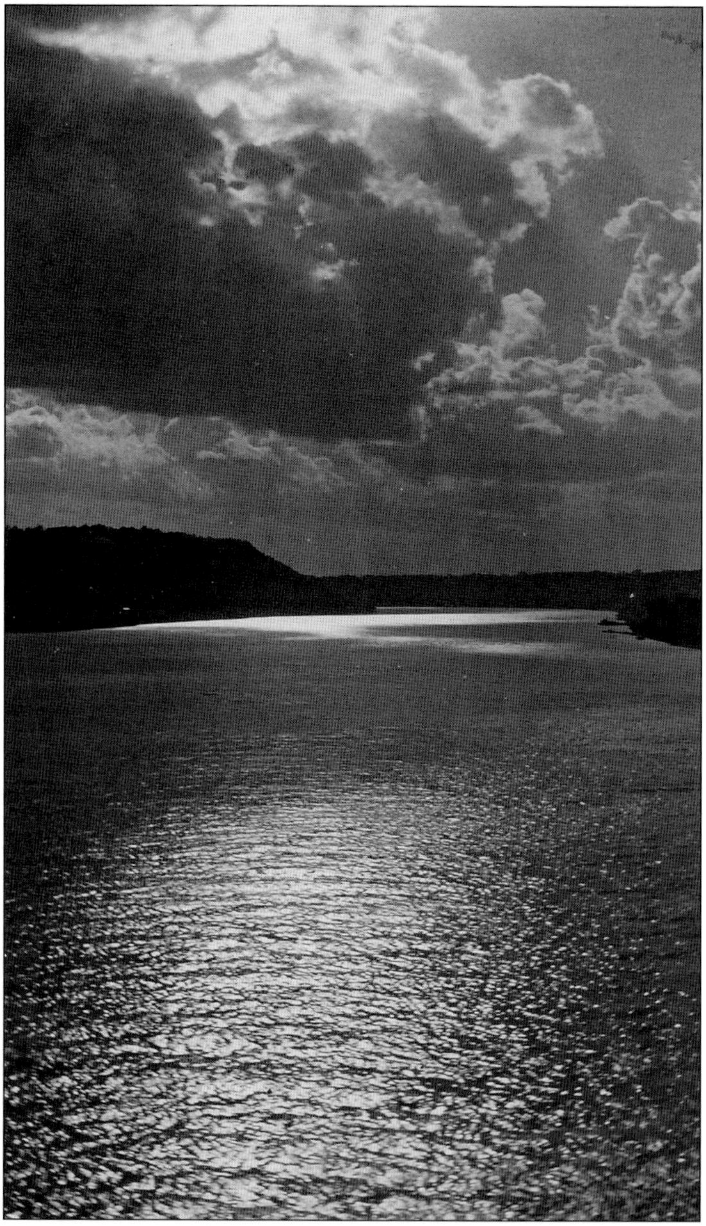

In the Beginning was Water. All of Indiana was covered with oceans in prehistoric times. The seas afforded a hospitable place for small creatures to live. When sea animals died, their crusty bodies sank to the bottom of the water and settled, making layers. The seas drained and then came back repeatedly, causing more layers to be added. The Ohio River came later and was named Oyo ("beautiful river") by the Iroquois. Historians point to locations where Native Americans probably sent signals to each other up and down the river. An enormous curve near Hanover changes the flow of the river from east-west to north-south and in the past caused sediment to form large sandbars. At certain times of the year, people could wade or swim across the river. Native Americans, trappers, and explorers traveled on the river in boats and barges. Hanover's earliest European settlers crossed from Kentucky. A shallow river crossing also gave escaped slaves a start in the Underground Railroad. (Courtesy LC.)

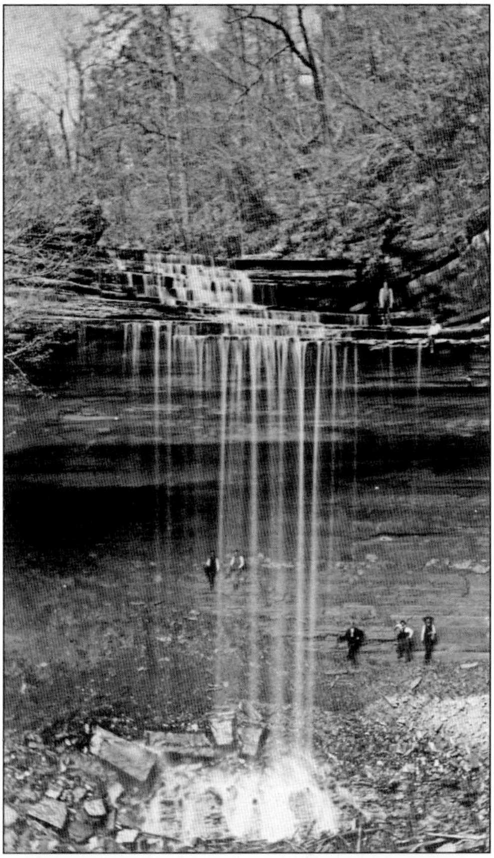

LAYERS OF SEA BOTTOM REVEALED. People explore at Clifty Falls around 1880. As water flows toward the Ohio River, rocks erode at different rates, creating waterfalls. This photograph shows multiple layers, which used to be sea bottoms. Pictured are, from left to right, (first row) ? Fisher, Andrew Young, and ? Webb; (second two) ? McKee, and Matt ? (third row)? Chaston and ? Wax. (Courtesy HCHA.)

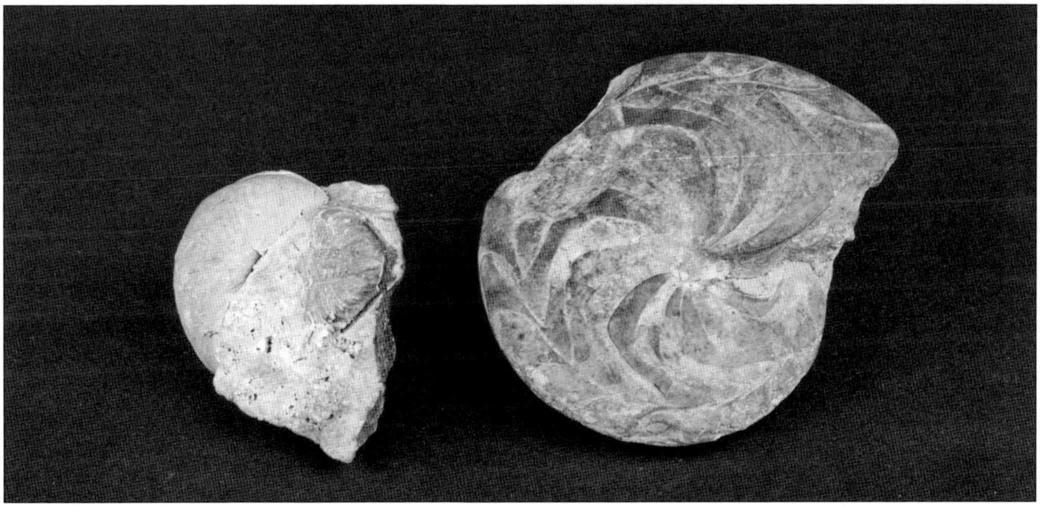

FOSSILS ABUNDANTLY DISTRIBUTED. A snail and trilobite share space on the left fossil and a Rockford Goniatite is seen on the right. All three types of fossilized animals have been found near Hanover. Their discovery gives clues about what kinds of plants and animals lived in Hanover before people came. Trilobites used to live in ancient oceans and are extinct. Modern-day relatives of goniatities include the chambered nautilus. (Photograph courtesy Hanging Rock Photography, Steve Rizzo.)

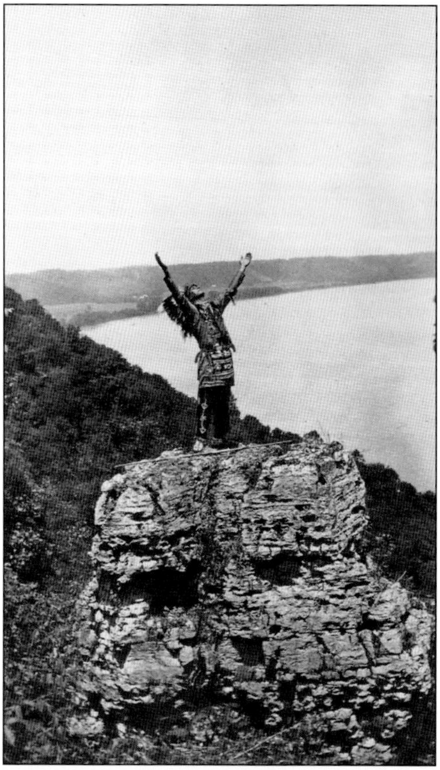

Native Americans Lived in Area. This photograph was taken around 1927, and it is not known whether the man in it is Native American or not. The tribal dress reflects a Great Plains tribe. Native Americans were living in Hanover thousands of years before Europeans arrived. By 1840, almost all Native Americans had gone or were run out of Southern Indiana. They left tens of thousands of artifacts behind. (Courtesy LC.)

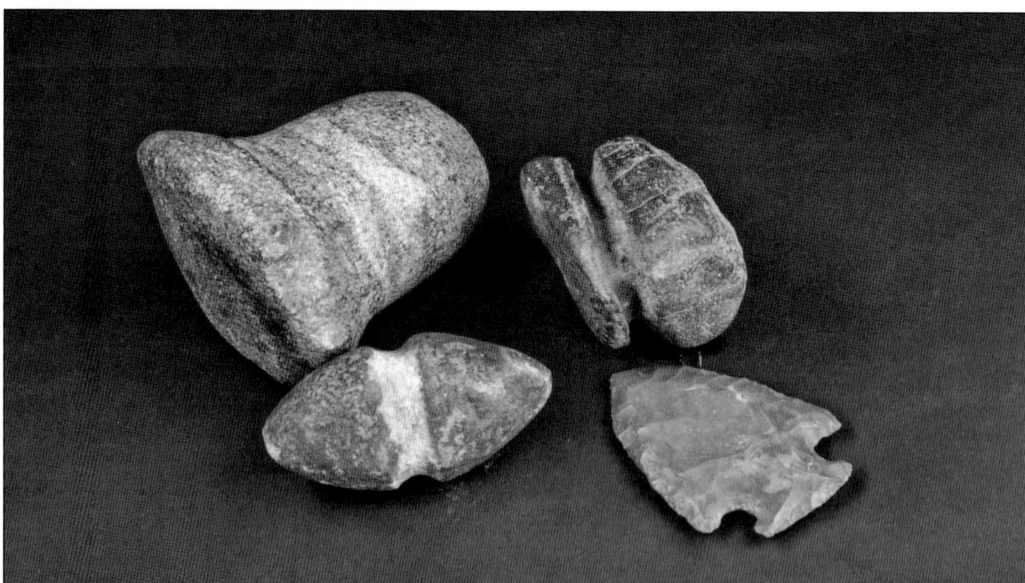

Artifacts Identify Native American Lands. These items were collected near Hanover. A bell pestle (8.5 by 9 centimeters) can be seen on the left. The full groove, war club head is 8.5 by 4 centimeters. The full grooved hammer stone is 8 by 4.5 centimeters. The corner-notched projectile point is 7.5 centimeters in length. The discovery of artifacts like these near mussel shells, fire-cracked rocks, animal bones, or pottery shards point to Native Americans—Hanover's first people. (Photograph courtesy Hanging Rock Photography, Steve Rizzo.)

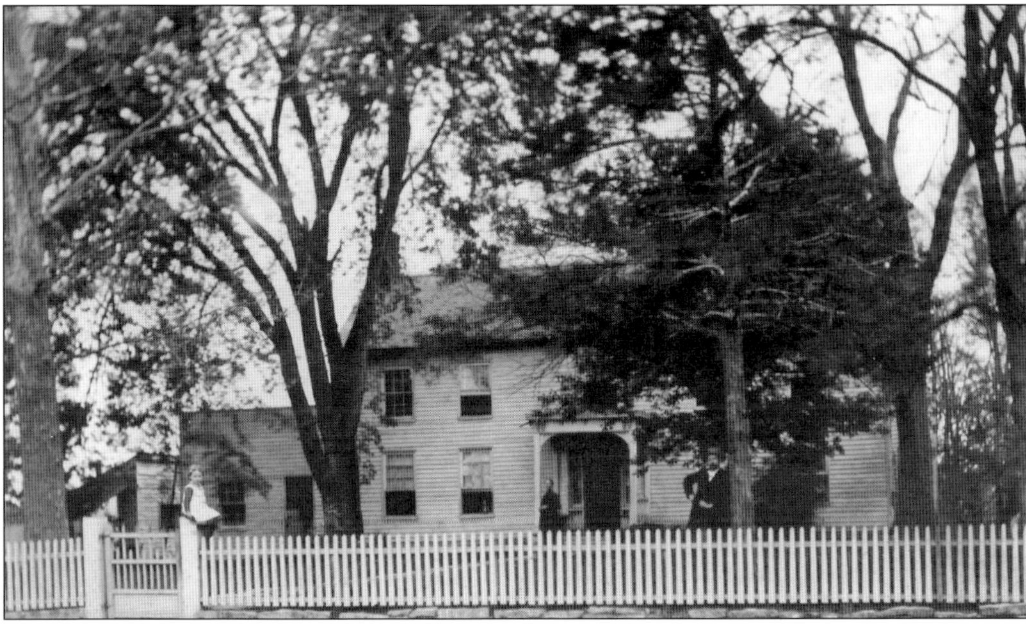

Log Home Still Stands. Hanover's first log house, built by Williamson Dunn in 1809, is tucked inside this two-story Federal structure, which was constructed around it. In this photograph, taken around 1885, Prof. Andrew Harvey Young leans against a tree in the right foreground. His wife, Mary Agnes Dunn Young, stands on the front porch and their daughter Jessie Dunn Young Adams sits on a fence post. (Courtesy Janet C. Cowen.)

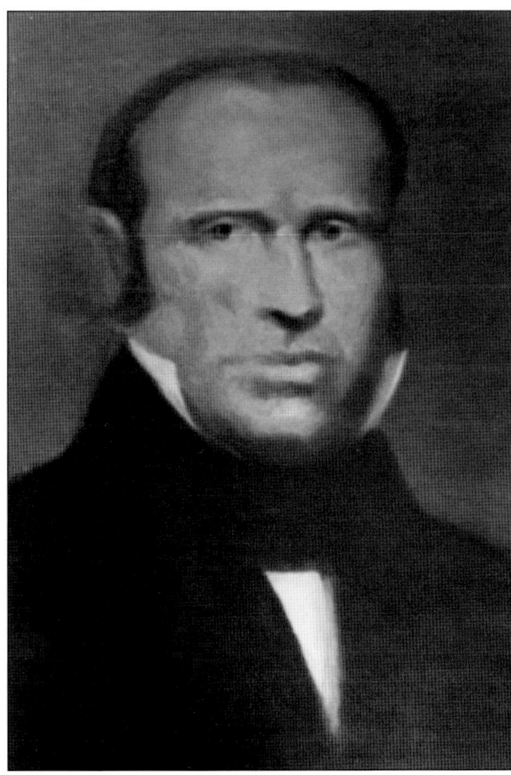

Williamson Dunn Settled in 1809. Dunn left Kentucky and helped found Hanover, which was first called "Dunn's Settlement." He gave up a political career to devote his time to his wife and 11 children. In addition to farming, Dunn served in the Indiana legislature, worked in land grant offices, rode as a ranger captain in the War of 1812, presided as a judge, and served as a church elder. (Courtesy HC.)

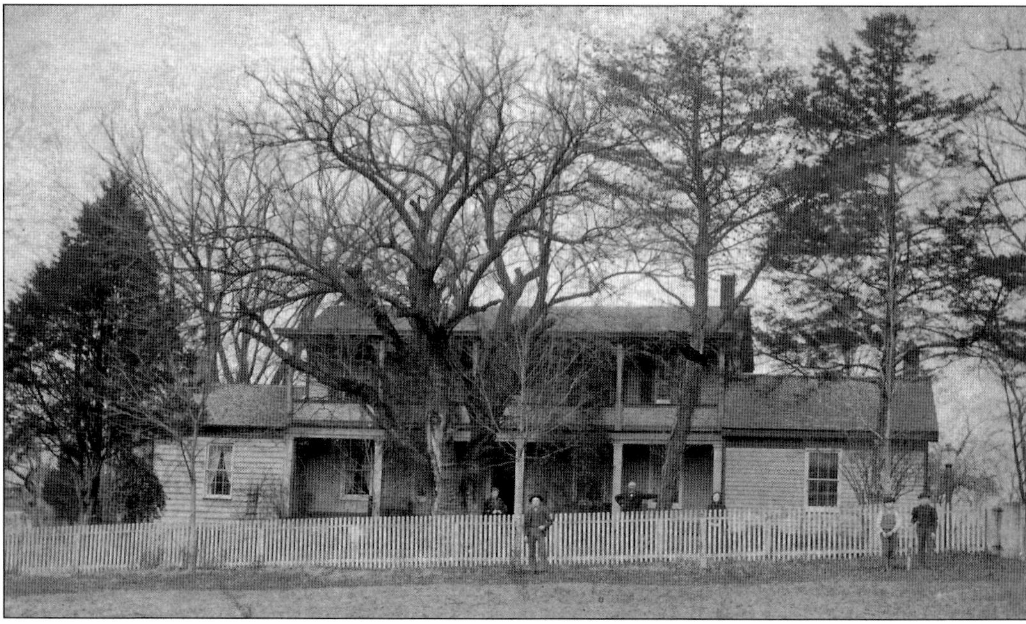

FOUNDER'S HOUSE LISTED. Ethel E. Crowe donated to Hanover College this rare image of the Crowe-Garritt House taken before 1860. The residence is included on the National Register of Historic Places. Dr. John Finley Crowe has a hand on the tree. People born in the house are listed on the back of the picture. They are Sarah Crowe Garritt; her children Lelia, Madge, and Joe; Joe's daughter Mary in August 1897; and Madge's daughter Sadie in September 1897. (Courtesy HC.)

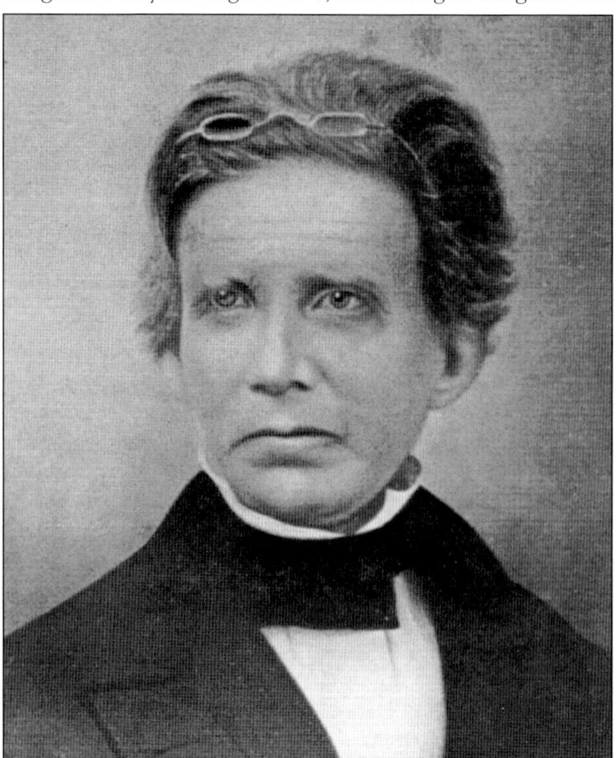

JOHN FINLEY CROWE FOUNDED SCHOOL. A reverend and doctor, John Finley Crowe served the Hanover Presbyterian Church. He also founded a school in Hanover in 1827, which became Hanover College. Crowe is credited with giving the first $100 of $380, which was raised to build a classroom. A second building for a theological professor was built by the students and citizens themselves from trees they cut and put together. (Courtesy HC.)

PROFESSOR TAUGHT FOR 50 YEARS. Joshua Bolles Garritt graduated from Hanover College in 1853. He married Sadie Crowe. They had three children, Leila, Madge, and Joshua C. Garritt taught Latin and Greek at Hanover College for 50 years, longer than any other person. He was an ordained Presbyterian minister and earned a master of science degree from Hanover College, a doctor of philosophy degree from the College of Wooster, and a doctor of laws degree from the University of Kentucky. (Courtesy HC.)

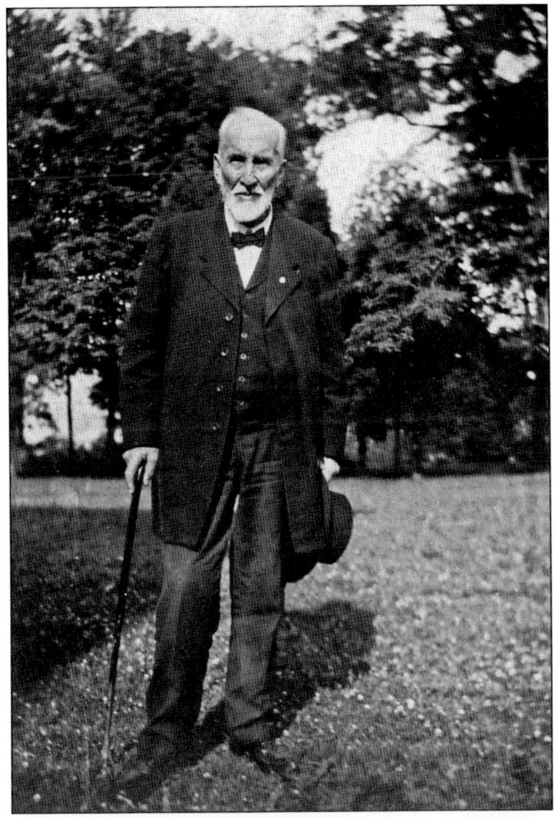

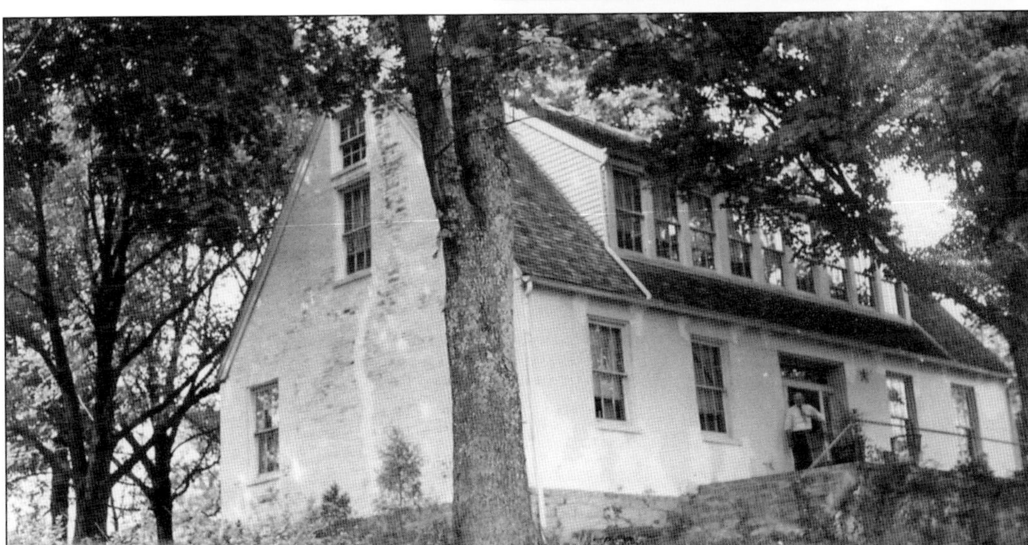

HOUSE BUILT BY EARLY SETTLER. The house pictured above was located on land called Logan's Point, which overlooks a magnificent view of the Ohio River. George Logan visited the area in 1801 and came back and built this house in 1817. He settled in and was instrumental in the founding of Hanover, Hanover College, and Hanover Presbyterian Church. Logan lived to 91. The house was destroyed by fire in 1979. (Courtesy LC.)

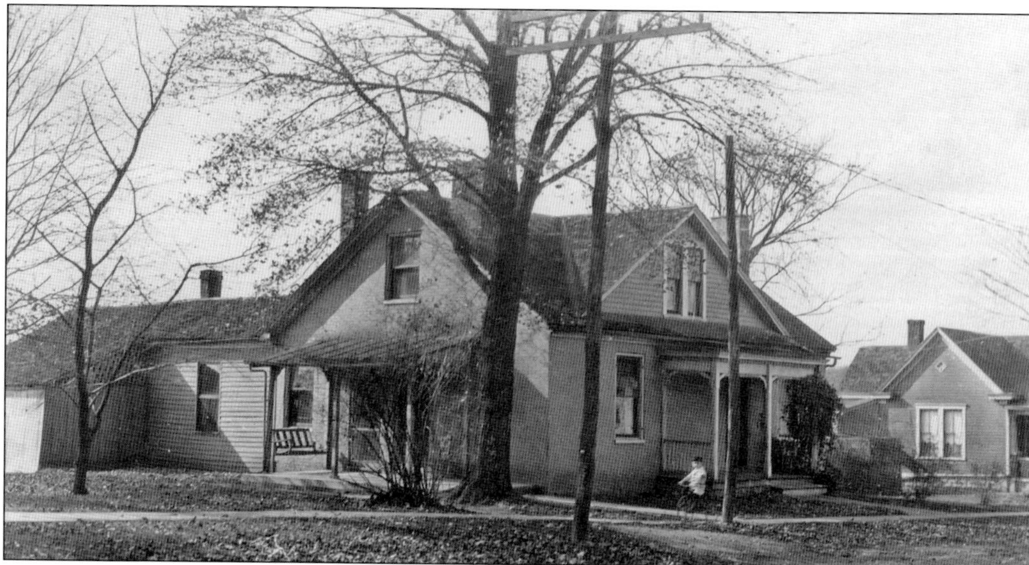

House Holds History. John and Martha Smyth built the home pictured above around 1838. The house was owned in the 1860s by Prof. John Scott and his wife, Mary. Their daughter Caroline married future U.S. president Benjamin Harrison. Some years later, after Caroline's death, Harrison married Mary Dimmick, who was Caroline's niece. Dimmick probably lived in this house as a girl. The home is owned today by Bob and Grace Ireland. Bob has lovingly helped restore at least 15 historic Hanover homes. (Courtesy Bob Ireland.)

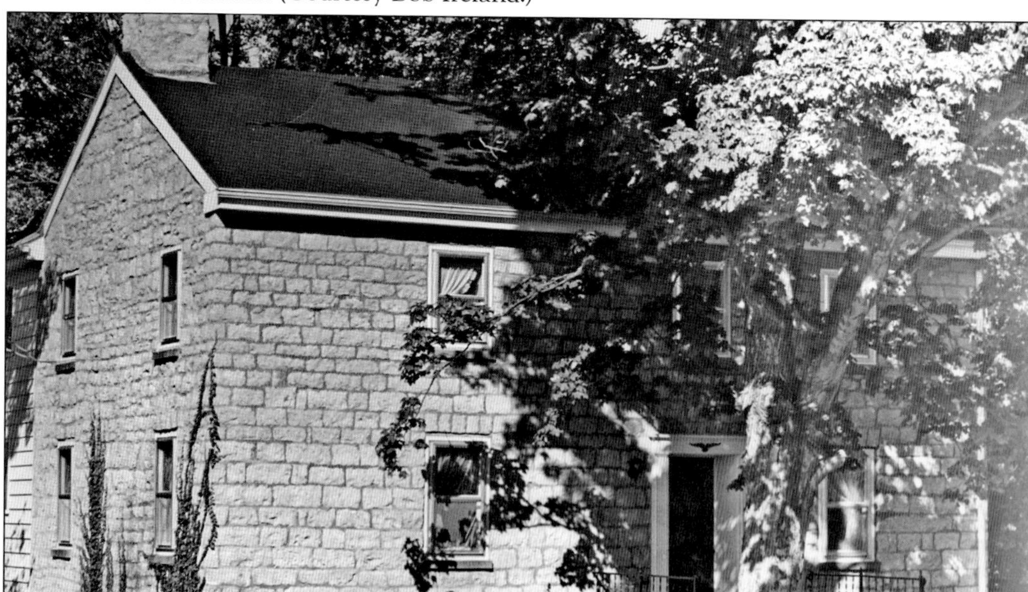

Property Dates to 1812. John Paul and George Shannon secured with a land grant the property this home stands on for David H. Maxwell and his wife, Mary Dunn, when David was away in the War of 1812. They sold the property to Amos Butler in 1818. He built this stone house using quarried stone instead of creek stone, which makes it singular in the Hanover area. (Courtesy JC.)

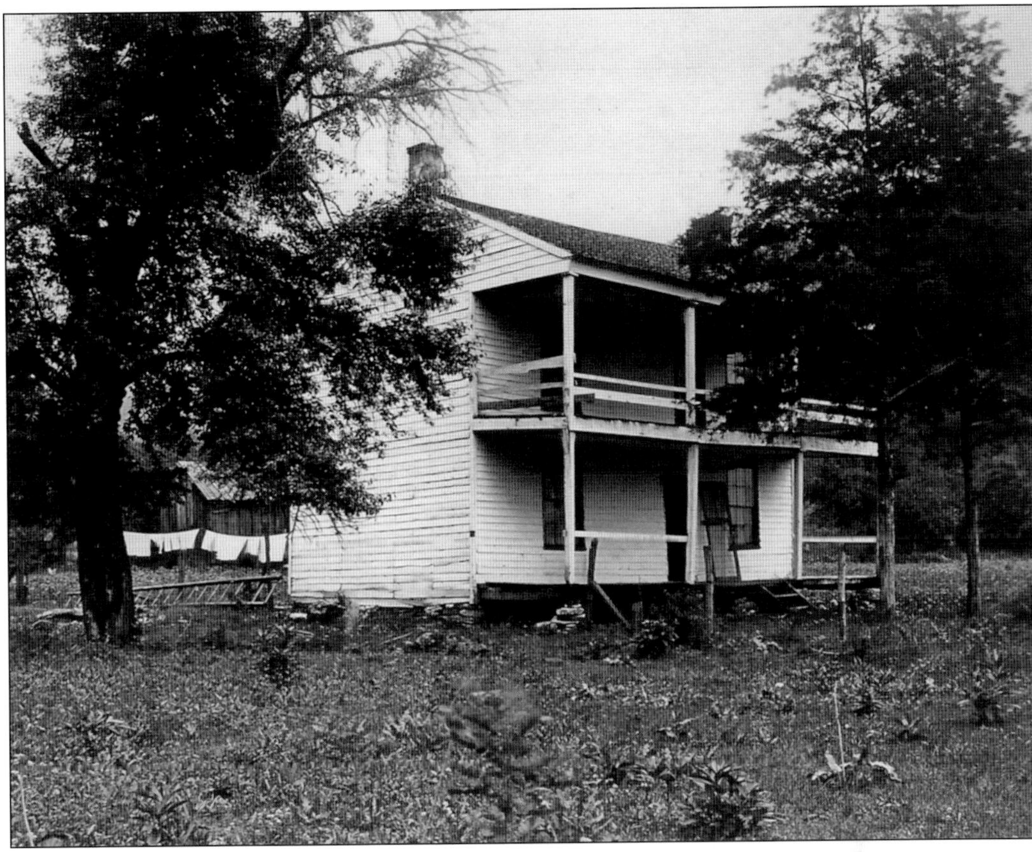

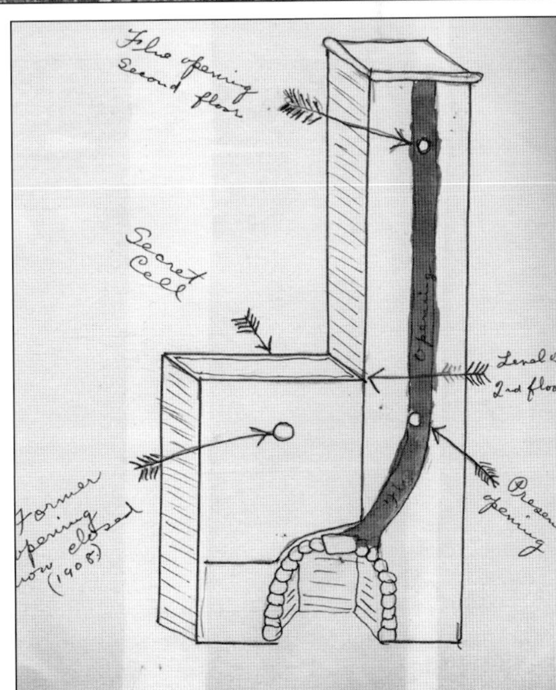

Runaway Slaves Hide in House. These images were found together in an archival collection of houses in or near Hanover. Local historians are not sure where the house stood. According to archival information, "John B. Todd built this house in the 1830s." Todd constructed a hiding space in the chimney, which could not be seen from the outside. Escaped slaves hid in this secret cell before continuing their run for Canada on the Underground Railroad. They crossed the Ohio River from the Kentucky side at the direction of Todd's brother, who waited for a signal. Todd would either bang a code on a kettle or leave a lamp burning in an upstairs window. Both signals meant "all is well," and the slaves would then be ferried across the river. When there was no immediate danger, the slaves stayed in an upstairs room that had a flue which opened into the secret cell. If needed, they could silently move floor boards and get into the hiding place. (Both, courtesy LC.)

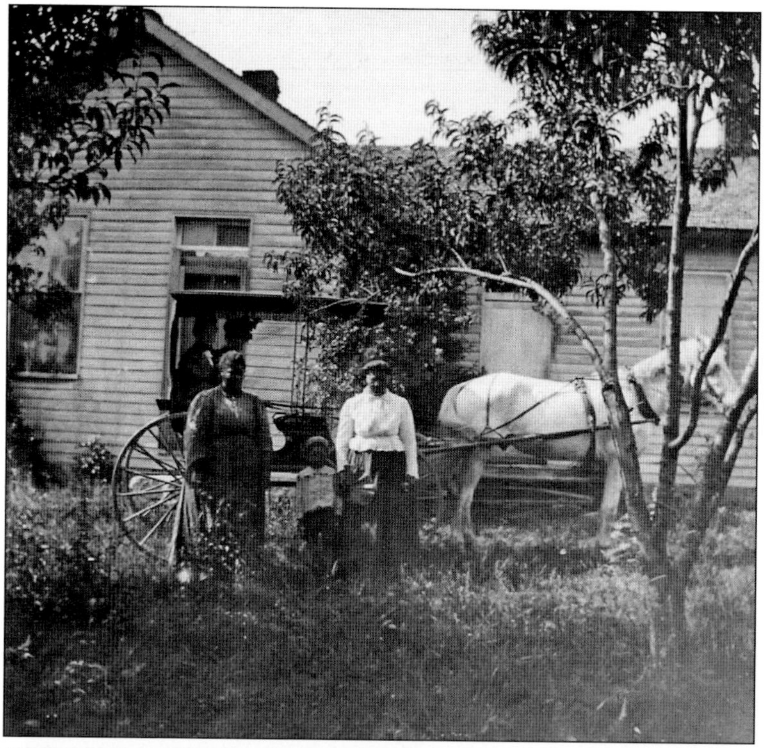

WOMEN GET READY FOR RIDE. In the front row and on the left, Della Vincent stands with her unidentified daughter-in-law and an unidentified child. Martha Elizabeth McFarland Dunn and her daughter Mary Agnes Dunn sit in the wagon. Martha married John Houston Dunn, Williamson Dunn's son. This picture was taken about 1909 on the east side of the Dunn home. (Courtesy Janet C. Cowen.)

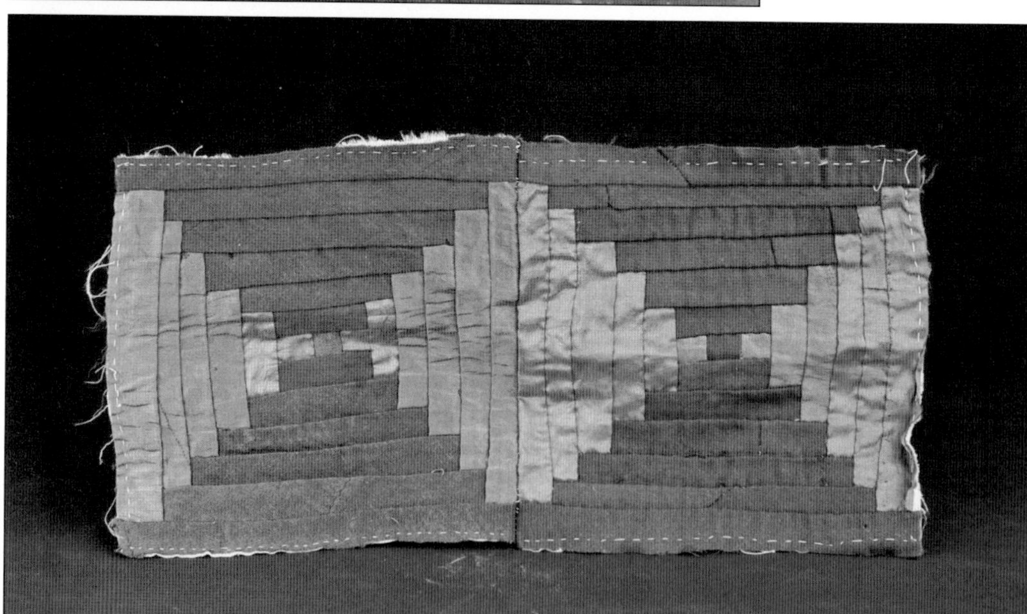

QUILTS UTILIZE SMALLEST FABRIC SCRAPS. Pioneers wasted nothing, including leftover fabric. Fibers were spun into yarn at a spinning wheel and the yarn was woven into fabric on a loom. Fabric was fashioned into clothing and other household items. Quilts came next, made from the fabric scraps. This quilt fragment, designed in the log cabin pattern, is thought to have been pieced by Hanover settler Martha Elizabeth McFarland Dunn (1827–1913). (Courtesy Janet C. Cowen; photograph courtesy Hanging Rock Photography, Steve Rizzo.)

Two

Around Town

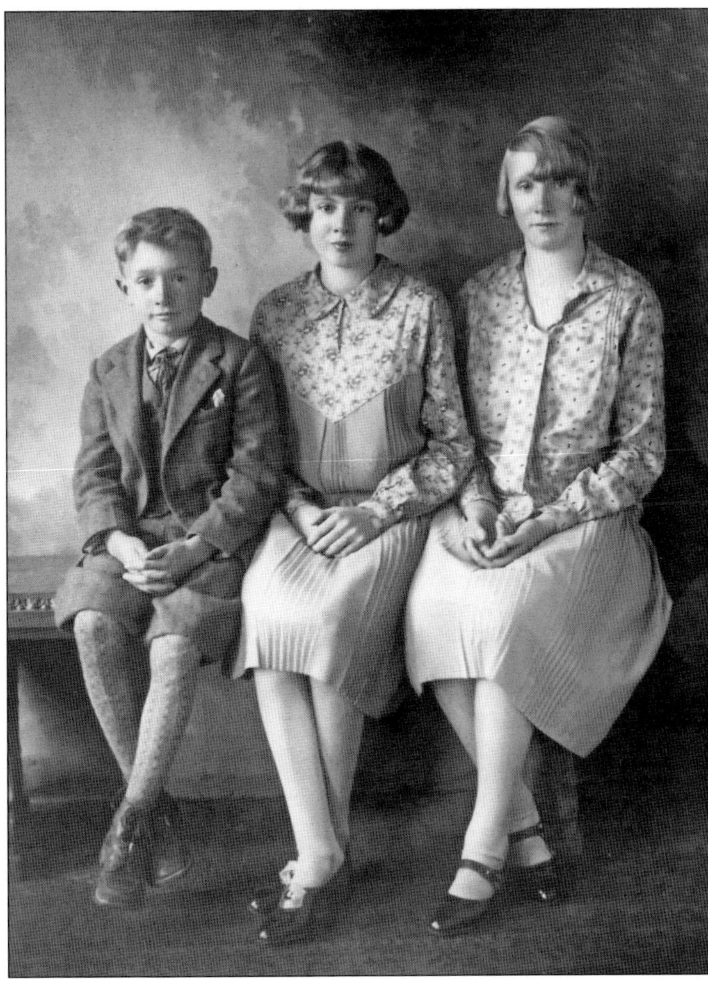

Adams Children Grew up Farming. From left to right, Thomas Harvey Adams, Mary Elizabeth Adams Lenzini Doyle, and Martha Dunn Adams Yeh pose for a photograph around 1929. The children lived and worked on their parents' farm at the corner of LaGrange and Riverview Roads. All three served as officers in the military: Tom as a U.S. Navy pilot and Mary and Martha as U.S. Army nurses. (Courtesy Janet C. Cowen.)

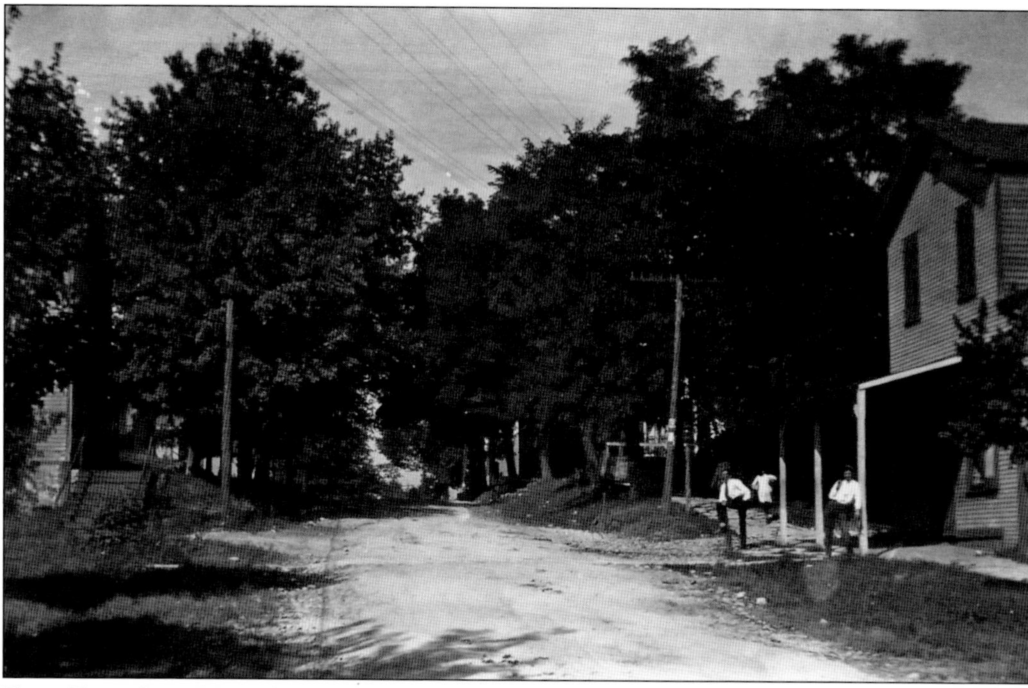

TALL TREES LINE MAIN STREET. Main Street in Hanover was lined with towering trees around 1915 when this picture was taken. To the right of the trees was one of two cisterns where residents got clean water. This picture was taken at the corner of Main and Locust Streets looking west uphill toward Main Cross. (Courtesy HC.)

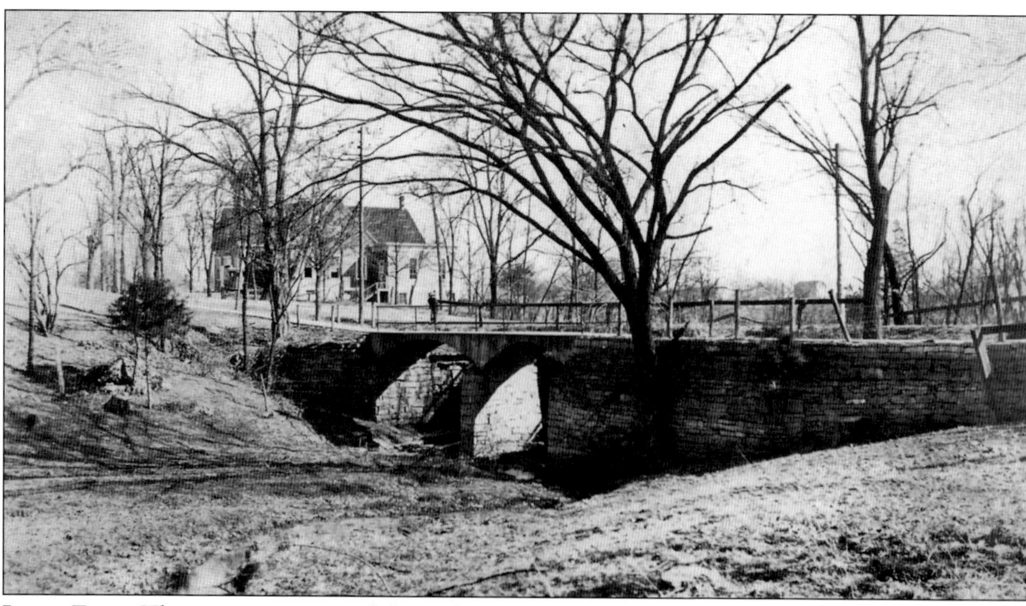

LOOK EAST. This picture postcard from the Hanover College archives shows what was called "the old footbridge" and "the Little Red Schoolhouse," which was later a community center. The bridge was taken down and a large culvert was put in. Where the water is in the foreground there is now a garden. (Courtesy HC.)

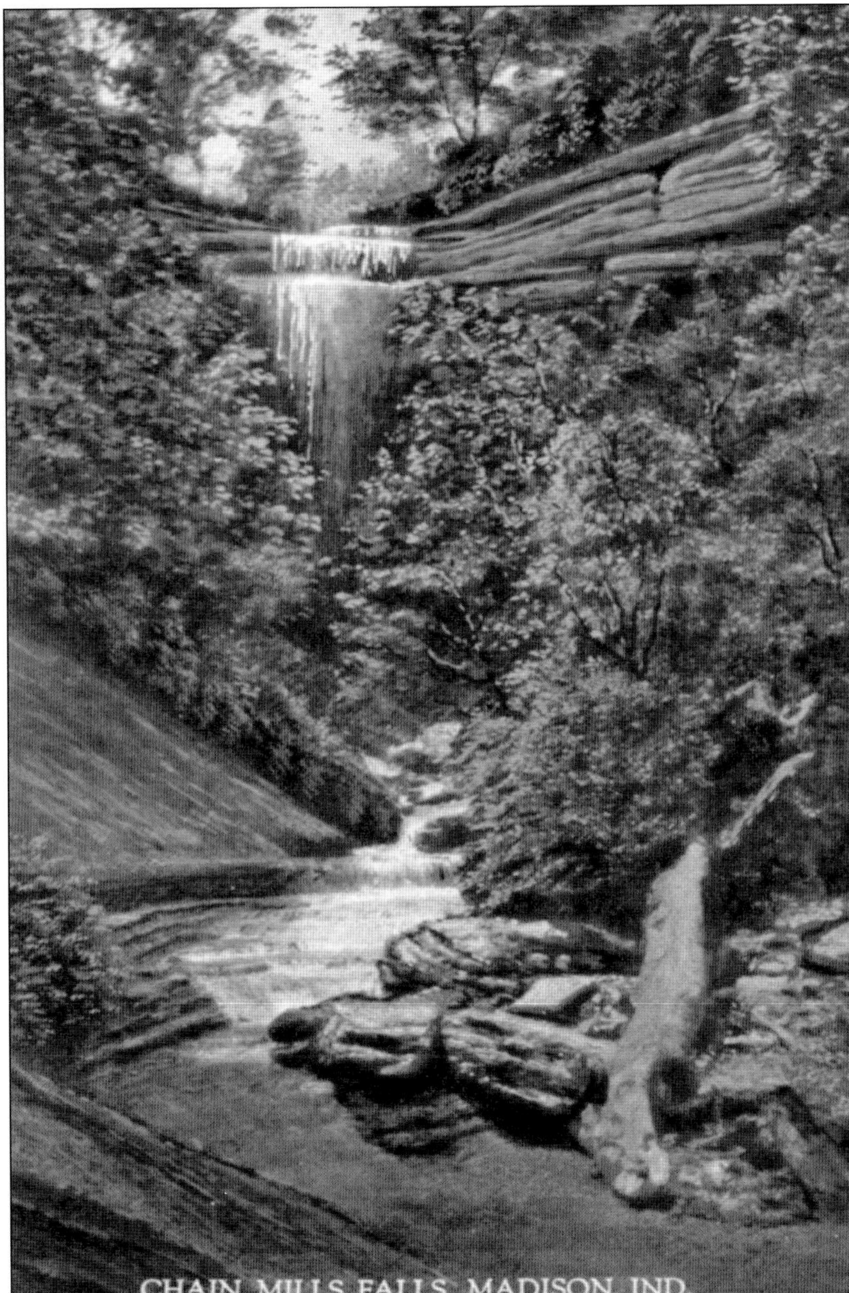

WATER FALLS PLENTIFULLY. Waterfalls in the Hanover area vary in height, from a few feet to almost 200 feet. They have historically provided a place to get clean water, bathe, wash clothing, take and paint pictures, study rock forms and nature, throw parties, and run machinery. One falls famous for running machinery was the Old Chain Mill Falls pictured in the historic postcard above. Two brothers named Gordon rigged up a continuous chain studded with cow horns in 1815 to power a system to grind grain. Over the years, the cow horns were replaced by square wooden buckets. According to local historians, the following are the names of Hanover's falls: Deadman, Horseshoe, Crowe, Butler, Chain Mill, Fremont, and Hart's (sometimes spelled Heart's). (Courtesy JC.)

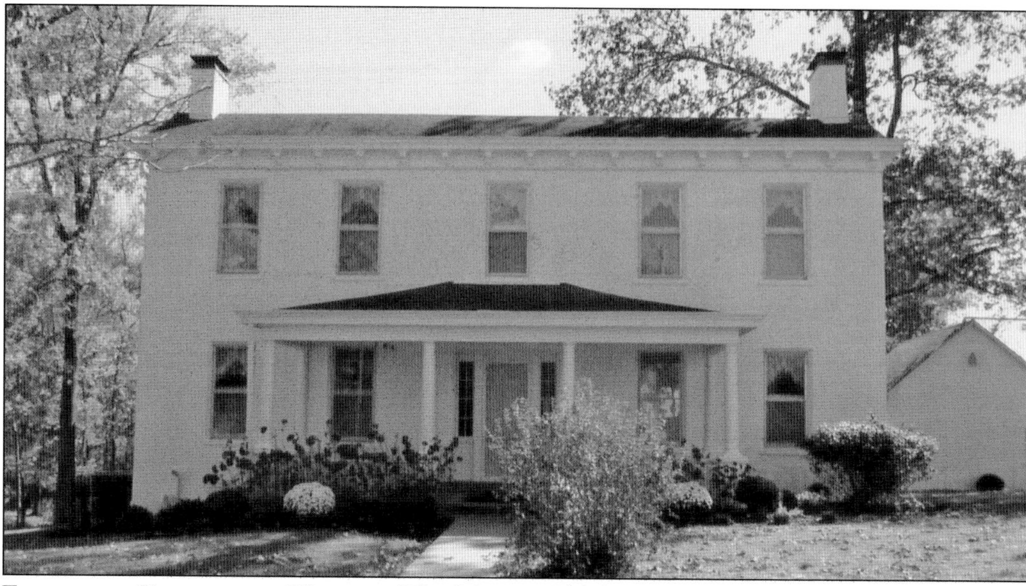

Farmhouse Filled with History. The Mouser-Oldaker-Green Home stands just outside of Hanover on State Road 56 on the way to Madison. It was built about 1840 by William Edwards. The current owners of the property are Gene and Sarah Green. They have carefully restored the home, which is designated as a Hoosier Homestead Farm. The property has been in Sarah's family since 1899. (Courtesy Gene and Sarah Green.)

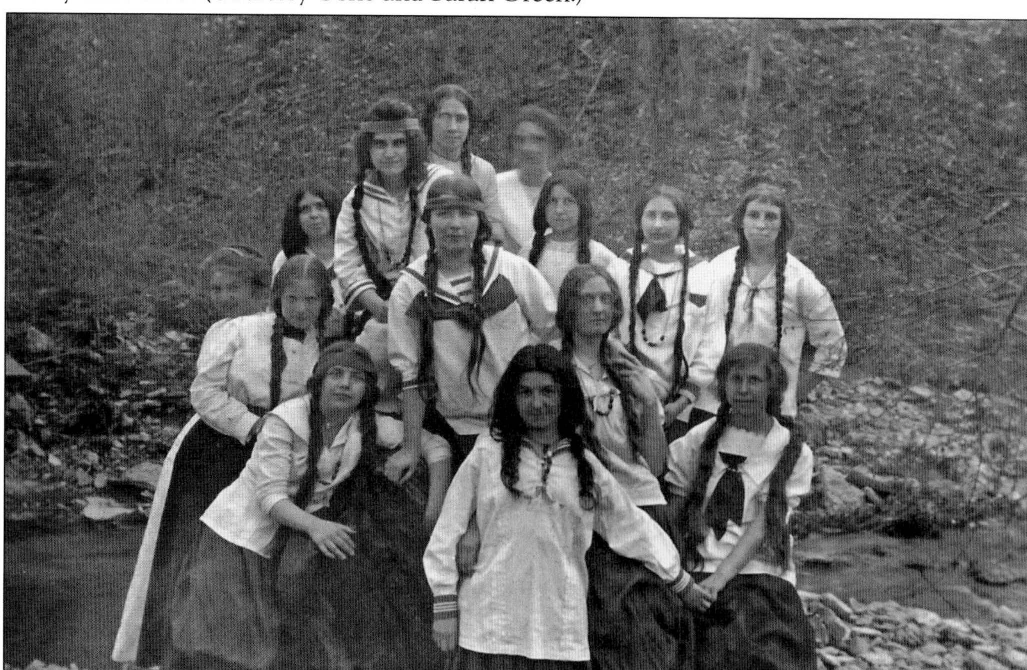

Young Women Visit Happy Valley. People hiked into Happy Valley, east of Hanover College, to enjoy the outdoors as well as study rocks, waterfalls, plants, and animals. Camp Fire Girls pose in the valley in this 1913 photograph. None of the campers in this archival photograph are named but their leader's name is given as Mrs. Phelps. (Courtesy HC.)

Mary Sits with Jeanette. Hanover native Mary Cook Cosby was one-quarter Native American through her maternal grandmother. Mary holds her daughter Jeanette Cook Cosby. Mary is the grandmother of Hanover resident Wanda Jean Cosby Lacy. Lacy reports her mother, Freda, saw Native Americans near Hanover on Highway 256 when she was a child. Freda turned 100 in 2010. (Courtesy John D. and Freda Cosby Johnson family.)

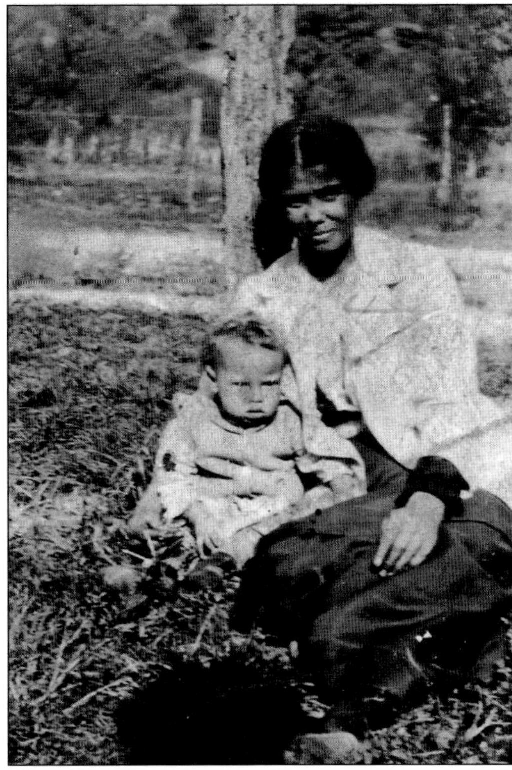

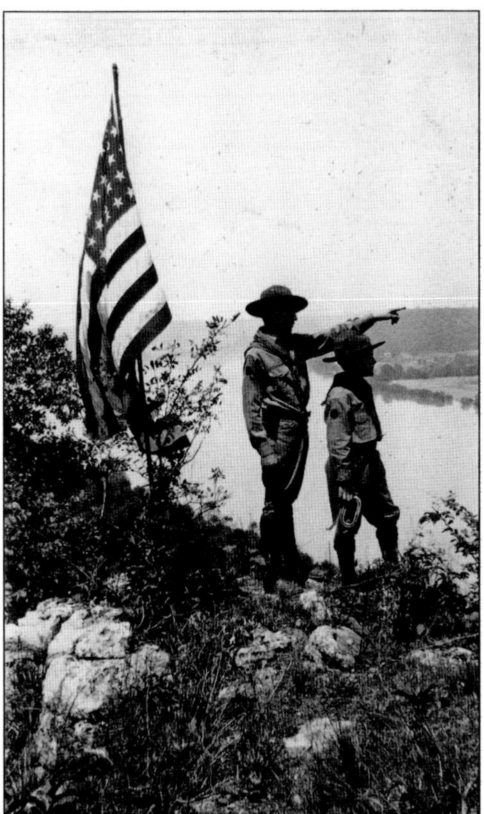

Boy Scouts Look over Ohio River. In this image from about 1927, two unidentified Boy Scouts have planted an American flag into the bluff overlooking the Ohio River. One scout points to Kentucky across the river and the other holds a bugle. (Courtesy LC.)

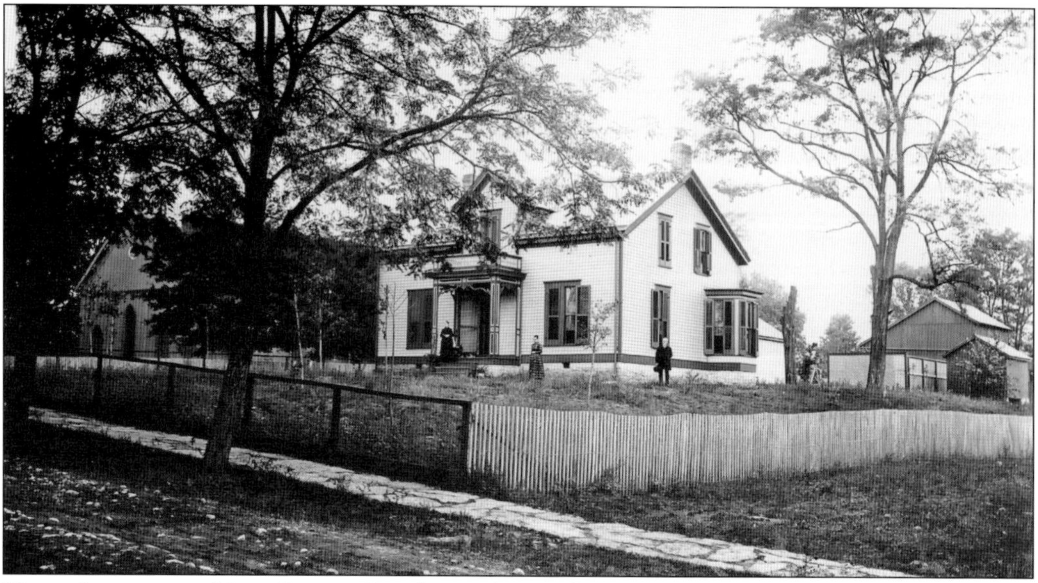

House Located on Main Street. Family members gathered outside their house for this photograph taken in the late 1800s. At one time, the residence was called the A. Y. Moore House. A notation of the back of the image reads, "Home of Miss Ella Moore—next door to Presbyterian Church." In the 1920s, the house was owned by the Ramsey family. (Courtesy HC.)

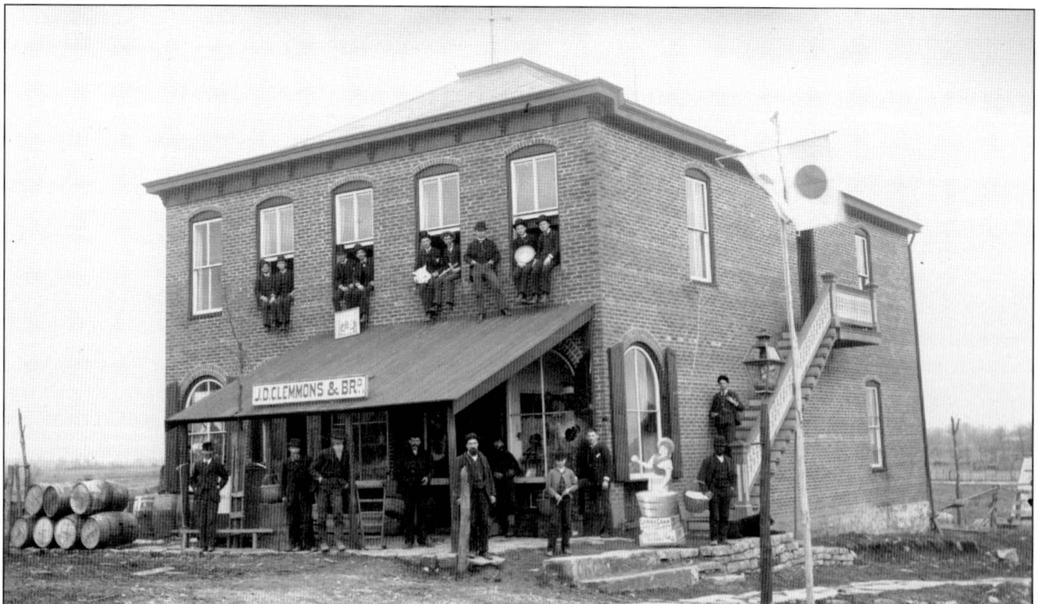

Men Hang Out. Men presumably from Hanover College gather at the "J. D. Clemmons & Bro." building at the corner of Main Street and Madison Avenue. The building was reported by Frank Baker to have been constructed in 1884. The upstairs was used for boarding and as a meeting place for fraternities and sororities. J. Clark Hill and his son Dean Clark Hill ran a general store in the building for 60 years. In the 1950s, the building housed the town post office and a bank in the 1960s and 1970s. Today the building is devoted to apartments. (Courtesy HC.)

WOMAN MARRIED COUNTRY DOCTOR. Mary Magdeline Russell (1850–1928) married Hanover doctor Charles A. Burdsall (1850–1947) in the last quarter of the 1800s. Her great-grandsons report a unique finding: she was part Native American and her brother-in-law fought Native Americans. This formal photograph shows interesting details of jewelry, a scarf, and a moiré satin dress. (Courtesy Young family.)

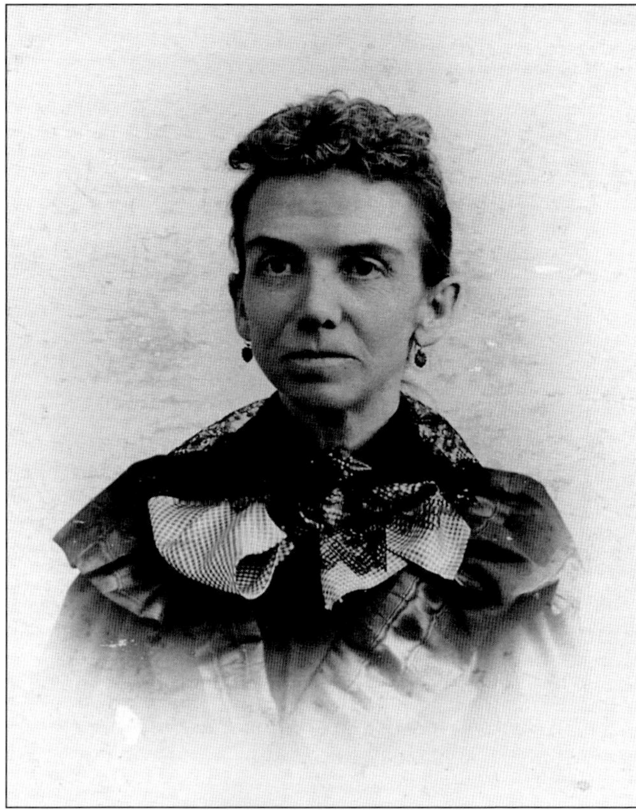

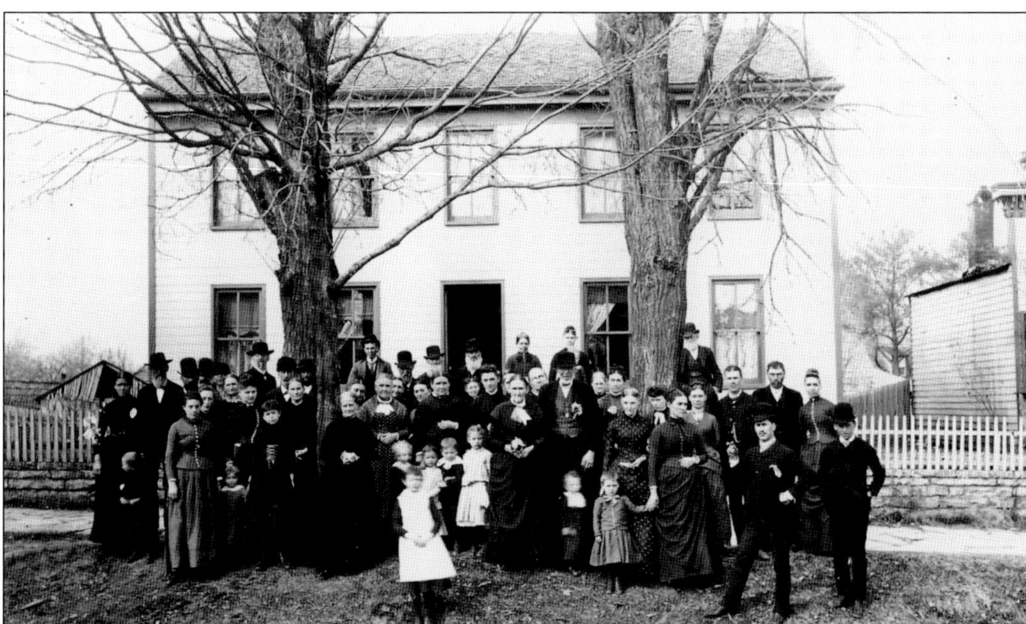

GROUP OF PEOPLE GATHER. An unknown group gathers in front of what is called "Todd's House" in the above photograph discovered in the Hanover College archives. While the image is undated, hats and clothes worn suggest the late 1800s. (Courtesy HC.)

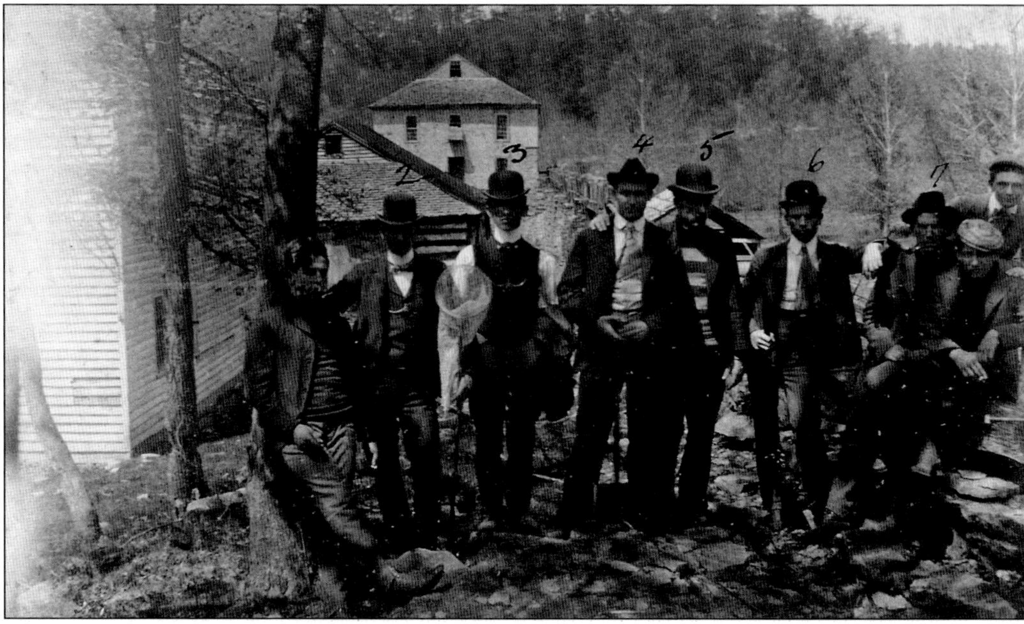

"Mill Race on Burdy's Farm." Nine men gather on Burdy's Farm in May 1900. Local historians suggest the building in the background is probably the Chain Mill Falls structure. While this archival photograph is labeled as a race, it also includes a notation about a zoological excursion. One man holds an insect net, another a shovel, and a third a shotgun. Pictured from left to right are, by last name only, Hawley, Runyon, Allen, Tilson, Marlsel, Roark, unidentified, Benson, and Rigers. (Courtesy JC.)

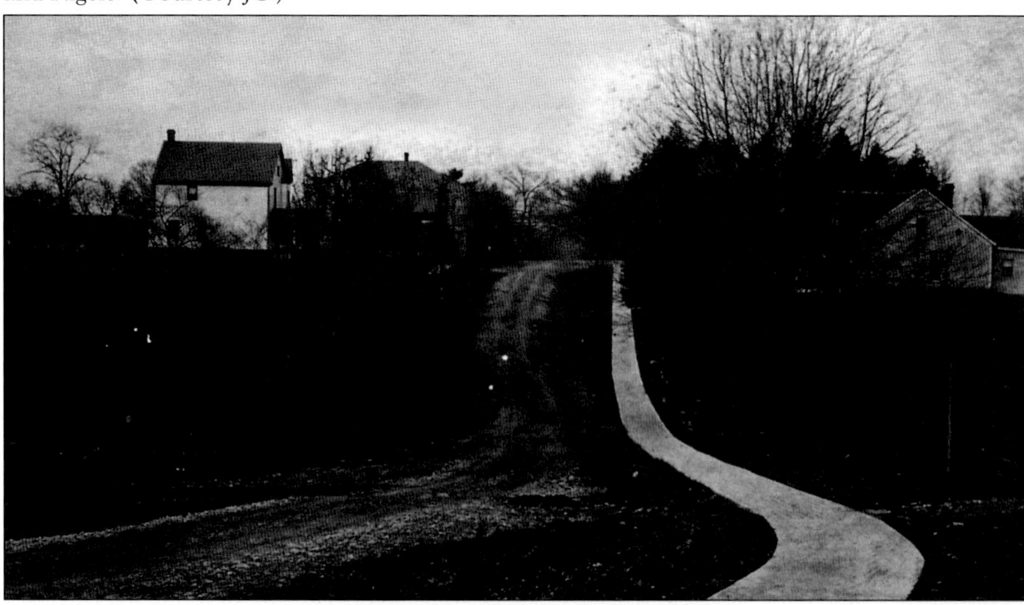

Sidewalk Poured Next to Dirt Road. People celebrated when the new sidewalk leading to Main Street between the college and town was completed. Students often lived in town as boarders. The walk between the town and college could be dusty as well as muddy when the ground was wet or snow had fallen. However, the road was not paved so horses and carriages still traveled through the dirt. (Courtesy HC.)

Grandmother Holds Her Grand Girl. Bess Jo Moore was one year old when this photograph was taken of her and her grandmother Bessie V. Hart in 1922. Hart bought the home now owned by Bob and Grace Ireland in 1921, and it was sold by her estate in 1944. It is thought that Hart was a schoolteacher. Moore lived in Wisconsin. (Courtesy Bob Ireland.)

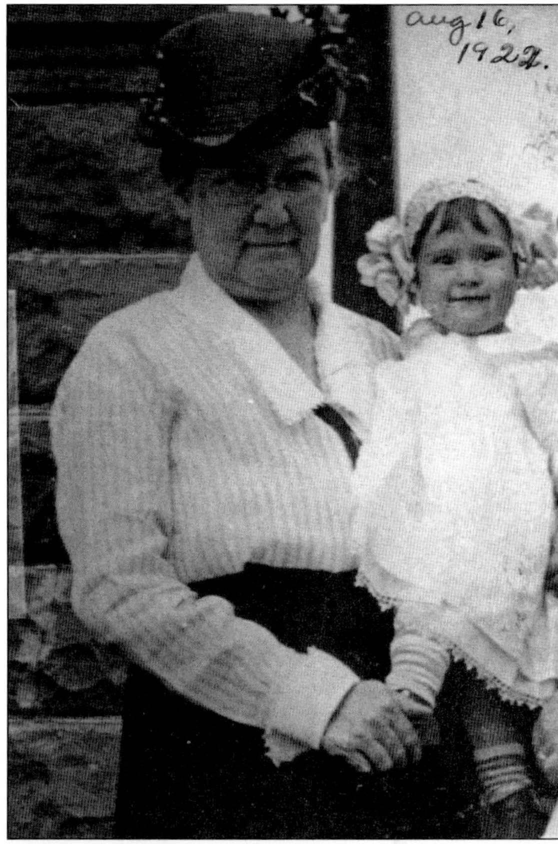

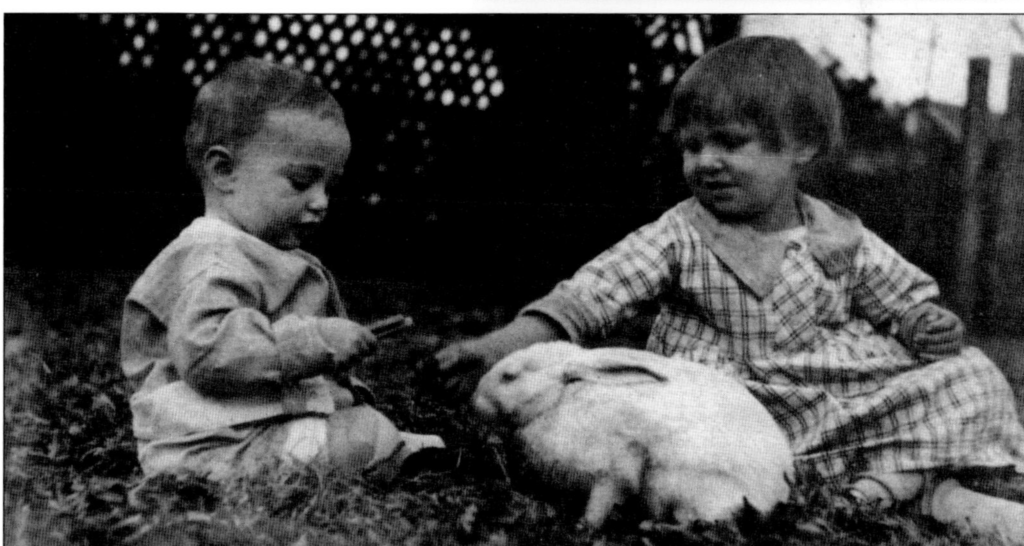

Children Feed Their Bunny. Clifford and Wilma McDonald grew up on a farm in Hanover. Clifford ran a grocery store in Kentucky most of his life. Wilma was born in 1915 and married Cecil Moore, a farmer. In addition to farming, Wilma also worked at Mills Department Store in Madison. (Courtesy William L. Moore family.)

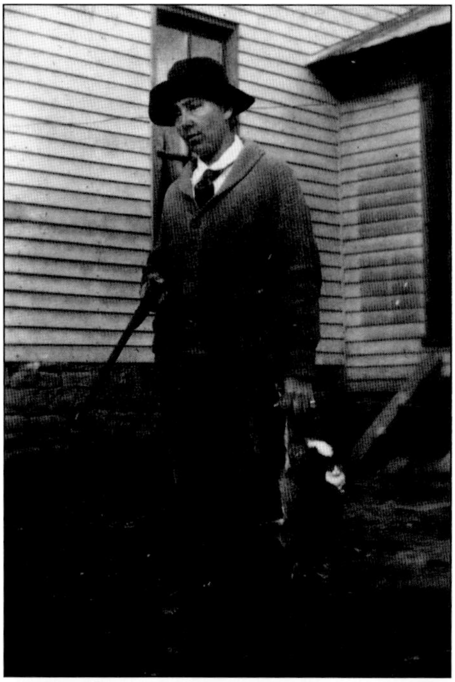

Grandma Finds Supper. Georgia Binger Means shot two rabbits and plans to cook them. According to her granddaughter, the meal would have included fried rabbit, potatoes, gravy, tomatoes, and biscuits. Means was a good cook and used an iron skillet to fry. She played the guitar and taught Sunday school at the New Prospect Baptist Church. (Courtesy D/M.)

Boarding Meant Sharing. Rooming arrangements in the 1800s were dramatically different than in modern times. People expected to share rooms and beds with others, sometimes with people they did not even know. In this photograph from the Hanover College archives, two men have been photographed in the late 1800s sleeping in their rooming house near campus. (Courtesy HC.)

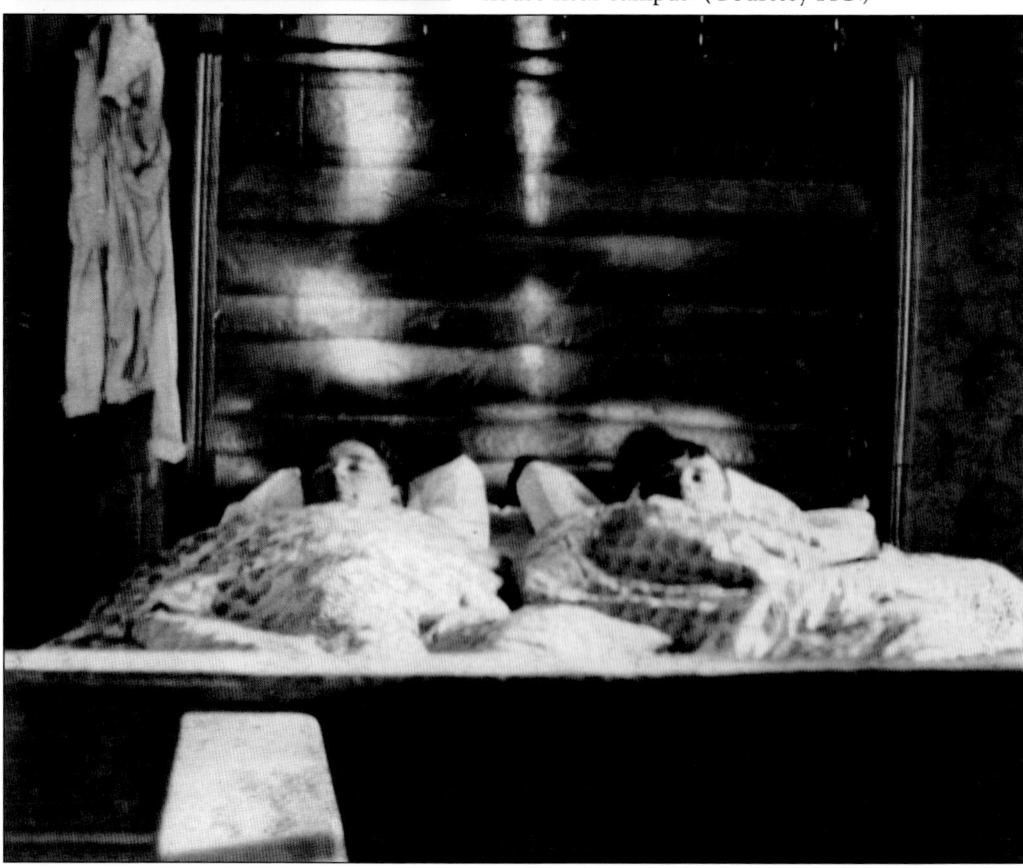

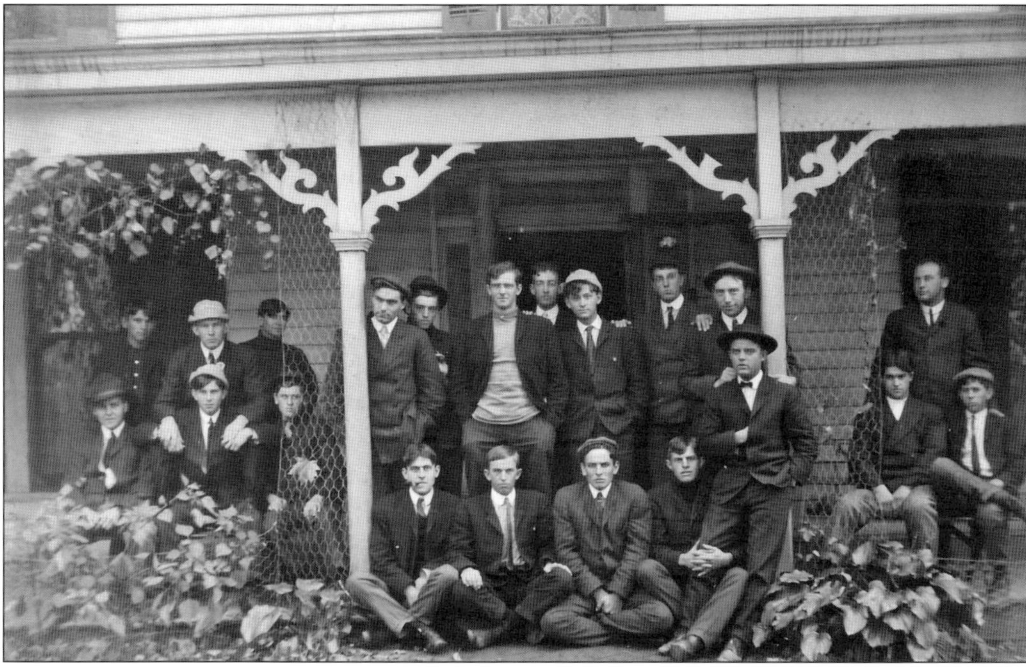

Fraternity Men Boarded with Sutherlands. In the 1890s, Phi Gamma Delta fraternity members ate together at what was called Sutherland's Boarding House. Local historians call this house the Finnigan/Moore House today. At a later time, Tom and Mary Finnigan owned and lived in the home. The men in the picture are not identified except for the third man from the left in the first row whose last name was Gore. (Courtesy Lee Bruther.)

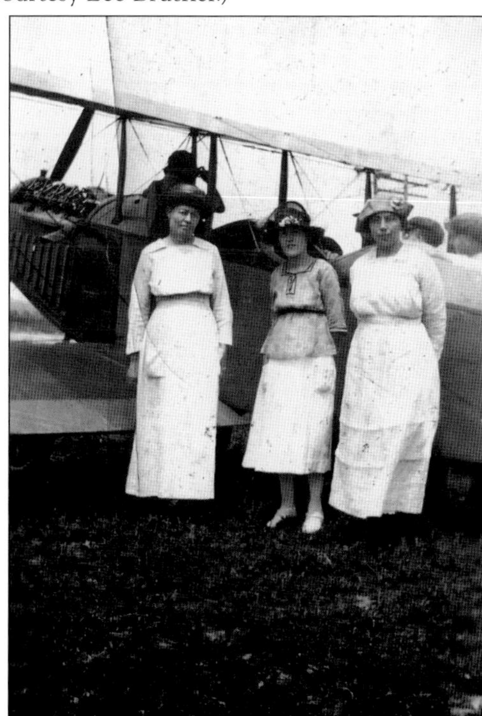

Flying was All the Rage. Georgia Means (who appears on the previous page with the rabbits) joined friends for a day of flying or at least hanging around airplanes in the 1920s, perhaps at Saluda Bottoms. These Hanover women are, from left to right, Means, Pearl Bruther, and Mattie Bruther. (Courtesy D/M.)

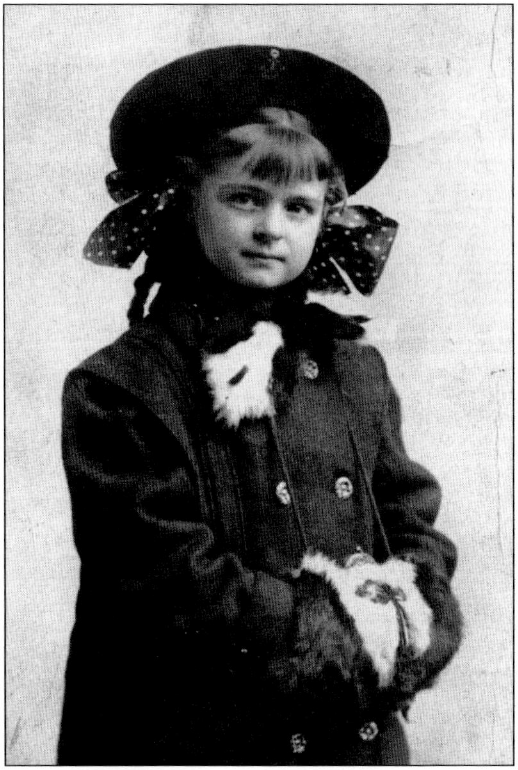

Girl Becomes Librarian. When people talk about Hanover College's librarian, "Miss Fitton," they smile and say she was a wonderful person. Mary Louise Fitton served from 1928 until 1966 and was popular with her family as well. The following appears on the back of the photograph at left: "A Merry Christmas to Anna from Katharine Fitton. Do you think Mary Louise has grown much 'in looks' "? (Courtesy HC.)

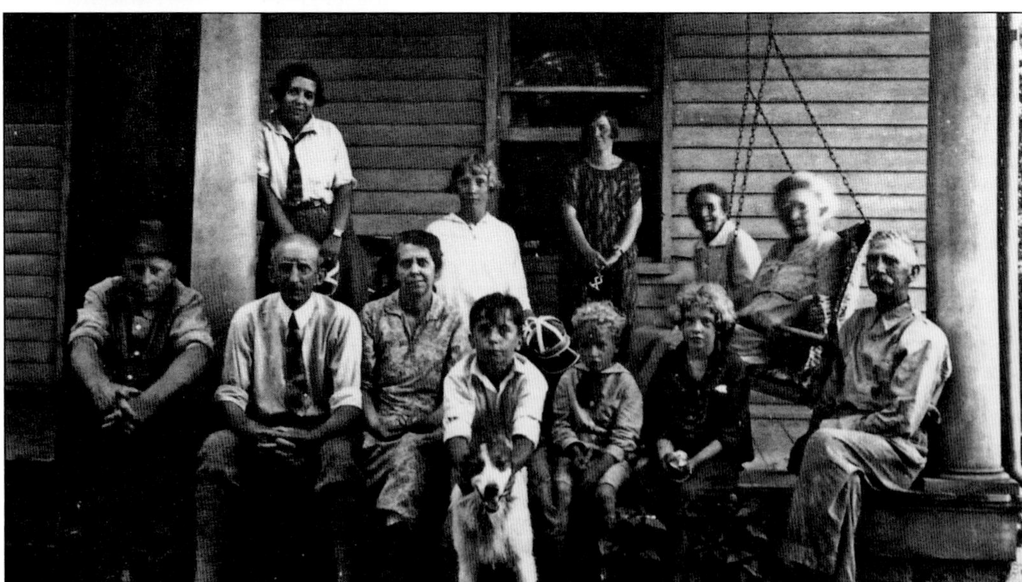

Family Gets Together in 1925. Elizabeth Adams raised three boys on a Civil War widow's pension. Pictured are, from left to right, (first row) Frank Raymond Adams, John Harris Adams, Etta Viola Dillon Adams, John Thomas Stewart Adams, Skipper the dog, Thomas Harvey Adams, Mary Elizabeth Adams Lenzini Doyle, and John Adams; (second row) Elizabeth ?, Martha Dunn Adams Yeh, Mildred ?, Mollie Archer, and Elizabeth Lysandra Harris Adams. (Courtesy Adams/Lenzini.)

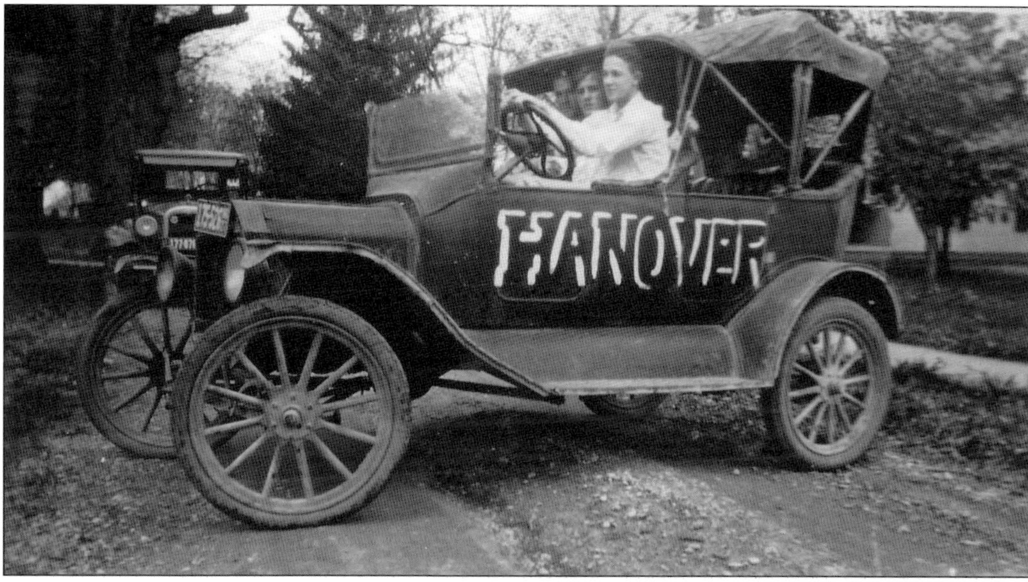

Men Go for a Spin. Bill Neighbert and two friends show off a vehicle called "Hanover" in the 1920s. The automobile, which looks very similar to a Model T, boasted a top speed of about 45 miles per hour. The ride was bumpy. An early automobile expert is said to have remarked that either tires or roads were going to have to get softer. Seems like tires won. (Courtesy LC.)

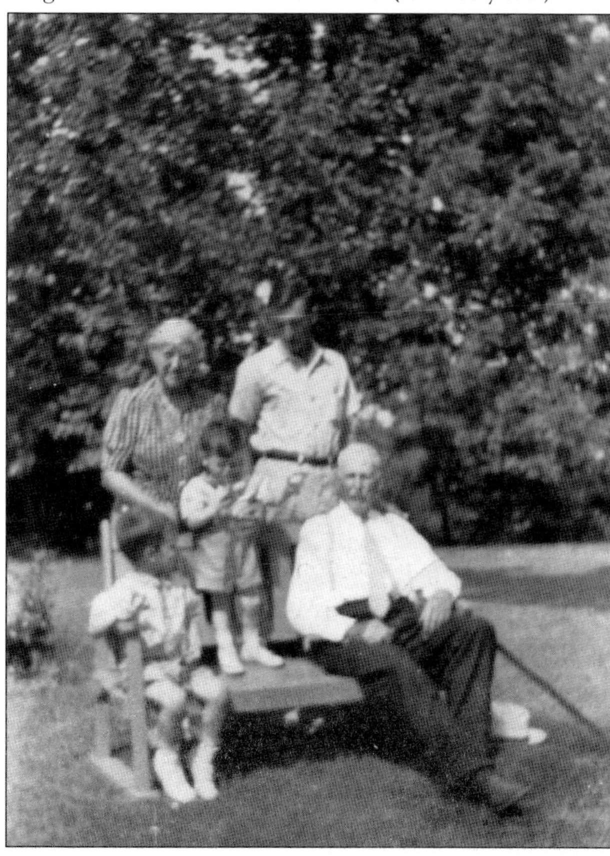

Family Gathers in Yard. Lora Burdsall Young ran a successful dairy business from the property she owned in Hanover, which was the original Williamson Dunn homestead. She is shown standing with her son John Burdsall. On the first row are her two grandsons, Robert, at left, and Jim. Her father, country doctor Charles A. Burdsall, sits next to his great-grandsons. (Courtesy Young family.)

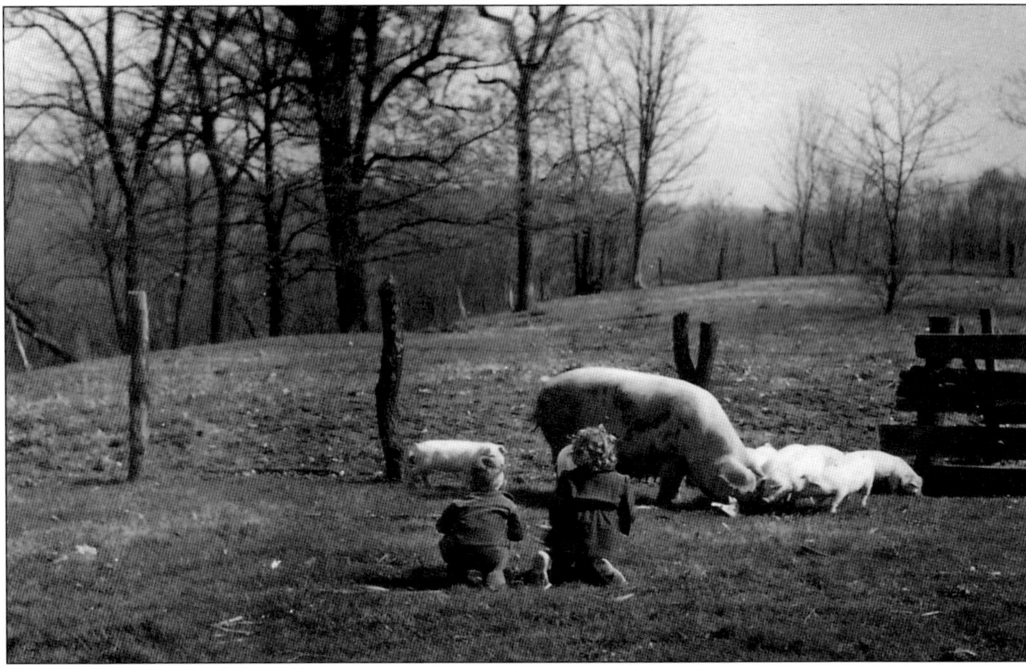

Hogs Eat as Children Watch. Mother hog and her piglets root around and eat food near their pen on the Robert Craig farm, which overlooked the Ohio River. Robert's grandson Carl Cowen Jr. and Robert's great-niece Martha Linda Lenzini watch. (Courtesy Janet C. Cowen.)

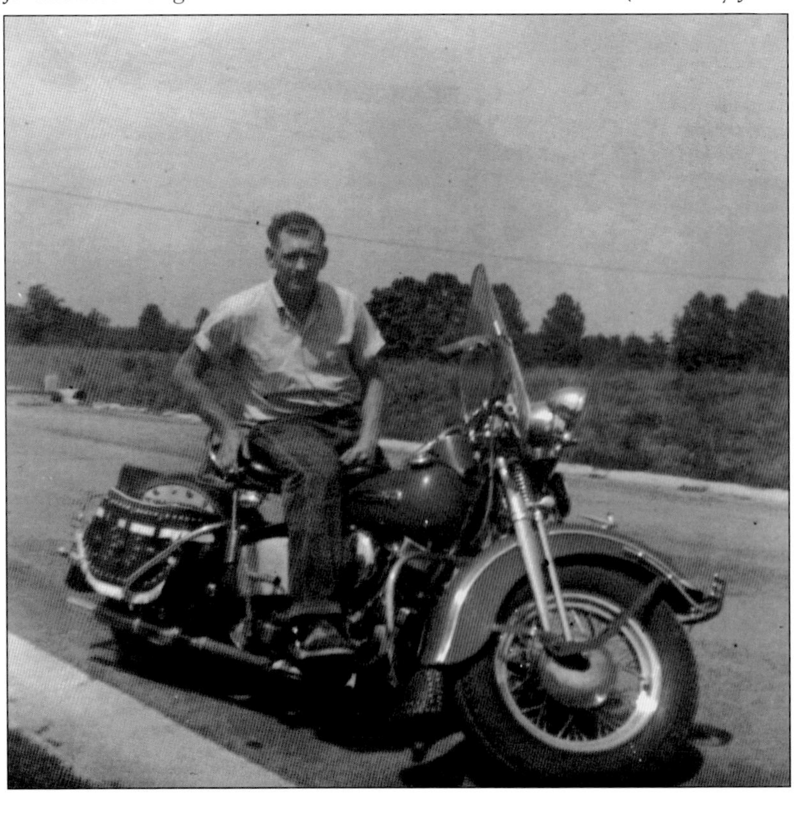

Everitt Rides His Harley. In the 1950s, Saluda resident Everitt William Elles rode what appears to be a Harley-Davidson FL with a Panhead V-twin engine. Elles was born in 1916, married Violet Risk Elles, and worked at Volz Chevrolet as the body shop manager for 30 years. (Courtesy William L. Moore family.)

STUDENT READIES FOR FUN. In 1938, college student Jim Davis stands in front of his automobile at the Hanover Confectionery (called the "Confec" by locals) in downtown Hanover where students gathered to have soft drinks, eat, and dance. This image was taken by fellow student Robert Craig. (Courtesy HC.)

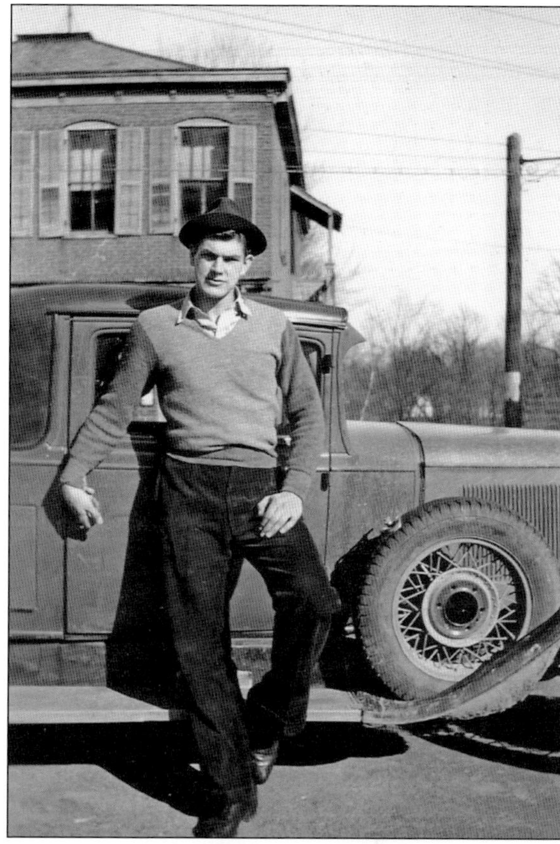

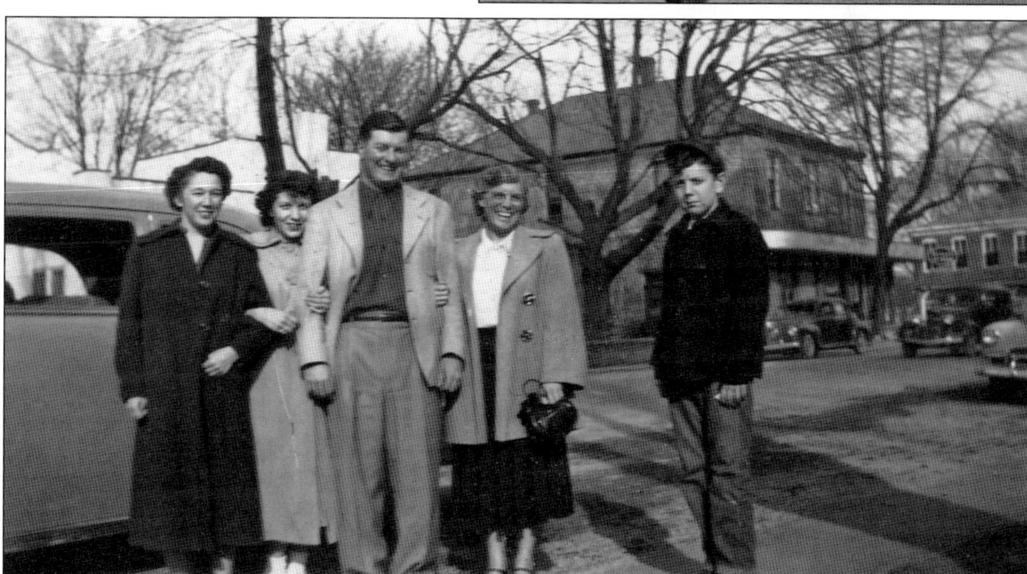

FRIENDS GATHER ON MAIN STREET. A group stands together with Cooper's Corner in the background in the 1940s. Dean Clark Hill's grocery can be seen on the far right. Pictured, from left to right, are Lottie Wood, June Gwyn Barnes, Perry Barnes, Rita Simmons, and Harley Byron Gwyn. Simmons taught elementary school in Hanover. (Courtesy Bob Ireland.)

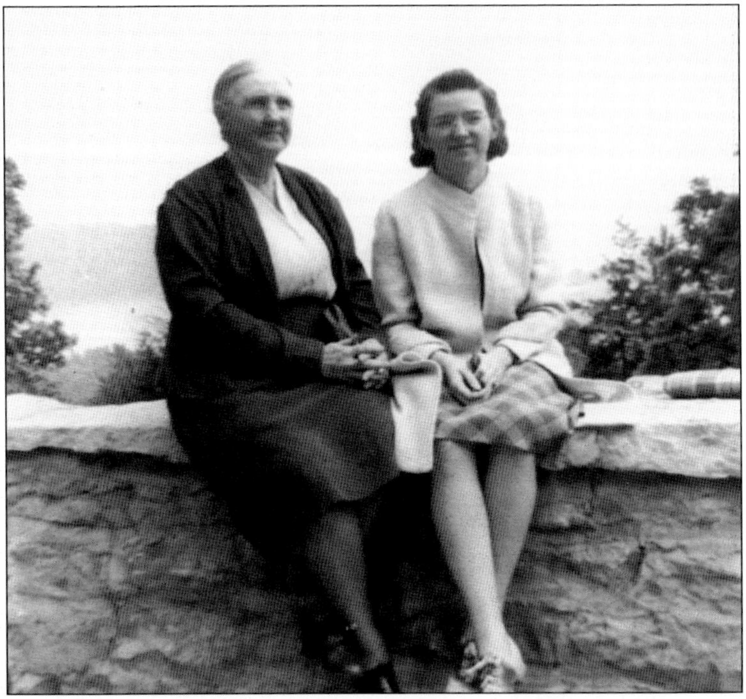

Two Generations Reflect at River. Mary Elizabeth ("May") Young Craig and her daughter Janet Catherine Craig Cowen sit on a wall at Hanover College. The spot overlooks the river at a place called "the Point." May graduated from Hanover in 1904 and Catherine in 1941. May worked as a successful farmer's wife, and Catherine taught school. After retiring from education, Catherine had more than 500 genealogy clients. (Courtesy Janet C. Cowen.)

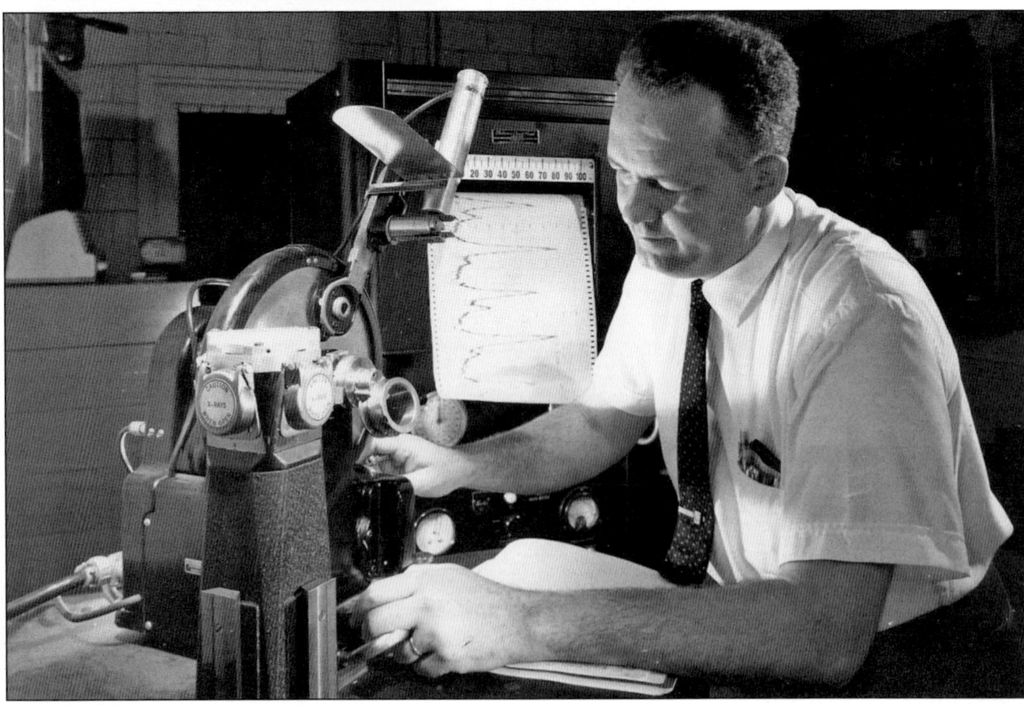

Link Belt Scientist Cowen Invents. Carl Cowen received his undergraduate degree from Hanover College in 1947. He earned a doctoral degree from Purdue University and served in the U.S. Navy before going to work at Link Belt in Indianapolis as a research scientist. After his retirement in 1983, he became deeply involved in genealogy research and moved back to Hanover. (Courtesy Janet C. Cowen.)

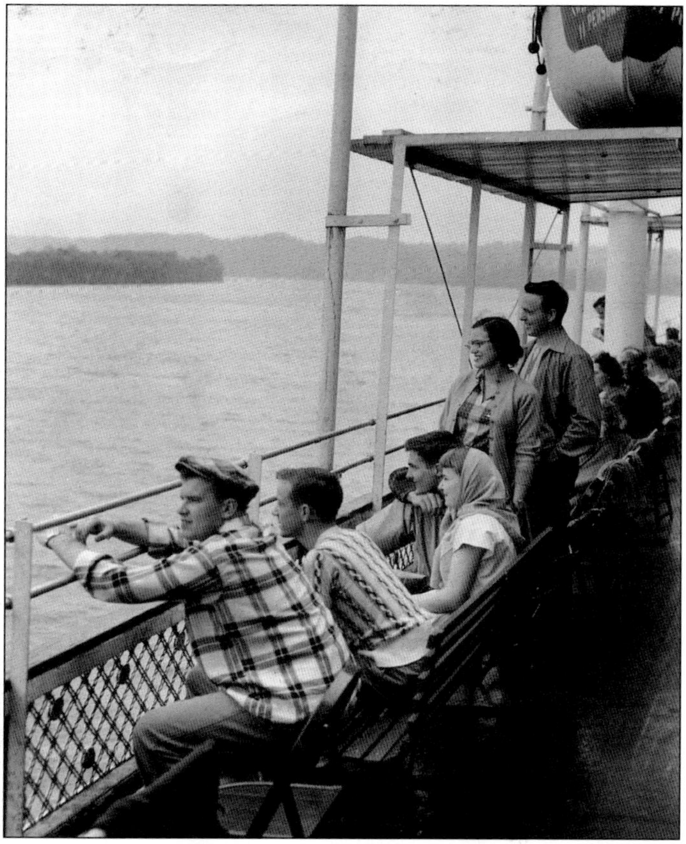

Residents, Students Cruise River. A peaceful day cruise on the Ohio River offered a long-anticipated, yearly treat for residents and these college students shown in the 1940s. For decades, Hanover students counted the annual trip, called the All College Boat Ride, as a highlight of the spring semester. Local citizens also participated in the annual rite. (Courtesy HC.)

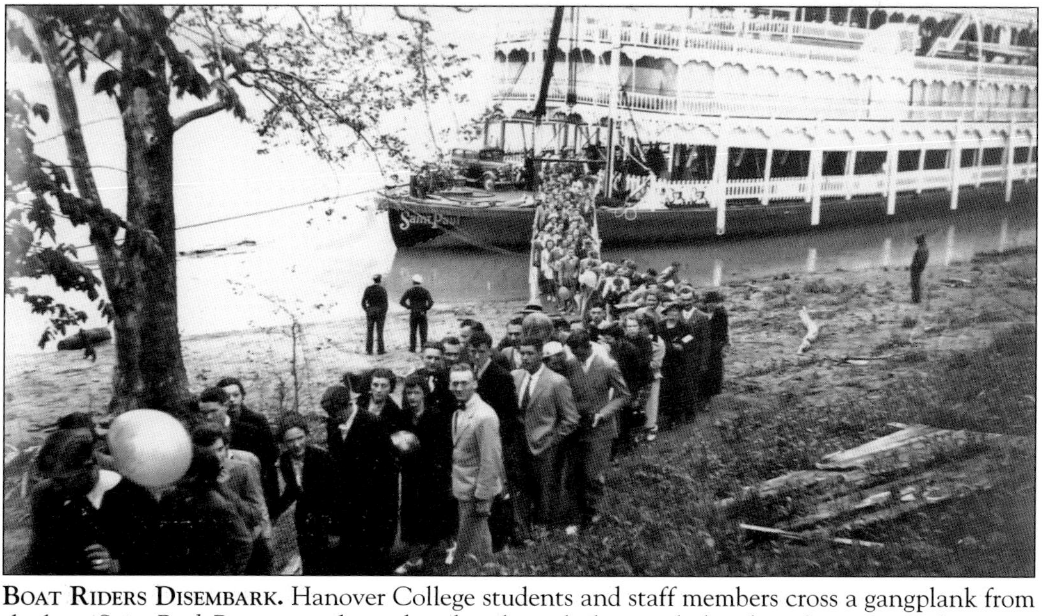

Boat Riders Disembark. Hanover College students and staff members cross a gangplank from the boat *Saint Paul*. Passengers dressed in their best clothes, including hats for some, in this 1930s image. Their day trip is completed and they look satisfied but are perhaps sad that the trip is over. (Courtesy HC.)

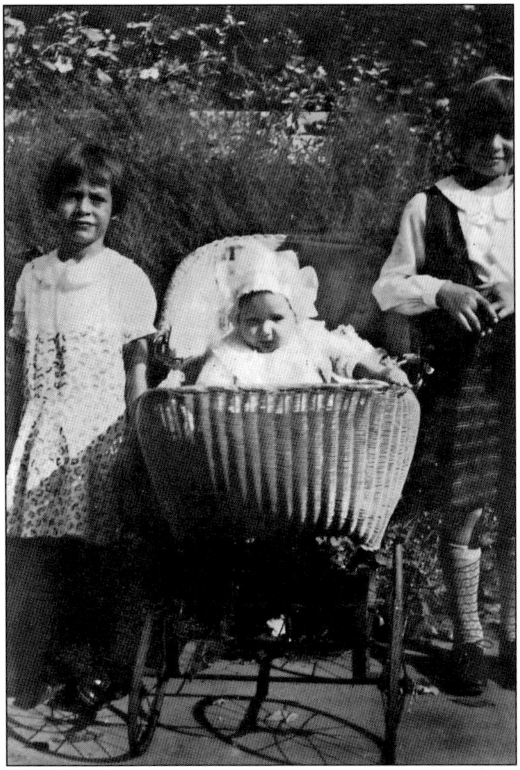

TEACHER SITS DURING OUTING. Marlyn Duke Finnegan sports a starched bonnet as she sits up in her baby carriage about 1932. She was born in Hanover, graduated from Hanover College, and taught English for 36 years in grades seven to 12. Marlyn's cousin Edna poses on the left with another cousin Doris on the right. Marlyn still has this carriage and uses it to display dolls. (Courtesy D/M.)

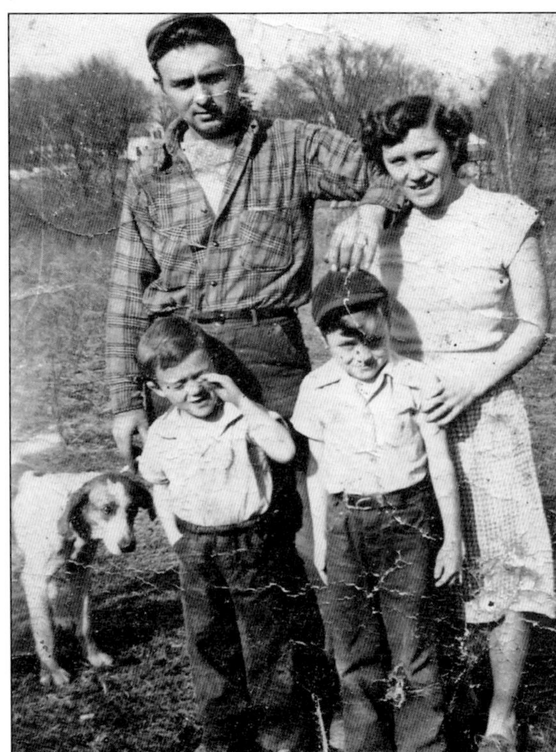

MARSH FAMILY GATHERS IN 1950. Robert Eugene Marsh stands on the left at the edge of the Neighbert orchard. His brother Charles ("Fred") Fredrick Marsh stands next to him wearing a Cub Scouts hat. Their father, Charles Henry Marsh, stands behind them with their mother, Ruth Ellen Larison Marsh. Their dog Whitie, a long-legged beagle, had a good nose for rabbits. Fred has studied Hanover history for decades and has a special interest in waterfalls. (Courtesy Marsh family.)

HANOVER GIRL POSES AROUND 1947. Lynne Cooper Abner sits in front of Cooper's Corner. She grew up in Hanover and her mother and father operated the Corner, a gathering place for students and adults alike. Lynne graduated from Hanover High School in 1956. She attended Hanover College and is married to Ernie Abner. (Courtesy Lynne Cooper Abner family.)

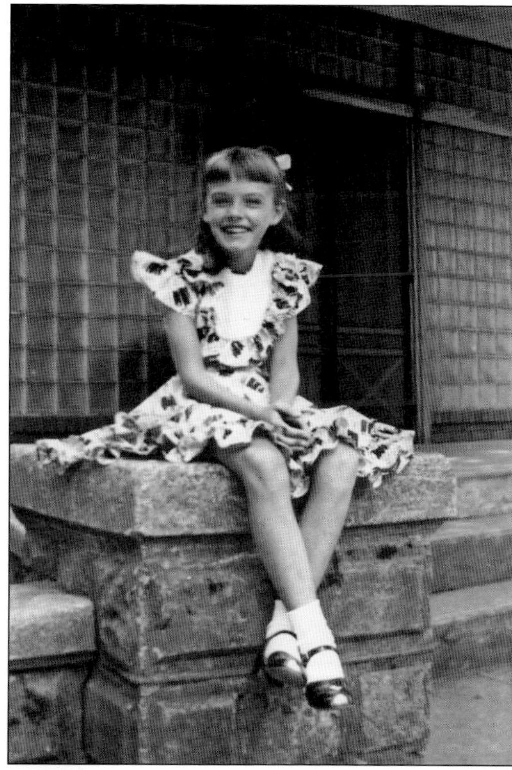

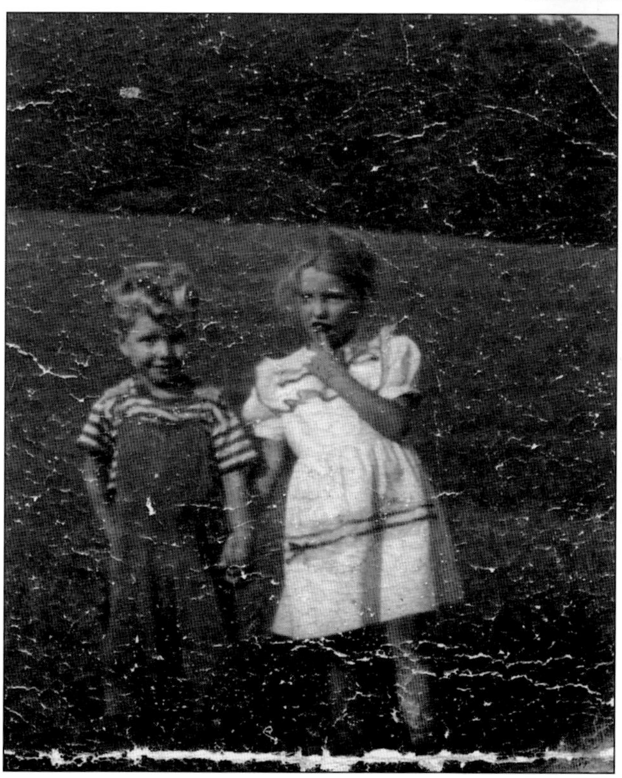

BROTHER AND SISTER FARMED. Local farmer Thermond Riley and his sister Dora Riley Kendricks hold hands in the late 1940s. Thermond and his wife, Marilyn Kingery, farmed on her family's 30-acre plot southwest of Hanover for 37 years. They had a son, Gregory Lee, who works in Madison. They grew tobacco, corn, wheat, and beans in addition to a large garden. (Courtesy Thermond Riley family.)

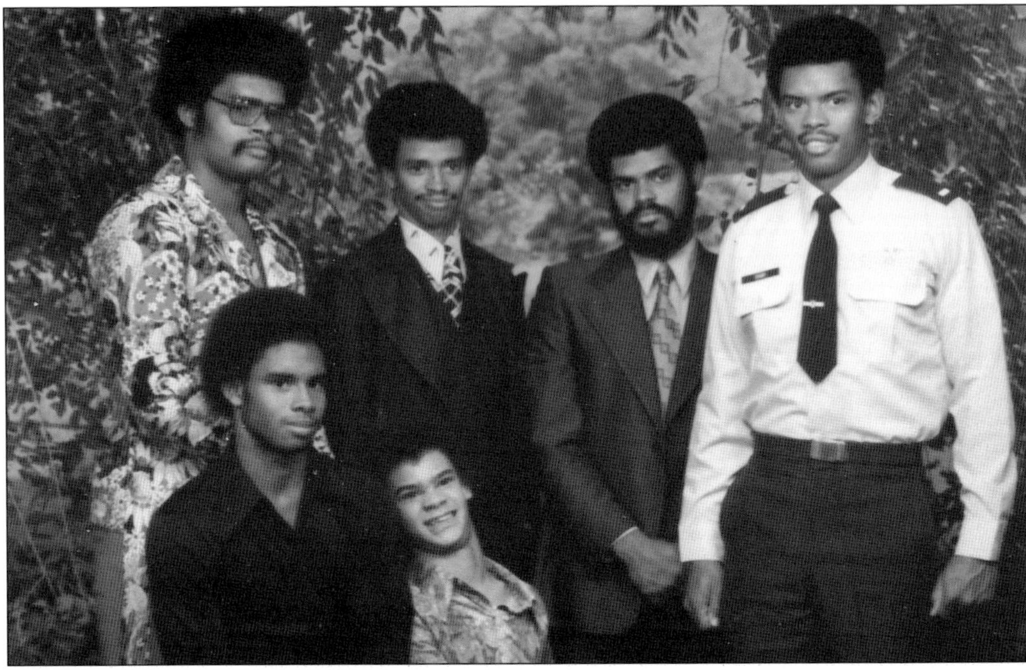

COSBY BROTHERS GATHER IN 1960S. All of the men pictured above were born in Hanover. Their father was Robert A. Cosby, who owned the Golden Rule Plumbing Company. Pictured are, from left to right, (first row) Isordor and Mark; (second row) Norman Gene, Eloyd, Robert Jr. ("Bobby"), and Rickey Joe, who retired from the U.S. Air Force as a pilot. (Courtesy John D. and Freda Johnson Cosby family.)

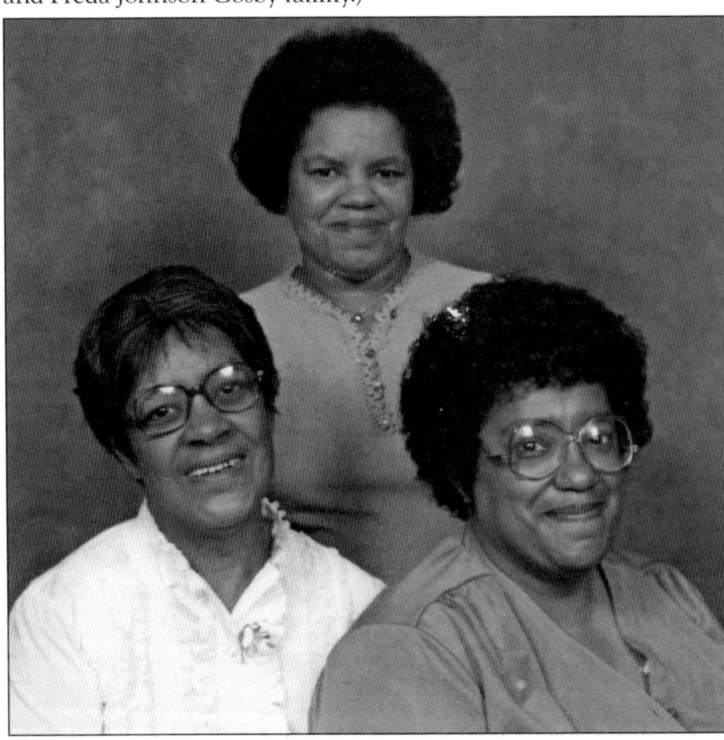

MOTHER AND DAUGHTERS POSE. Mother Freda Johnson Cosby, left, trained to become a registered nurse in Chicago. Wanda Cosby Lacy, center, was a certified nursing assistant and cosmetologist. Davidteen Cosby Watson, right, worked at Madison State Hospital. Freda still lives in Hanover and is 99 years old. (Courtesy John D. and Freda Johnson Cosby.)

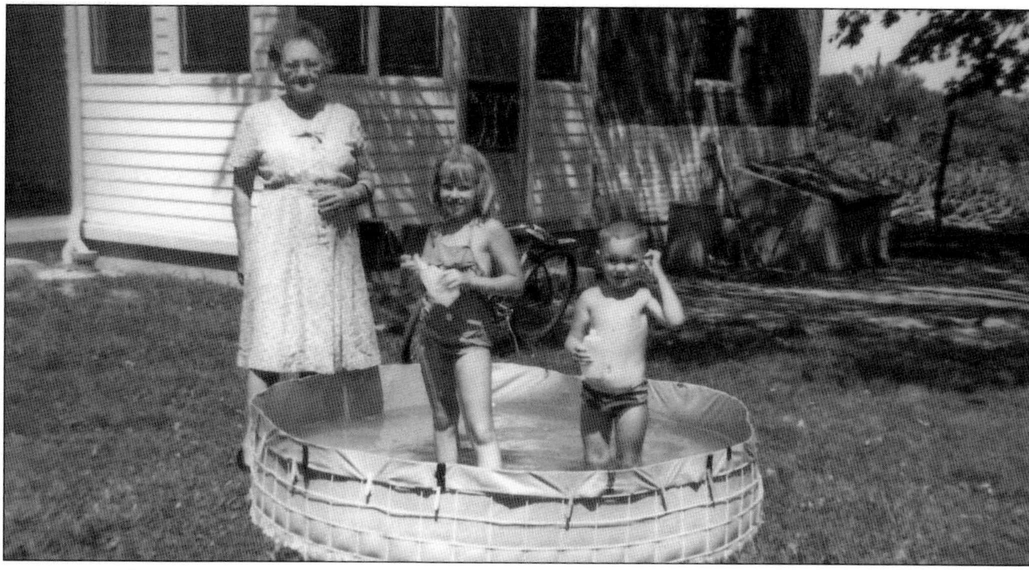

Children Cool off during Summer. Tom Hatton began keeping bees in 4-H. He now has about 200,000 honey bees in hives on the property seen above. In this photograph, Tom and his sister Patsy take time to splash around in July 1963. Their babysitter Clara Poland watches them. The house visible in the background started out as a three-room schoolhouse in 1826. (Courtesy Tom Hatton family.)

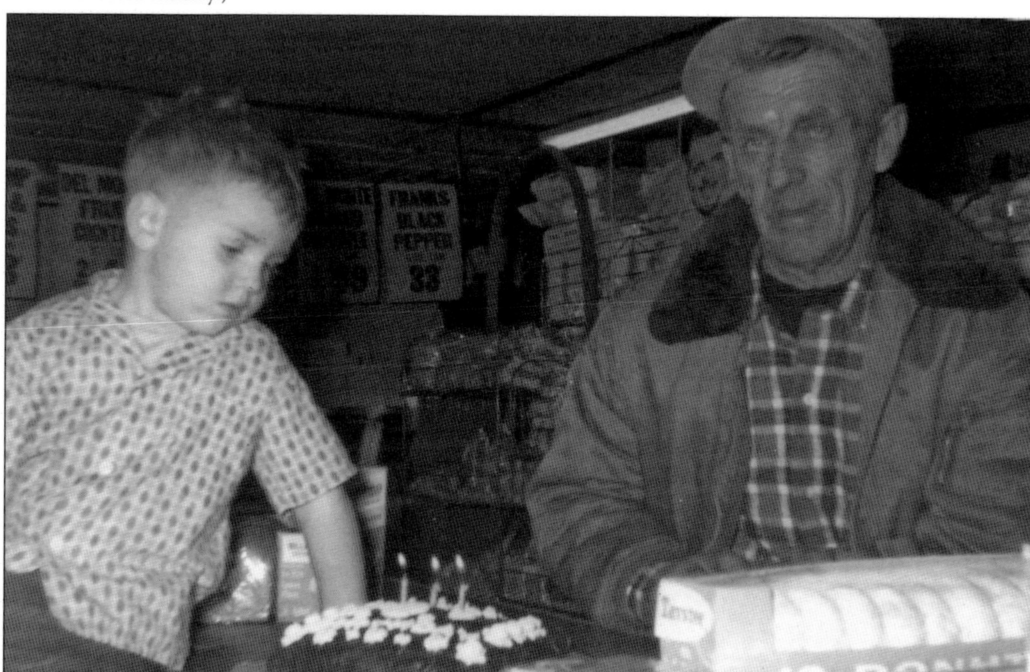

Third Birthday Celebrated. Judd Martin looks on as three-year-old Randy Cole checks out his birthday cake. Locals tell about a time when a farmer's cow got loose and came to Randy's bedroom window, stuck its head in, and gave Randy's face a big lick—perhaps the world's most unusual wake up call. As an adult, Randy rounded up an escaped baby buffalo on Main Cross Street. (Courtesy Cole family.)

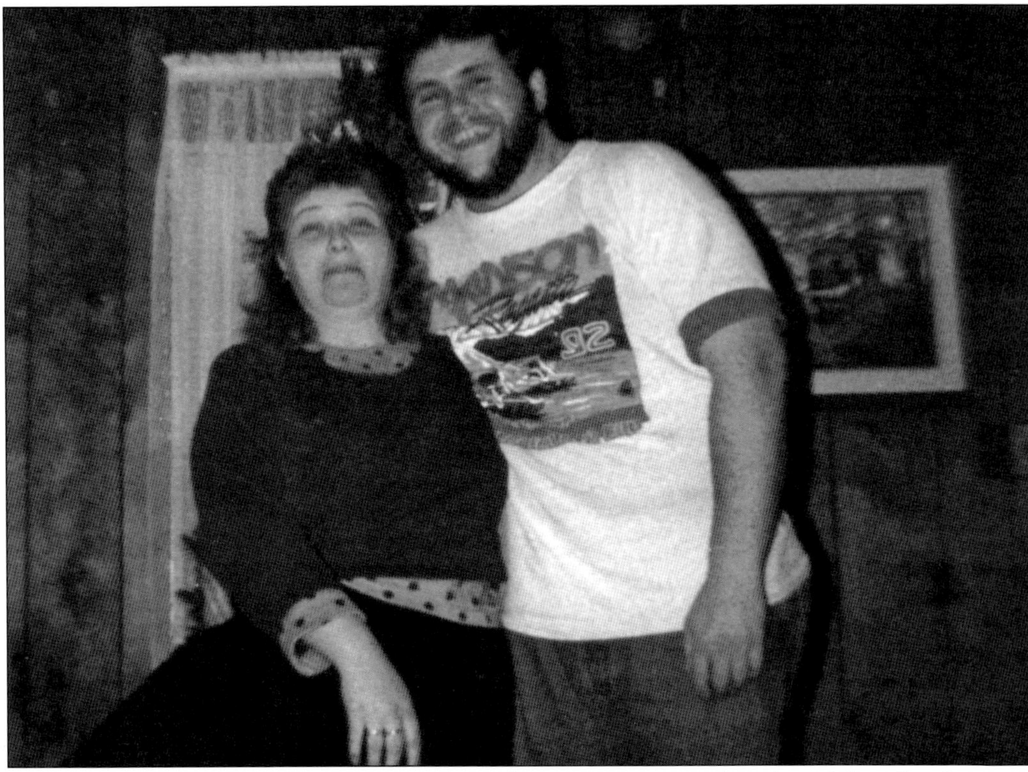

Husband and Wife Hug. Darrell Lee Lock was born in Hanover and graduated from Southwestern High School in 1980. He has been in business for himself for 30 years with Lock's Lawn Care. He and his wife, Lisa Kay Brooks, who is pictured above with Darrell, have six children. She works at Kroger. (Courtesy Lock family.)

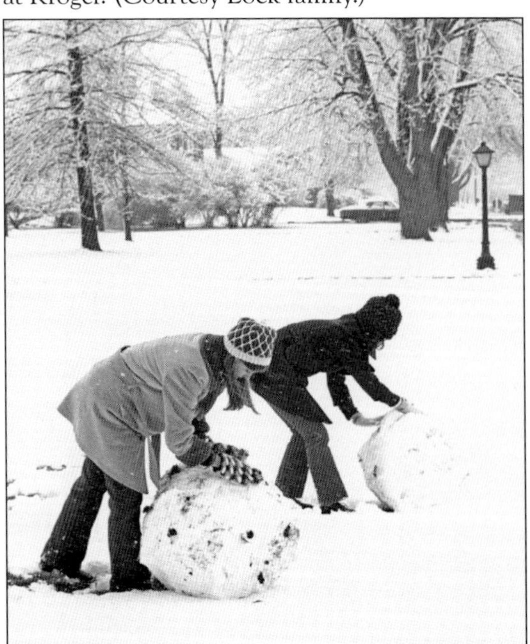

Snowfall Challenges Builders. Unidentified Hanover College students take time to roll snow into giant balls. Students were still expected to go to class when it snowed—and still are. They did receive two days off when the Ohio River flooded in 1937. (Courtesy HC.)

SWEETHEARTS MARRY. Donna Jean Dattilo and William "Bill" Paul Jackson married in 1959. They own their home in Hanover and Bill's business too, The Hanover Barber Shop. A farm of nearly 80 acres has been in Bill's family since 1844. The couple has four daughters: Julie Anna Jackson Berry, Paula Jean Jackson Berry, Laura Diane Jackson McCarty, and Mary Beth Jackson Boone. (Courtesy Bill Jackson Family.)

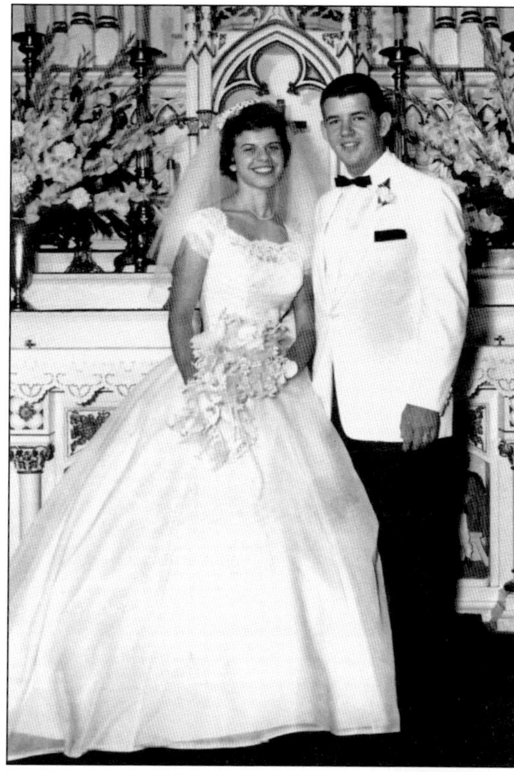

FAMILY FORMS BASEBALL TEAM. The Adams family had a lot of sons and a lot of athletic talent. They started a baseball team, pictured below. Shown in 1957 are, from left to right, (first row) Luther Adams, Newton "Newt" Adams (father), Albert Adams, Floyd Adams, and Donald Duke; (second row) Jack Weber, Melvin Adams, Jim Selig, Orville Selig, Bob Black, Clifford Adams, Willard Adams, and Robert Adams. (Courtesy Bill Jackson family.)

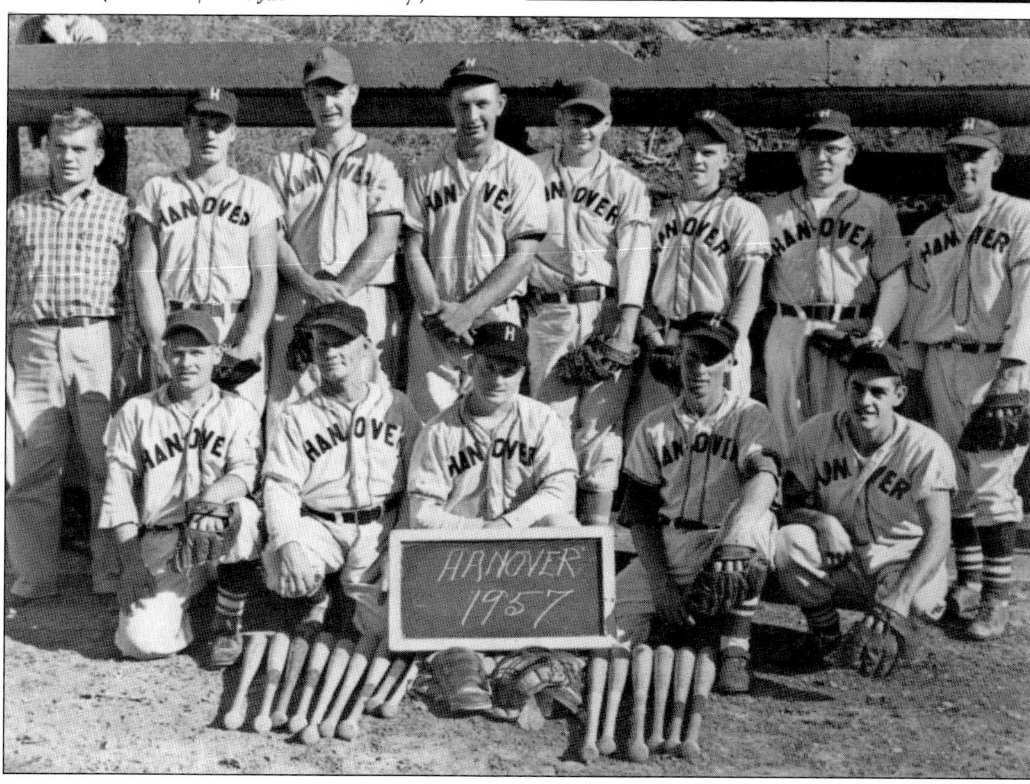

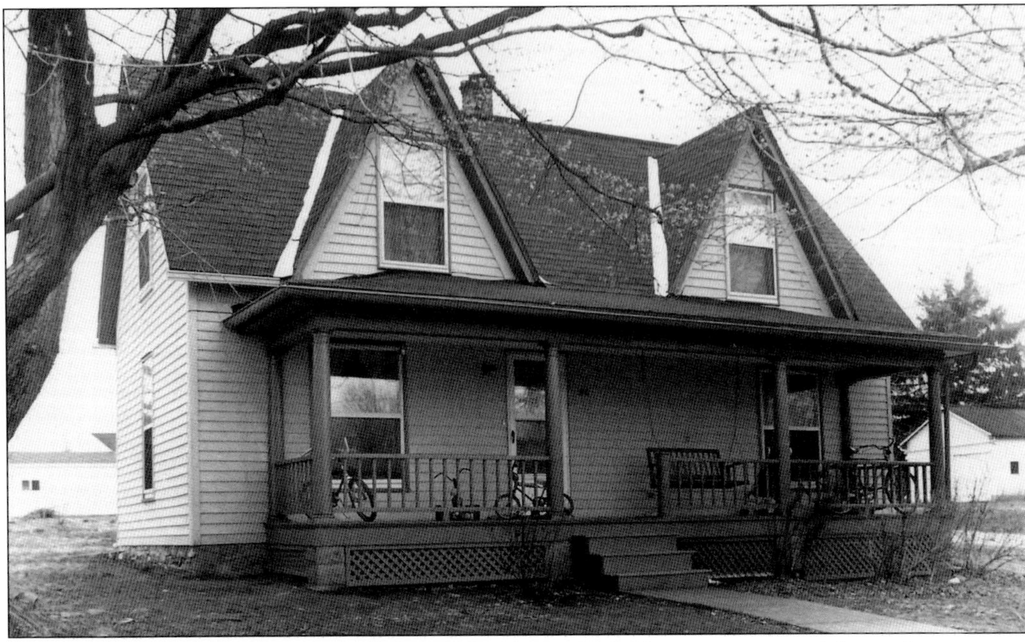

House Started as a School. The Corrie Saphenfield House was moved from the corner of Riverview Drive and Highway 56-62 to its present location in Hanover around 1900. Before becoming the back of the house pictured above, the building was a one-room schoolhouse named the Beech Grove School. The Corrie family added on to the room, creating a seven-room home. (Courtesy HC.)

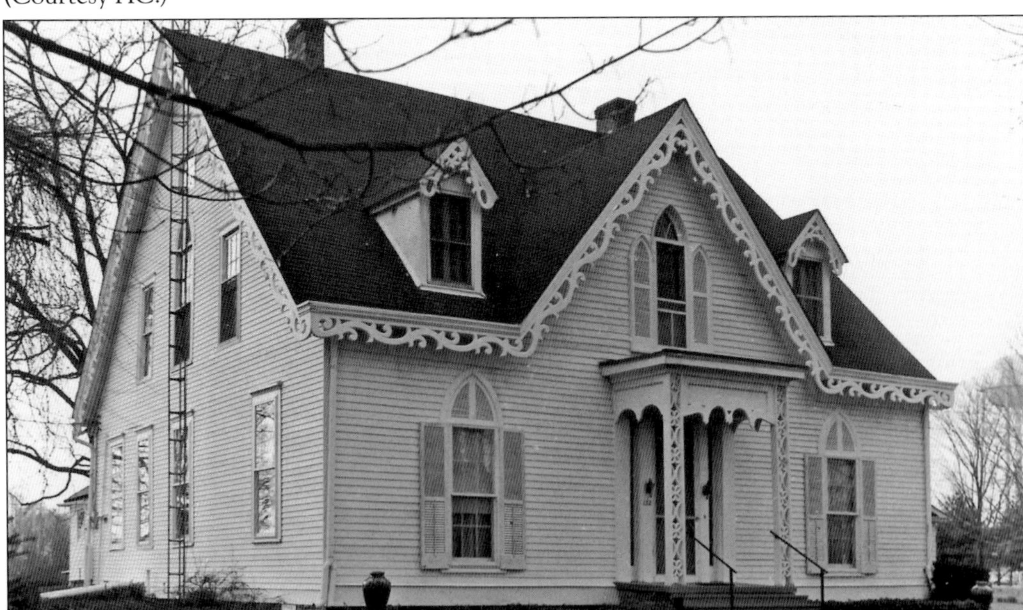

Rogers House Known as "Bird Haven." Built in 1858, the Henry Carter Rogers House, photographed here in 1977, was once a small hotel before the time of bed-and-breakfast operations. The Carpenter Gothic–style structure is one of only two such homes in Indiana according to today's owners, Bill and June Rogers. (Courtesy HC.)

Hanover Beach Famous for Serenity. Families have gathered for more than 100 years at Hanover Beach. Visitors sat in lounge chairs to talk and watch river traffic. A boat can be seen steaming upriver toward Cincinnati. Other boats included tugs pushing barges loaded with freight and pleasure craft. A local historian reports boat races took place. The dock afforded visitors a chance to sun, swim, and dive. (Courtesy LC.)

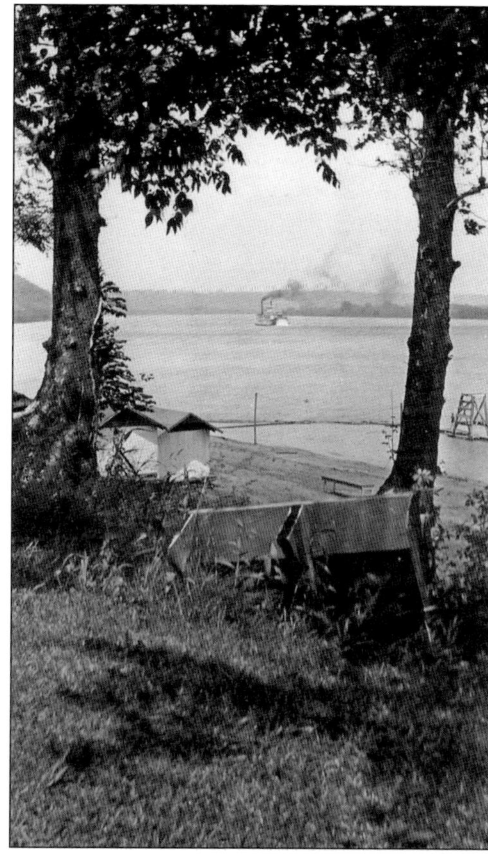

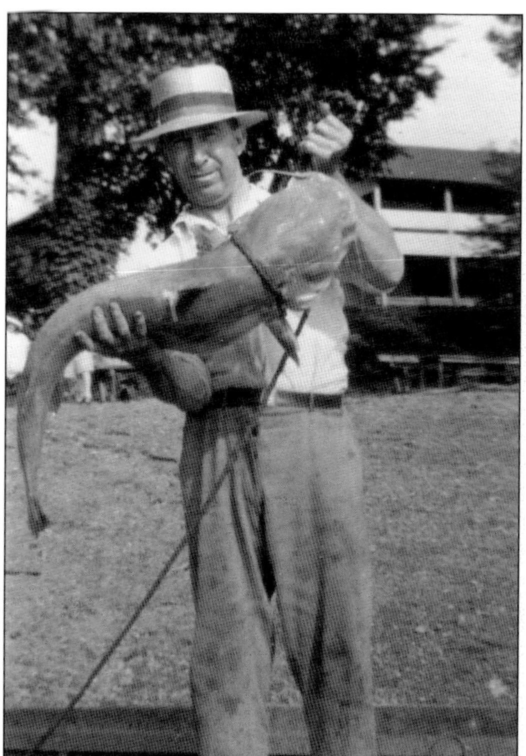

Man Shows off His Catch. Ed Andres holds a catfish he caught at Hanover Beach. A caption accompanying the photograph in the archives at the Jefferson County Historical Society reads, "Show it [the fish] to your Florida friends and tell them this is the size of the minnows in the Ohio River." Another unrelated fish story involves a catfish so big the entire Presbyterian church was fed in the 1920s. (Courtesy JC.)

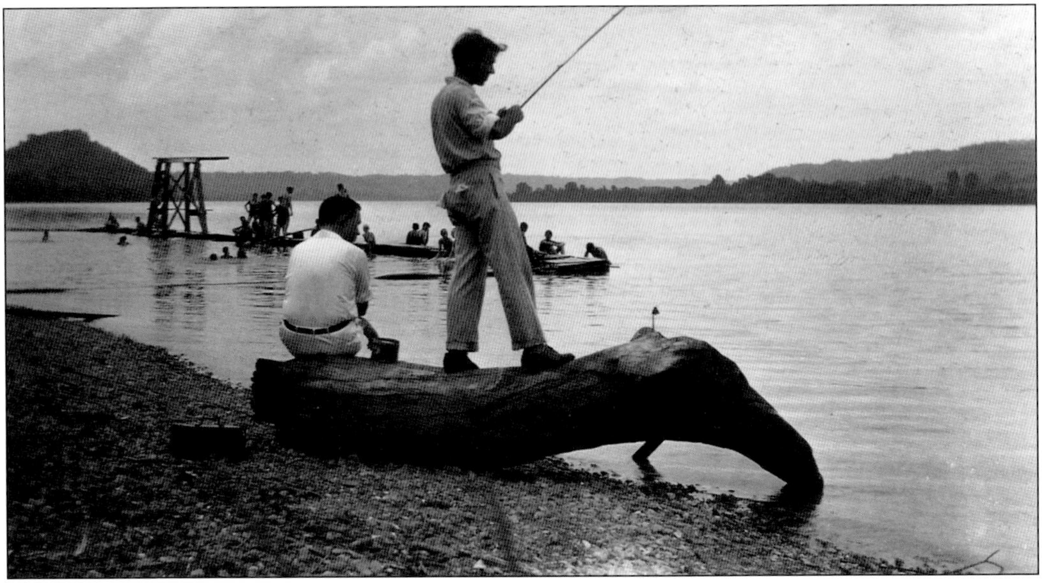

A Place to Swim, Fish, Hike. A man fishes in the Ohio River while his companion looks across the river toward Kentucky. In the background, a group of swimmers enjoy the water at Hanover Beach. Devil's Backbone can be seen on the far left. Children and adults alike considered climbing up the "backbone" to be a feat to be bragged about for years. (Courtesy LC.)

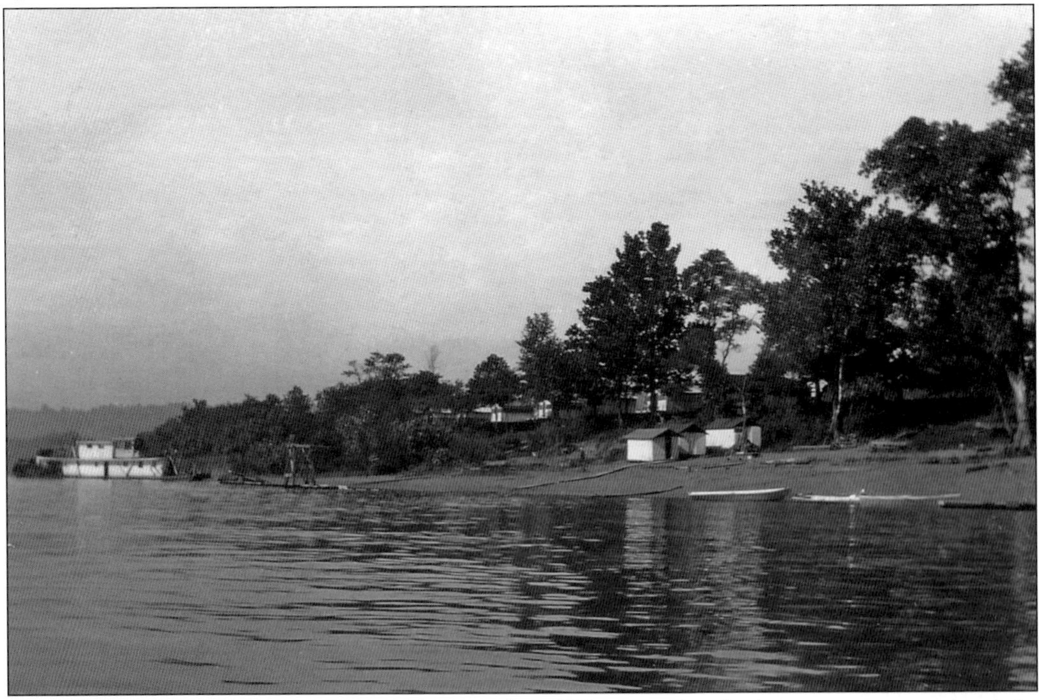

Peek to Beach from River. Most photographs of Hanover Beach show activities on land. In this unique photograph taken in the late 1920s or early 1930s, the reader can see some of the cottages nestled on the river bank, a dock, a powerboat, and some smaller boats used for paddling up and down the Ohio River. Some of the same people came each summer to enjoy the popular site. (Courtesy LC.)

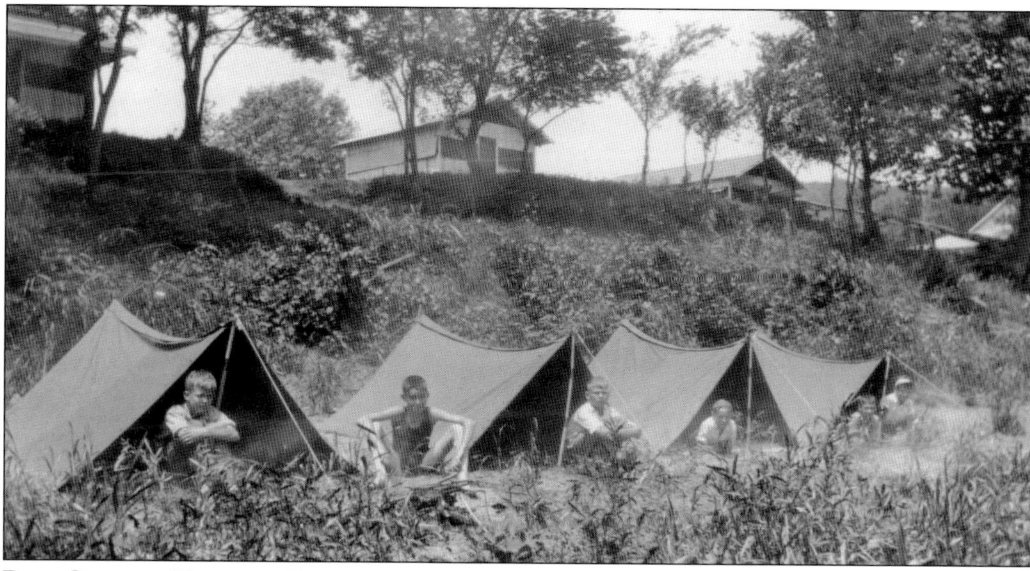

Boys Camp at Hanover Beach. A group of boys have pitched tents on the banks of the Ohio River in the late 1930s. Their other family members would have slept in the cabins up higher on the river bank behind the tents. The boys are identified as, from left to right, Robert Gourley, George Miller, unidentified, possibly Robert Cox, and two unidentified. Miller wrote newspaper columns for the *Madison Courier* in Jefferson County from 1964 until 1995. (Courtesy JC.)

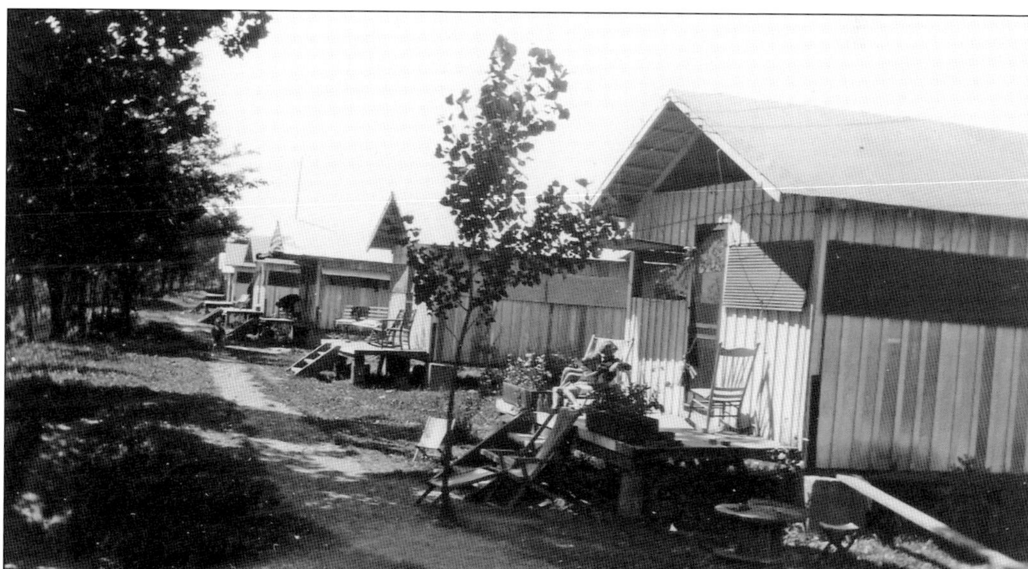

Cottages Offer Relaxation at Riverside. Seasonal cottages were enjoyed by owners and also rented to those who wanted a taste of leisurely river life at Hanover Beach. Visitors gathered for home-cooked meals at what was called the Lodge. The fare included an entrée of perhaps fish or chicken and vegetables from nearby farms. And there was the pie! Elle Rogers's pies were famously delicious. (Courtesy JC.)

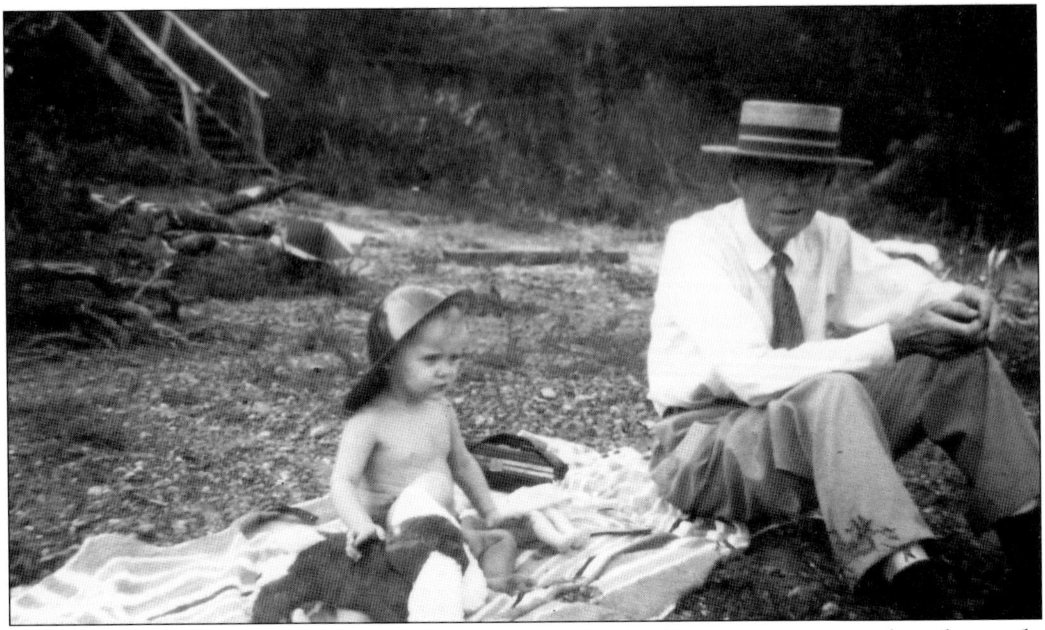

BELOVED DOCTOR RELAXES AT HANOVER BEACH. Dr. Carl Henning is remembered warmly by Hanover historians who were his patients. He is pictured above with an unidentified baby, perhaps a grandchild. Henning married Rispa Adelaide Robertson in 1912. He served as a doctor during World War I and was a member of the Jefferson County Medical Society. (Courtesy Marsh family.)

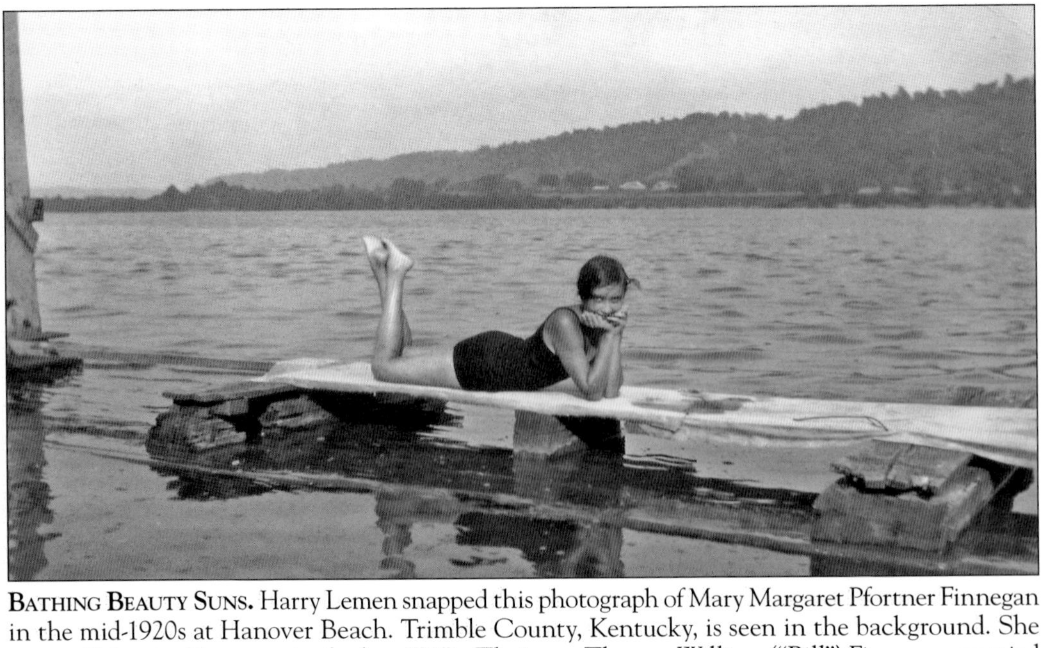

BATHING BEAUTY SUNS. Harry Lemen snapped this photograph of Mary Margaret Pfortner Finnegan in the mid-1920s at Hanover Beach. Trimble County, Kentucky, is seen in the background. She married Maurice Finnegan in the late 1920s. Their son Thomas William ("Bill") Finnegan married Marlyn Jean Duke in 1957. (Courtesy D/M.)

Three

Farming and Industry

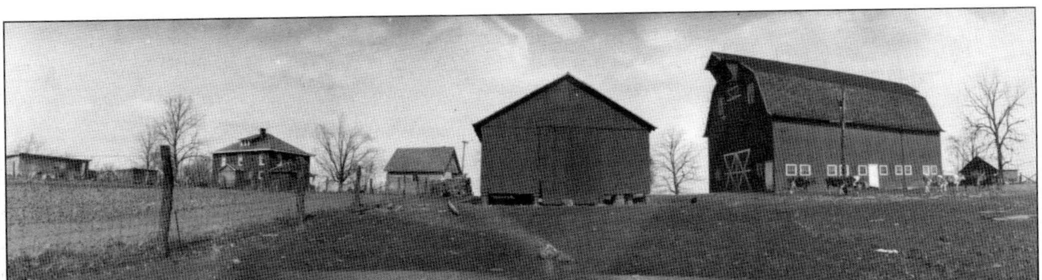

Early European Settlers Farmed. The work and business of Hanover in its first 100 years mostly had to do with farming and Hanover College. The picture above shows the Robert Joseph Craig Farm in the early 1930s. Farmers and farming as well as other workers through the years are featured in this chapter. (Courtesy HC.)

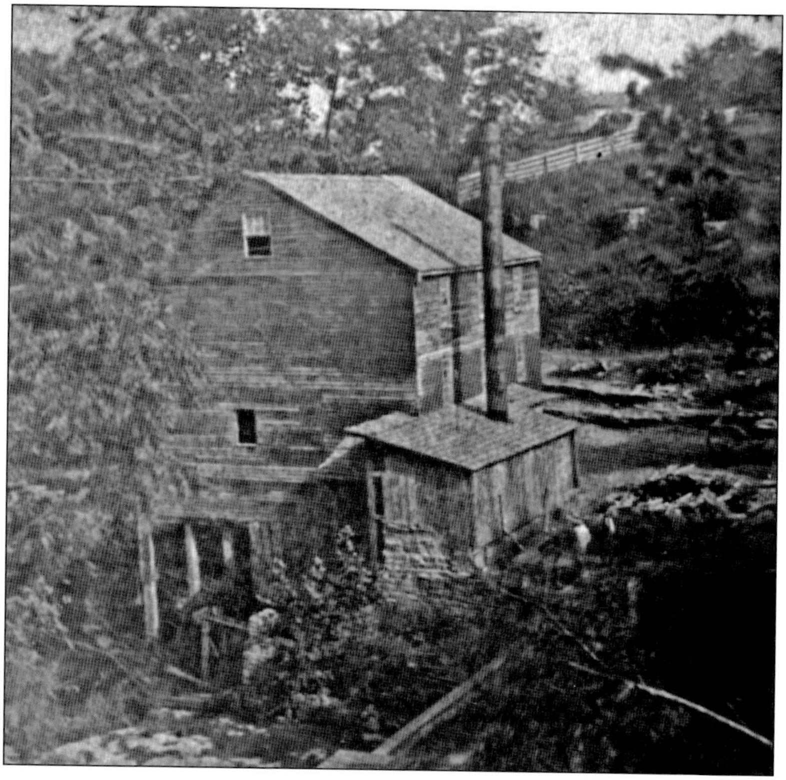

People Gather to Grind. The building associated with the gristmill called Chain Mill Falls can be seen in this faded, extremely rare image dating from the 1880s. The grinding of grain was done by harnessing the power of a stream and waterfall with a series of buckets on a chain, which turned a shaft. That shaft was geared to operate a 1-ton millstone about 4 feet in diameter and 8 inches thick. (Courtesy LC.)

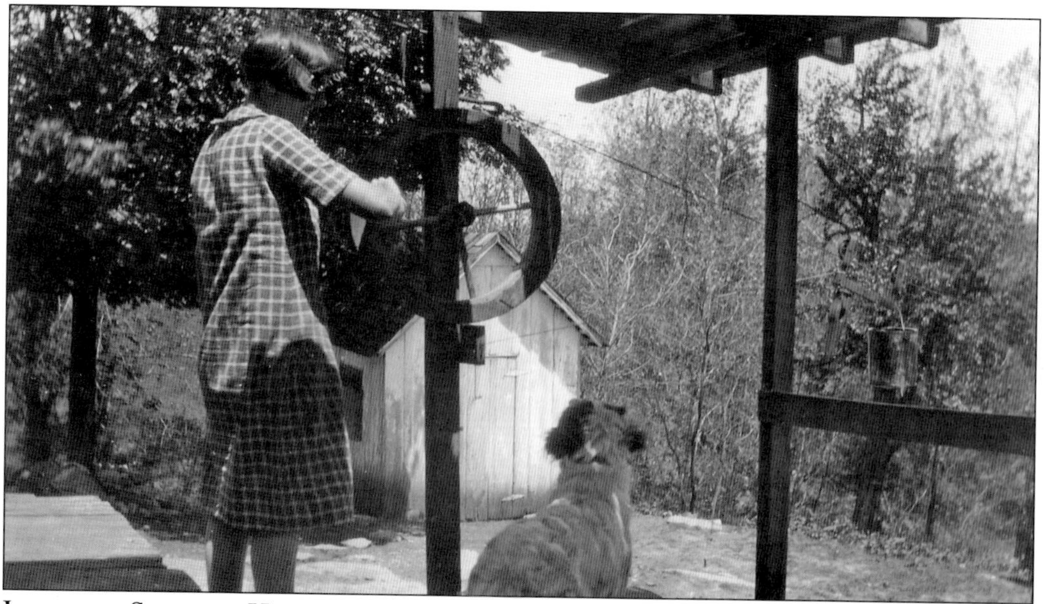

Invention Simplifies Housework. A pulley attached to a post made fetching water easier. In the early 1900s, the woman in this image, who may be Julia Spry, turns the wheel to move the bucket attached to the line in the right of the picture. The bucket was guided toward Chain Mill Falls, filled, and then pulled back to the house. (Courtesy LC.)

FARM FAMILY TAKES A BREAK. The Dukes and Means families provided most of the farm images used in this book. Not only were they hardworking farmers, they also took numerous, artfully-arranged photographs. Pictured in this 1920s photograph are, from left to right, (first row) Georgia Means, Ella Mae Means Bruther, and Mittie Means; (second row) Andy Means and Louis ("Lou") Means. (Courtesy D/M.)

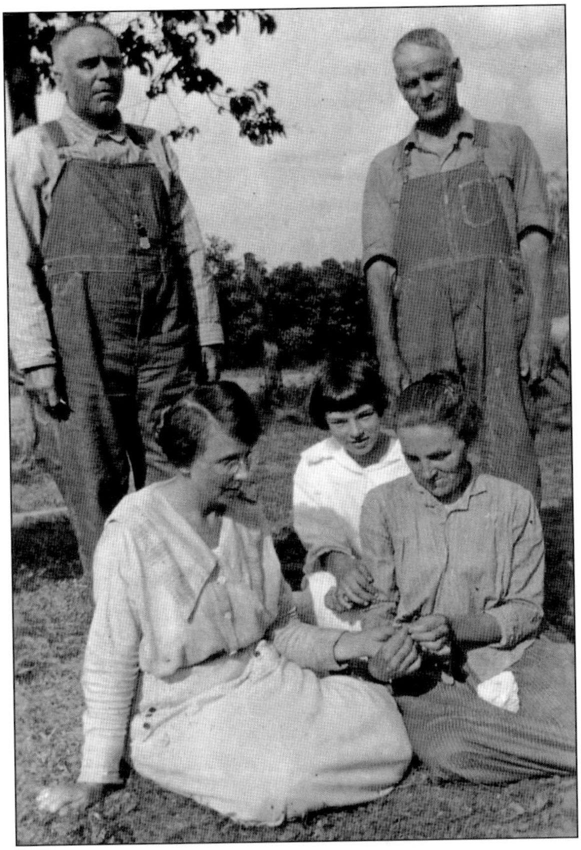

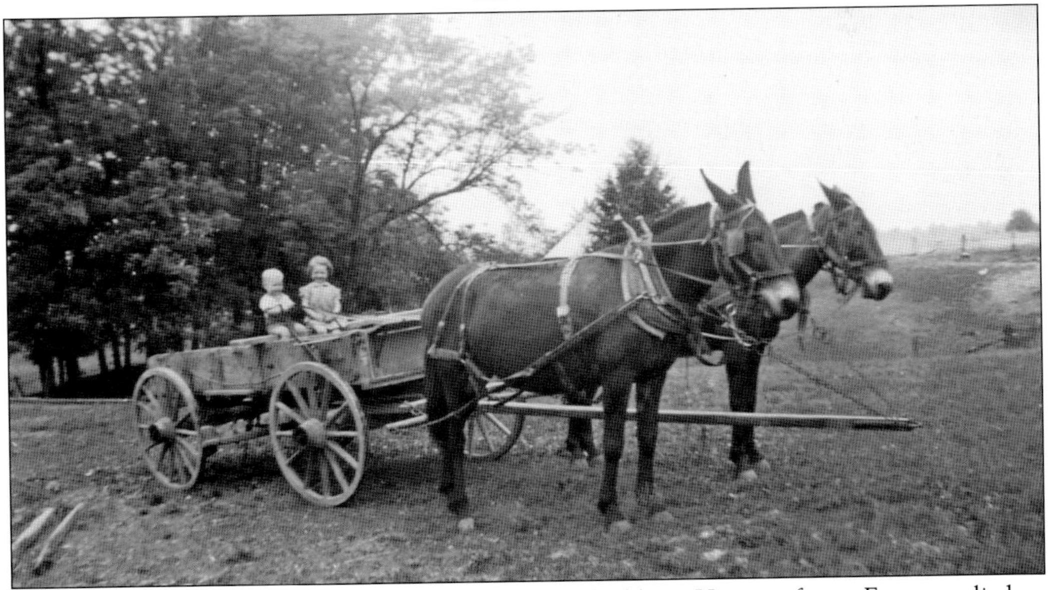

FARMS DEPEND ON MULES. Mules and horses were invaluable on Hanover farms. Farmers relied on them to help with difficult work and invested a lot of resources to keep them healthy and happy. Bill and Betty Moore pretend to drive their mules Kate and Jerry in the late 1930s. (Courtesy William L. Moore family.)

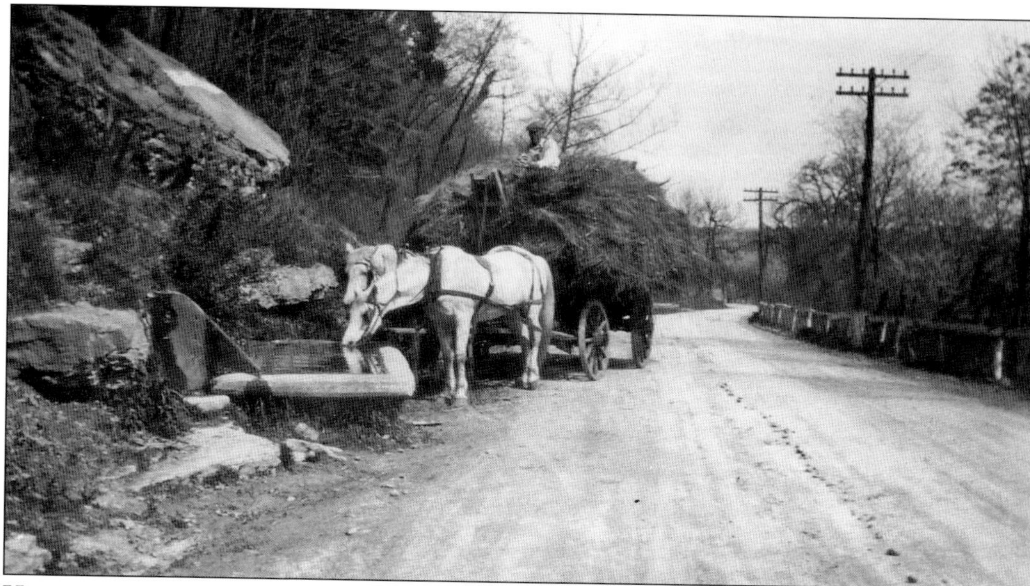

Horses Drink at Their Trough. A farmer stops to let his horses drink from a trough on Hanover Hill Road (Highway 56) in the 1920s. The horse trough has been eliminated because now cars, not horses, zip back and forth between Hanover and Madison. (Courtesy LC.)

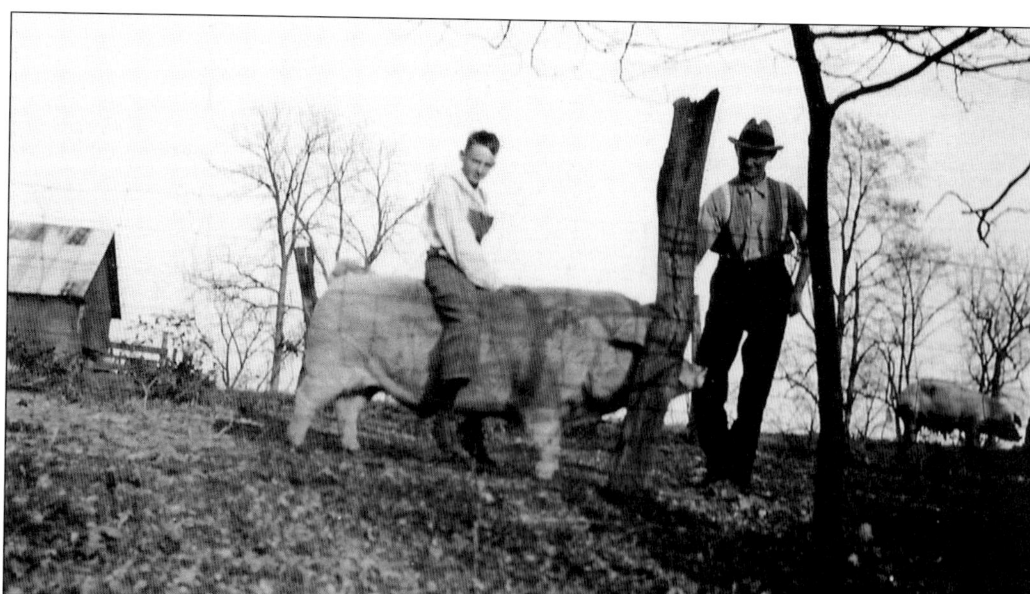

Farmer Rides Hog. Robert Craig Sr. watches as his son Robert Jr. sits on the back of one of their prize hogs in 1929. Robert Sr. was recognized as Indiana's Farmer of the Year in about 1924 for his innovation and success. Robert Jr. graduated from Hanover College in 1935, served in the U.S. Army, and operated a Marathon service station in Hanover for more than 25 years. (Courtesy Craig/Cowen family.)

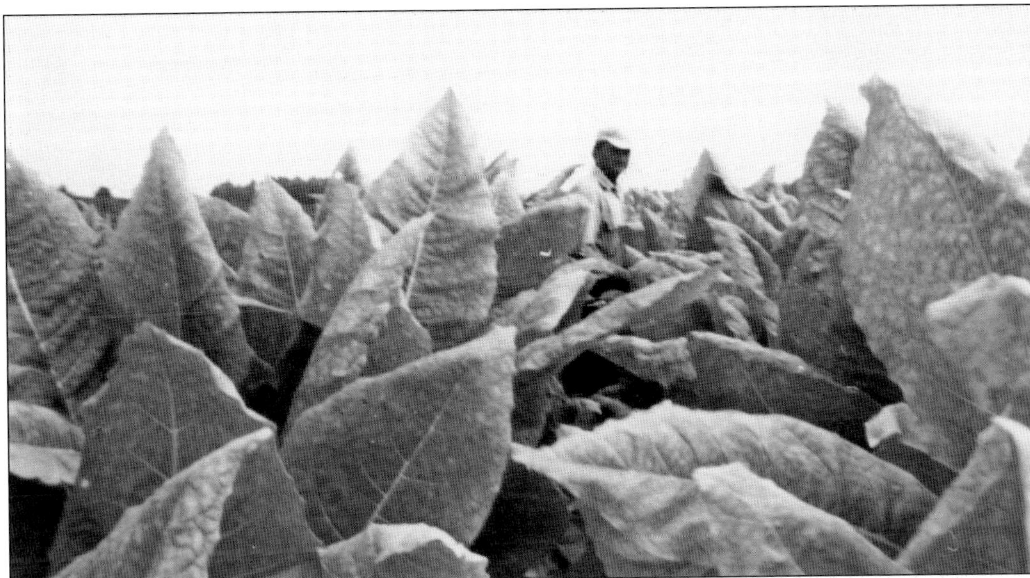

TOBACCO ENDURES AS CASH CROP. Freddie Harrell stands in his tobacco patch in the 1930s. His farm was west of Wirt, about 9 miles from Hanover. Of all the crops a farmer could plant, a successful tobacco crop would bring the highest cash return per acre. Getting tobacco ready to cut took a lot of hard work, much of it by hand. (Courtesy Bill and Janice Sanders.)

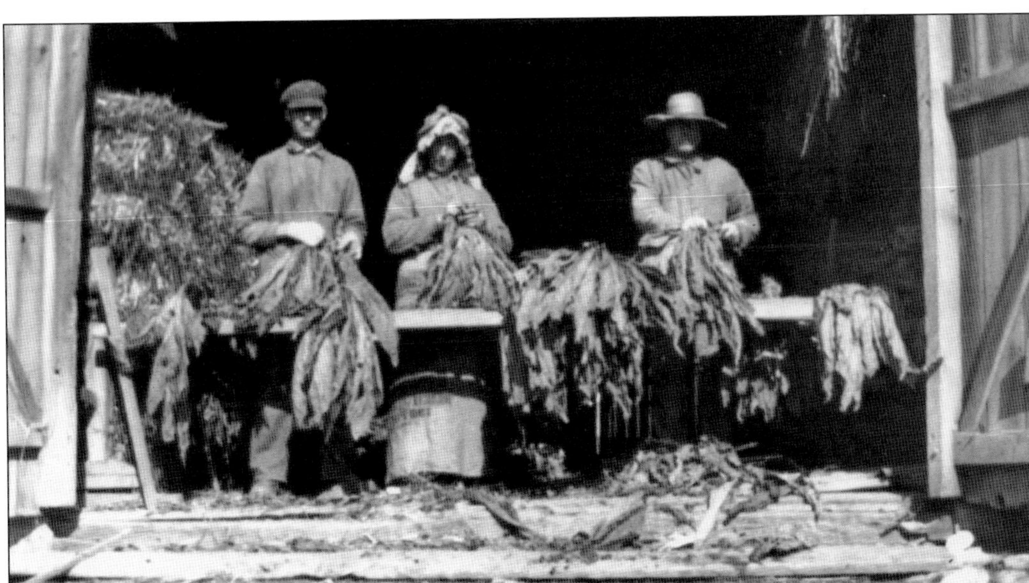

TOBACCO GRADING TAKES SKILL. From left to right, Roy Beach, Georgia Means, and Andrew Means strip tobacco off drying poles around 1920 and grade it according to the bottom leaves. Six or seven grades included from the "lugs" (the best) to the "trash" (the most raggedy). The better the grade, the more the tobacco sold for. (Courtesy D/M.)

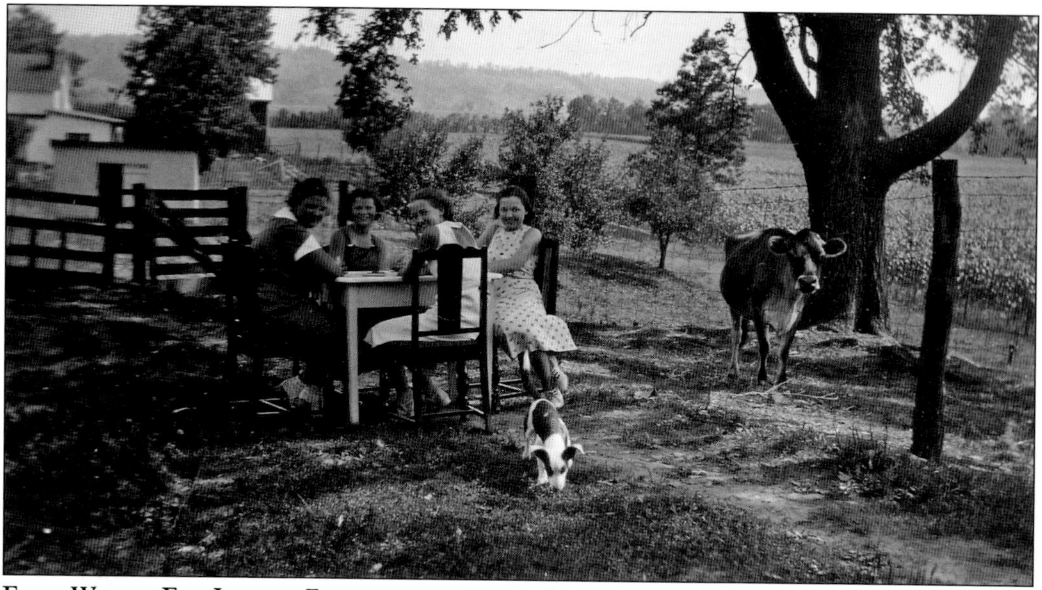

Farm Women Eat Lunch. Farm women stop working to eat a quick lunch. Their picture was snapped in the 1920s by Harry Lemen, who often drove around taking pictures. The dog is sniffing in the grass or getting ready to charge at Harry. Even the cow is curious! While the identities of the women are not known, they represent the spirit of Midwestern people—hardworking, friendly, and gentle. (Courtesy LC.)

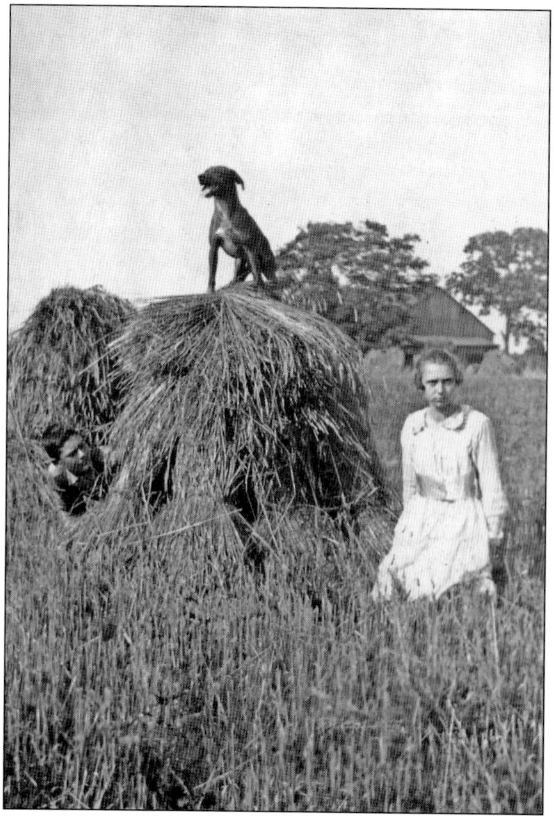

Dog Keeps Watch. Roy Beach peeps around a pile of hay on the Means Farm around 1915. Pearl Means is looking at the camera. Hay was stored in a barn and used to feed animals during the winter. Freddie the dog is perched on top of the pile. (Courtesy D/M.)

Young Farmer Stands in Corn. Around 1930, Roy Beach looks over the corn crop as he holds a hoe. Corn grown in large fields like this was often used for silage, which is what is eaten by cattle and hogs after it has been processed. (Courtesy D/M.)

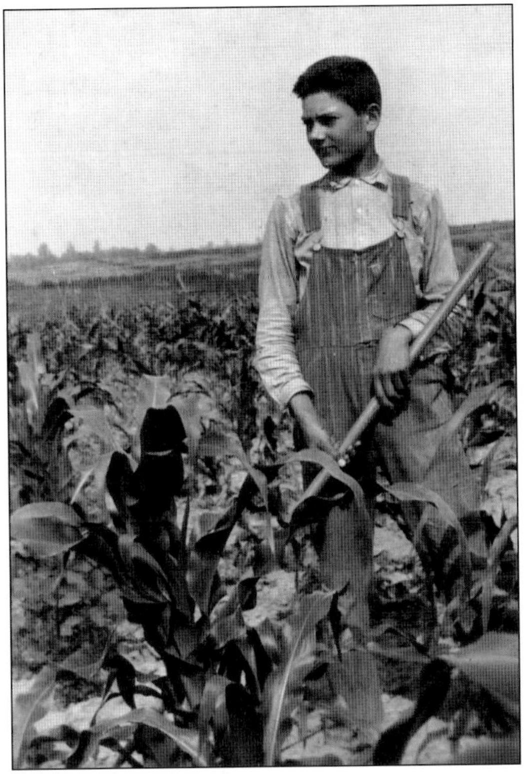

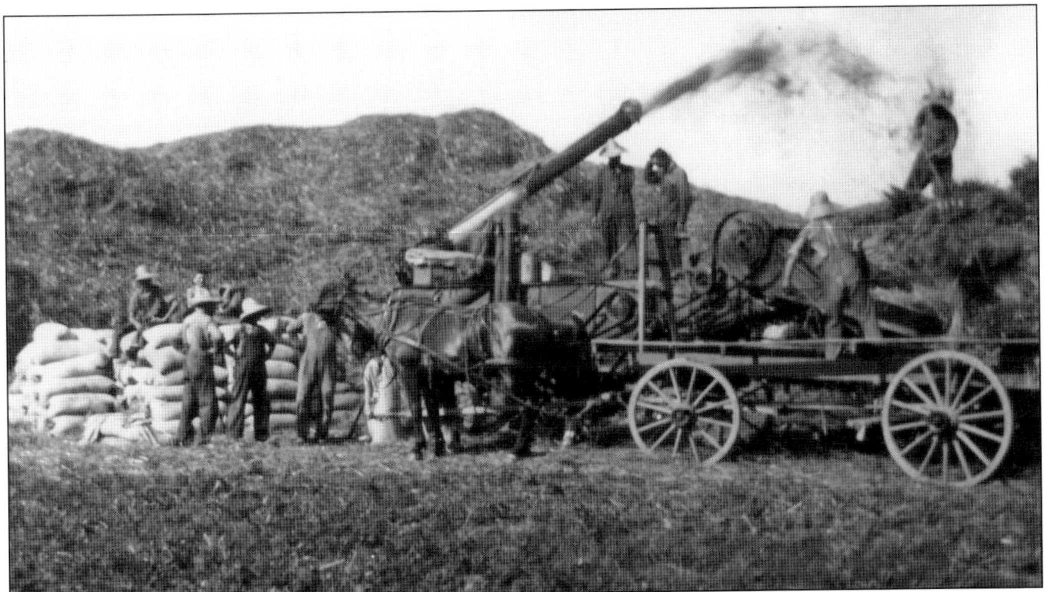

Threshers Work Hard. In this vintage 1920s image, threshers are separating wheat from the other plant residue and putting the wheat into sacks, which are stacked to the left in the photograph. An outside contractor who owned a threshing machine worked with farmers and their friends in teams to handle the demanding job. The expression "cooking for threshers" came from the meals provided by the farmer's wife and her relatives and friends. Threshers ate feasts of fried chicken, mashed potatoes, vegetables, homemade biscuits, pies, and cakes. (Courtesy D/M.)

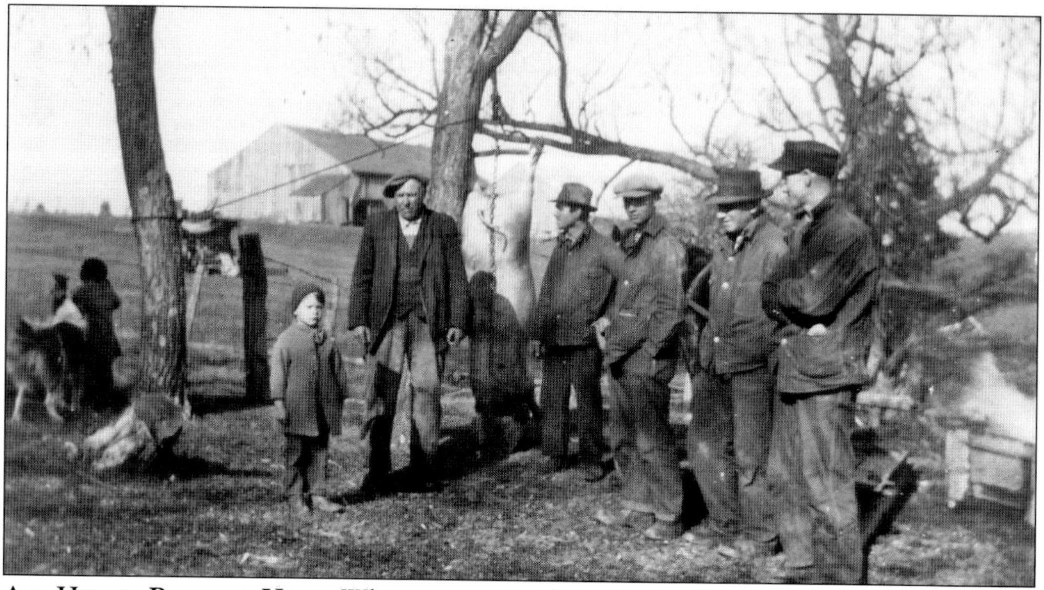

All Helped Butcher Hogs. When anyone butchered hogs, friends and family helped each other with the big job. From left to right, Raymond Duke, Andy Means, Clifford Duke, Clarence Baylor, Charlie Baylor, and George Fresh gathered at Andy Means's farm around 1920. (Courtesy D/M.)

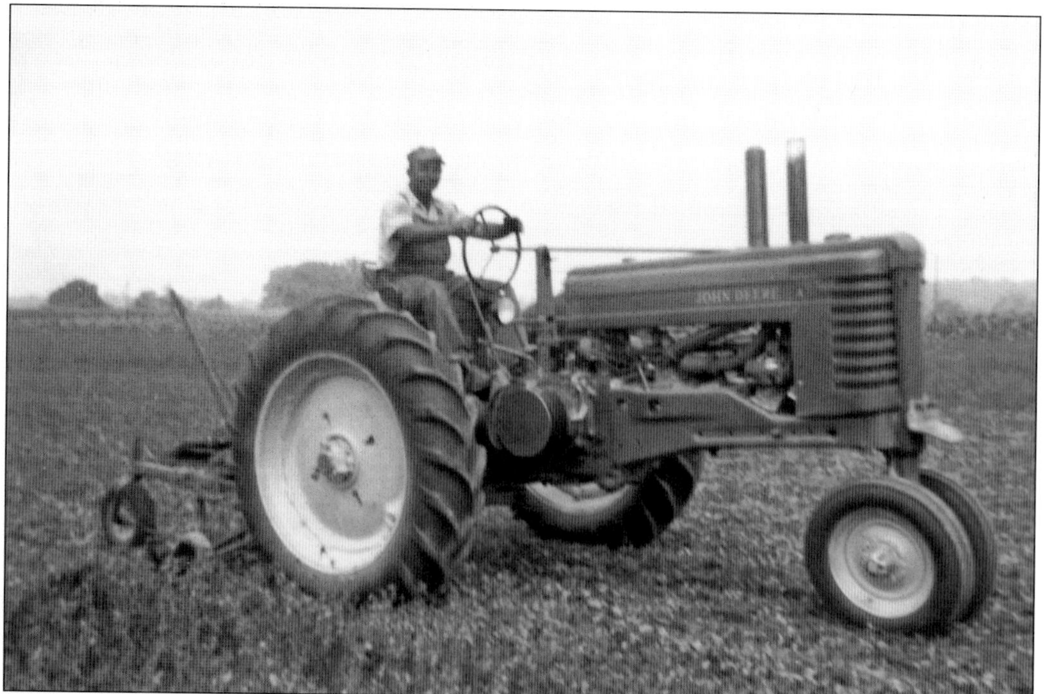

Farmer Plows with John Deere. B. T. Brawner rides his John Deere "A" bought in 1949. He is mowing hay with a No. 5 John Deere mower. He and his son Paul Joe Brawner worked what is now a four-generation farm of 641 acres called Brawner Farms. The organic farm is operated today by Greg and Teresa, B. T.'s grandson and granddaughter-in-law, and their son Gregory. (Courtesy B. T. Brawner family.)

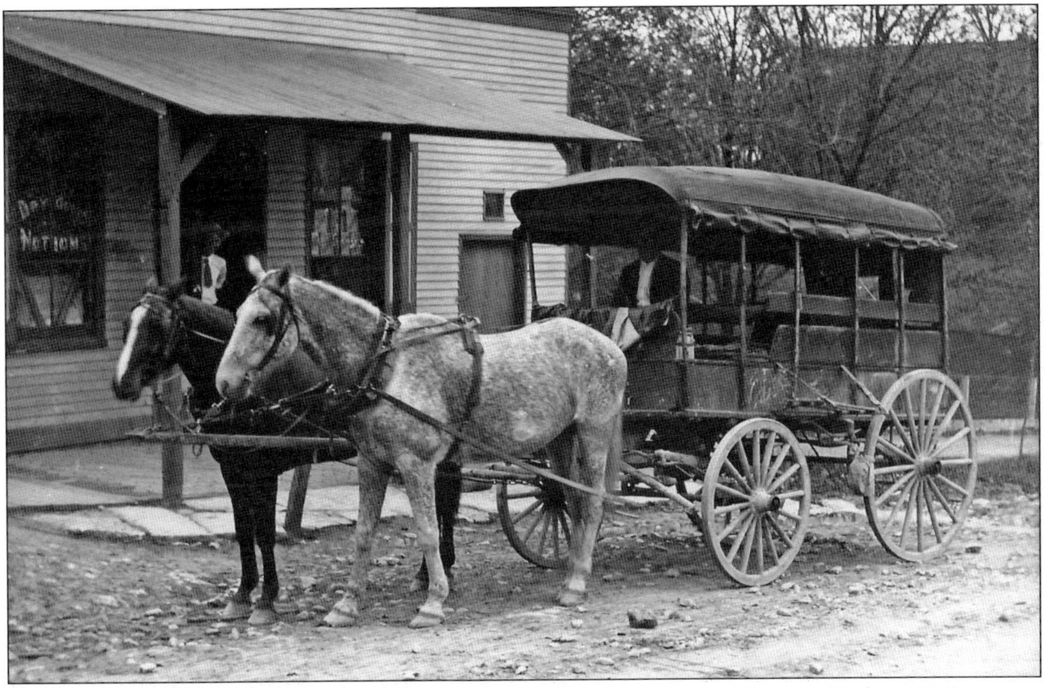

Hacks Transport. Public transportation was a given before automobiles. In this late 1800s image, one of the town's wagons for hire, called a hack, is waiting in front of Park's Meat Market located on Main Street. Before the Parks owned the meat market, it was owned by the Stillhammer family. Other public transportation businesses were named according to archival records: Waddle and Rankin's rig, Uncle Billy Graham's wagon, and Monroe and Monroe hacks. (Courtesy HC.)

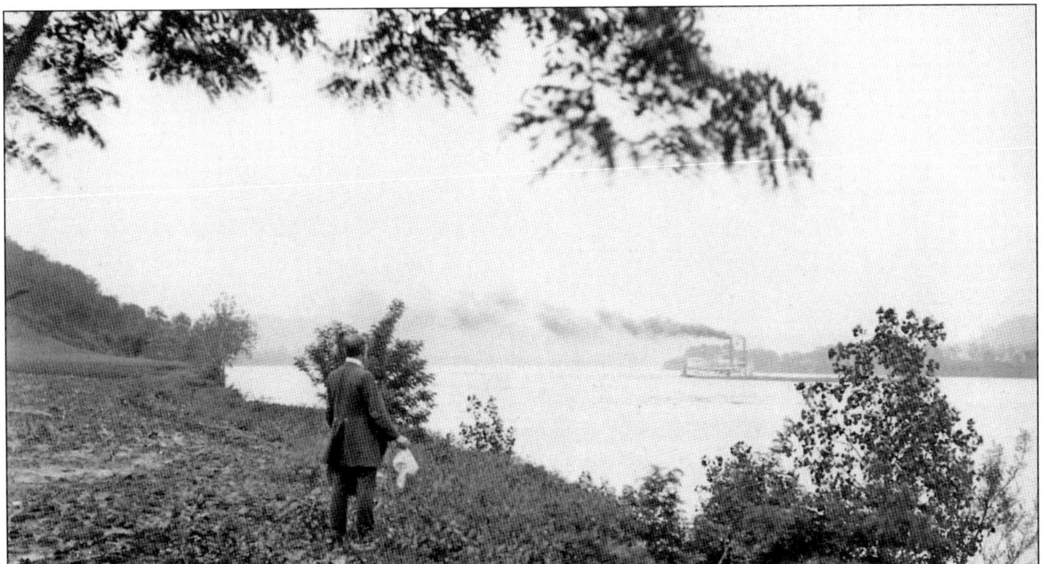

Man Flags down a Ride. People knew the fastest way to get to Cincinnati or Louisville was by steamboat. How did 1890s steamboat captains know a person wanted to board at Hanover Beach? A resident took a white handkerchief out and waved it furiously as a boat approached. The boat docked and lowered a wooden gangplank for the person. (Courtesy HC.)

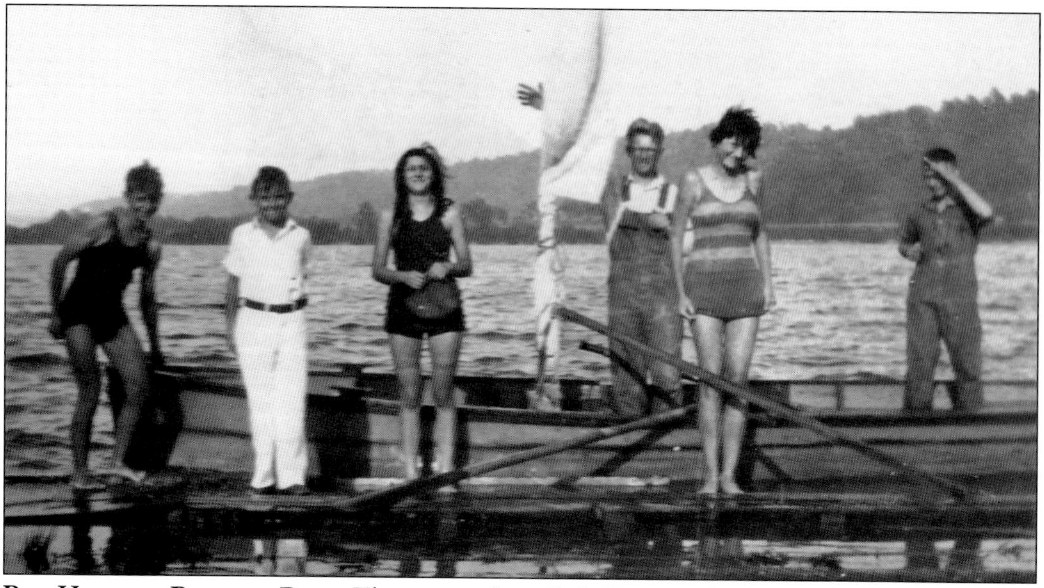

Bob Henning Builds a Boat. The street where Bob Henning built boats was named for the operation: Marine Street. Pictured above is the first boat Henning built in 1928 tied up to a dock at Hanover Beach. Those pictured are identified as the crew. They are, from left to right, Bill Zinzer, Kenny Kyle, Marjorie Nighbert, Orval Duke, Sarah Henning, and John Burdie Young. (Courtesy Bob Ireland.)

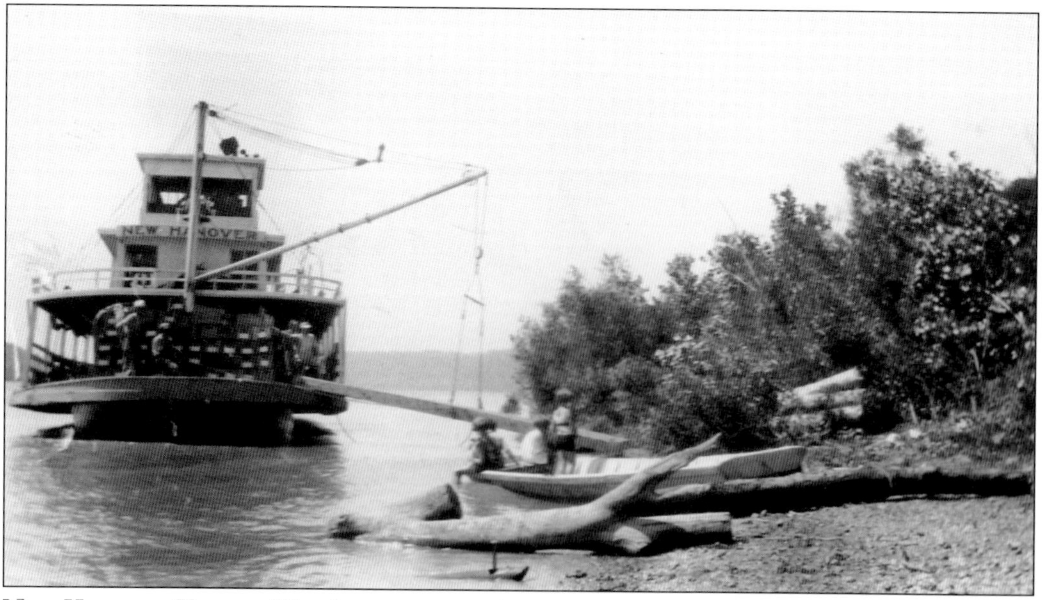

New Hanover Ties up. Riverboats generated enormous interest in the Hanover area. People traveled on them, and they were used to transport goods. The boat shown in the above image, taken in the 1920s was named the *New Hanover*. Apparently the boat dropped its gangplank at Hanover Beach to off-load cargo, which can be seen on the deck. Some riverboats from the area were made by the Turner family on land at the foot of Plowhandle Point. (Courtesy LC.)

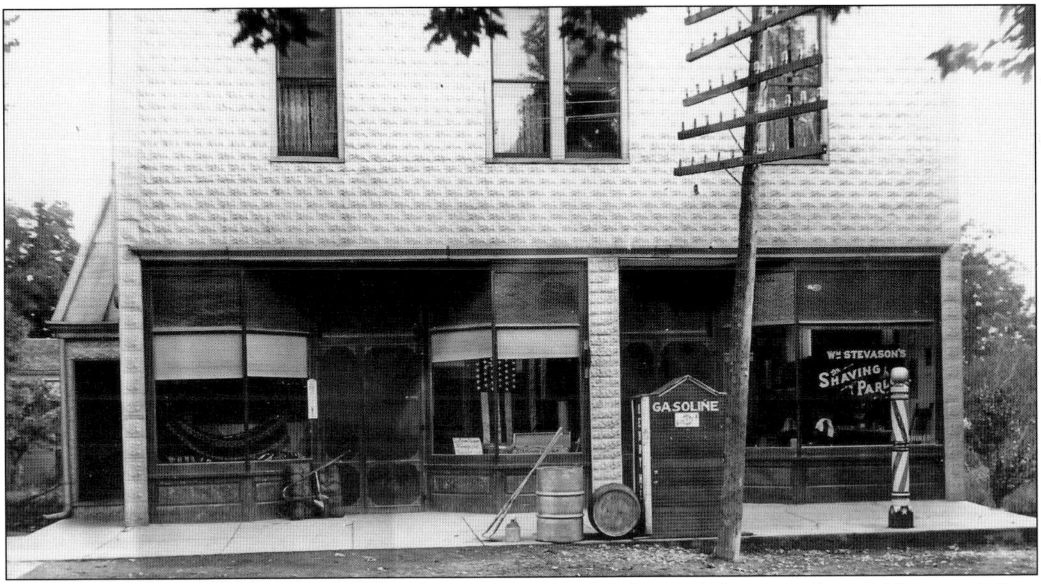

Building Destroyed by Tornado. The store to the left housed Finnegan's and Hanover's first telephone exchange in this image taken around 1927. The Jimmy Tafflinger family lived upstairs during World War II. Cecil Mier, his wife, Mary, and their daughter, Sara Mier Minor, lived in the upstairs in the 1950s. A 1974 tornado destroyed the building. A new structure housed several grocery stores over the years. (Courtesy JC.)

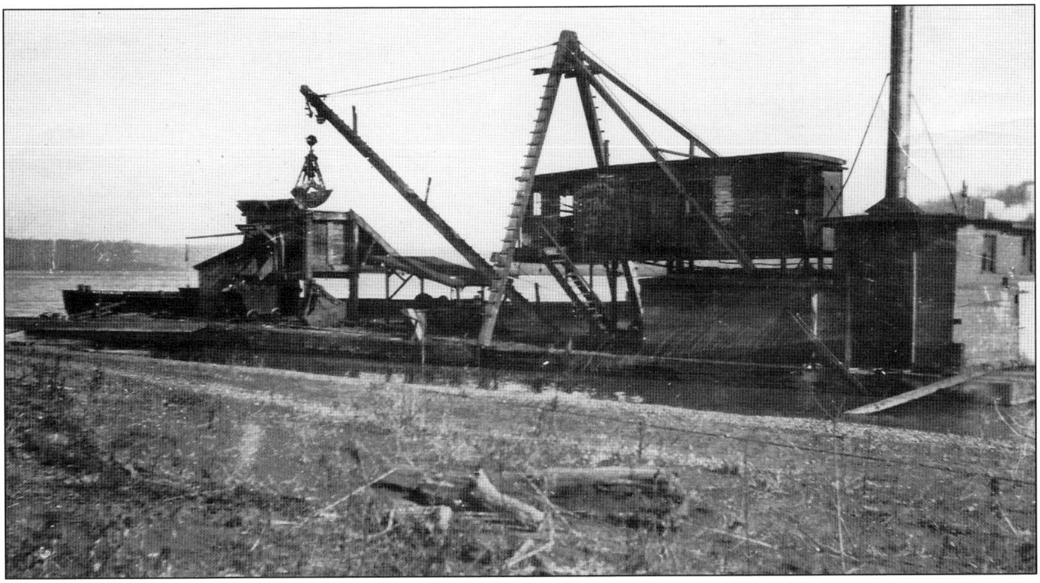

Coal Off-Loaded. In 1923, coal was used for keeping warm as well as cooking. A barge is shown tied up at the Hanover Coal Supply at Hanover Landing. The coal was off-loaded there and left in enormous mounds. In the early years, people drove their wagons to collect the coal. Later the coal was distributed from a structure at Main and Main Cross Streets. (Courtesy D/M.)

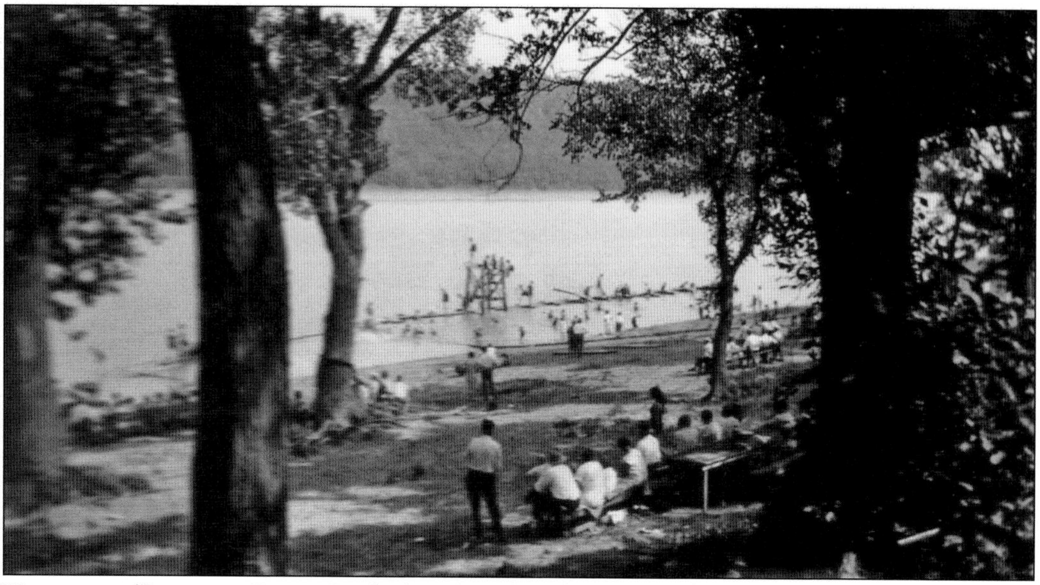

Hospitality Begins at Beach. In the late 1920s, Joseph Rogers and his family operated a beach and hotel called Hanover Beach on the river below Hanover. Guests could swim, dive, or take a rowboat out in the river. Additionally meals were served in a dining room. Guests gathered at riverside by campfires for conversation and toasted marshmallows in the evenings. (Courtesy LC.)

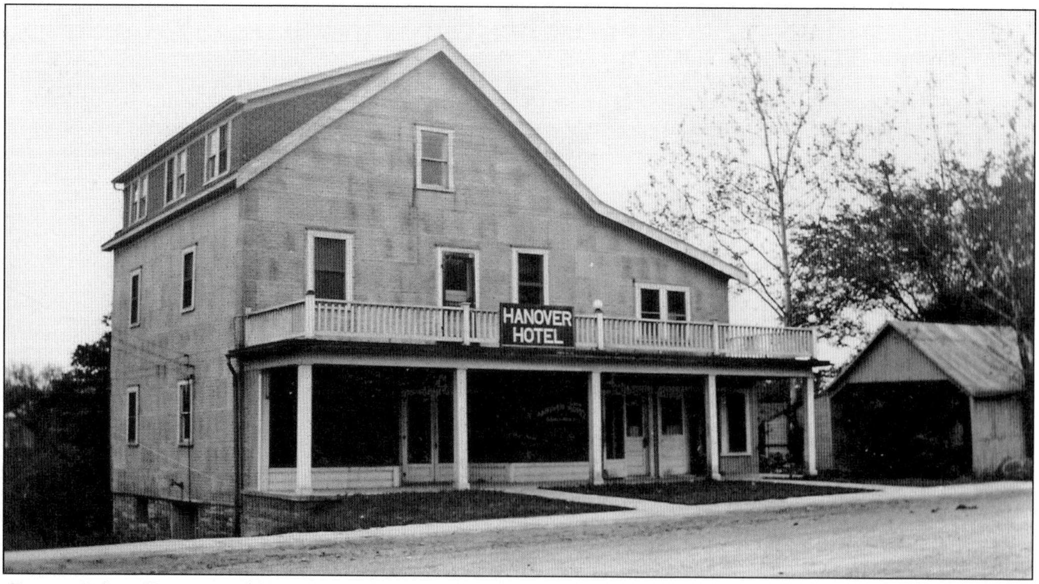

Chain Mill Becomes Hanover Hotel. The building pictured above around 1927 was moved to its present location on Madison Avenue, one block north of Main Street, between the late 1860s and early 1900s. Formerly the Chain Mill Falls structure, it served as a hotel, which closed in the 1940s. Subsequently it functioned as Amos Apartments (1952–1964) and Kirk Apartments (1964–1970), operated by Roberta and Carl Kirk. (Courtesy LC.)

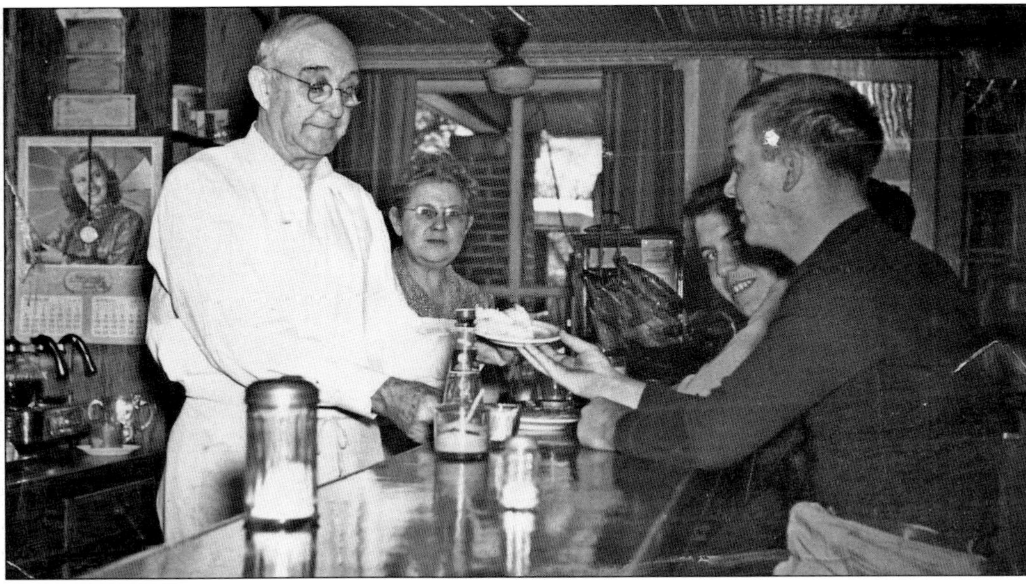

Home Found Away from Home. Jewel, left, and Maude Summers ran the Maude Summers Restaurant inside a log house that used to stand at the corner of Main Cross and Main Streets. They loved students and made their business one where all were welcome—college, high school, and townspeople. Some fellows even came up from Louisville to eat according to local historians. (Courtesy D/M.)

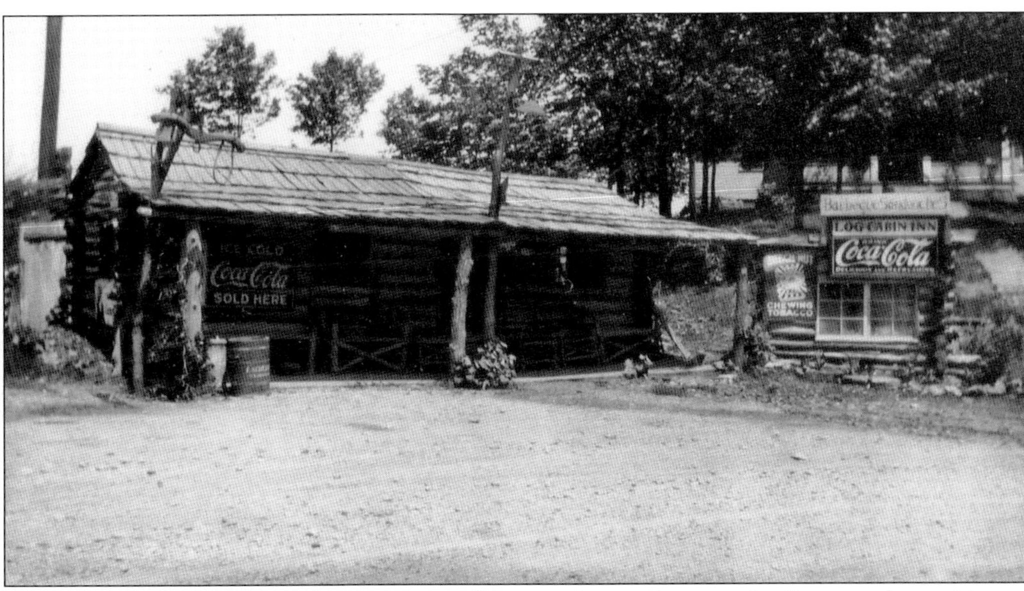

Stop for Refreshments. This image was discovered in a photograph album in the archives of the Jefferson County Historical Society Research Library. Included in a pictorial account of an automobile trip from Madison to Hanover and back, accompanying text said, "At the top of the Hanover Hill you stop at the Hanover Log Cabin Inn for some refreshments." The cabin was built on the south edge of the Grimes family home according to local historians. (Courtesy JC.)

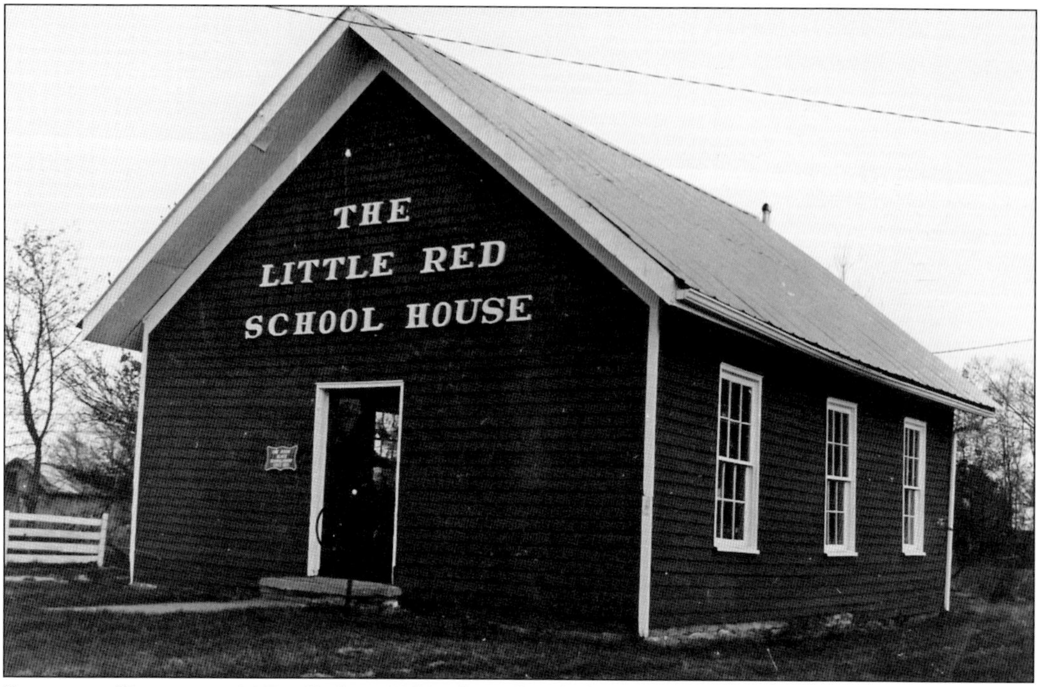

Building Dates to 1871. Before 1950, the school above was called the Hanover School, or historically the Hanover Colored School. In Indiana, the building holds the record as the state's oldest, surviving, segregated school. For almost 80 years, children in grades one through eight studied together inside the one-room schoolhouse. Now the building contains an antique store. (Courtesy HC.)

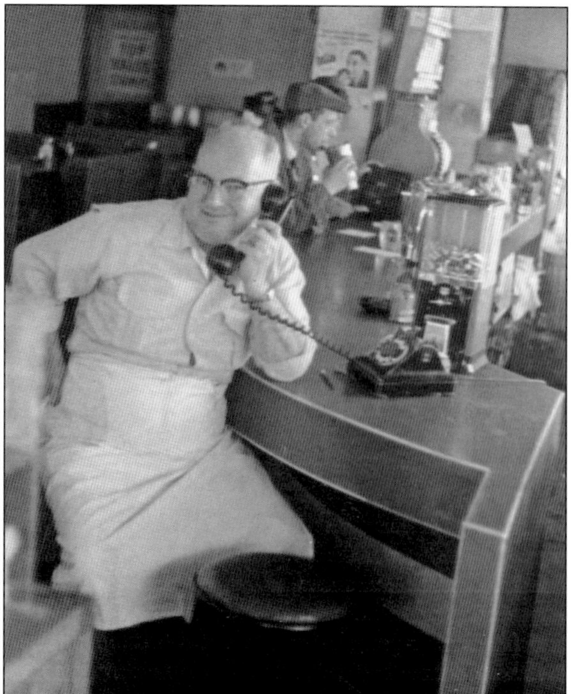

"Coop" Manages the Counter. Robert "Coop" Cooper operated Cooper's Corner from 1945 until 1961. It served as a popular hangout for high school and college students. Coop and his wife, Mary Ella ("Ellie") Weber Cooper, attended Hanover College in the 1930s. Coop said students returning to college from military service needed jobs. He employed a number of them and provided them places to live. (Courtesy Lynne Cooper Abner family.)

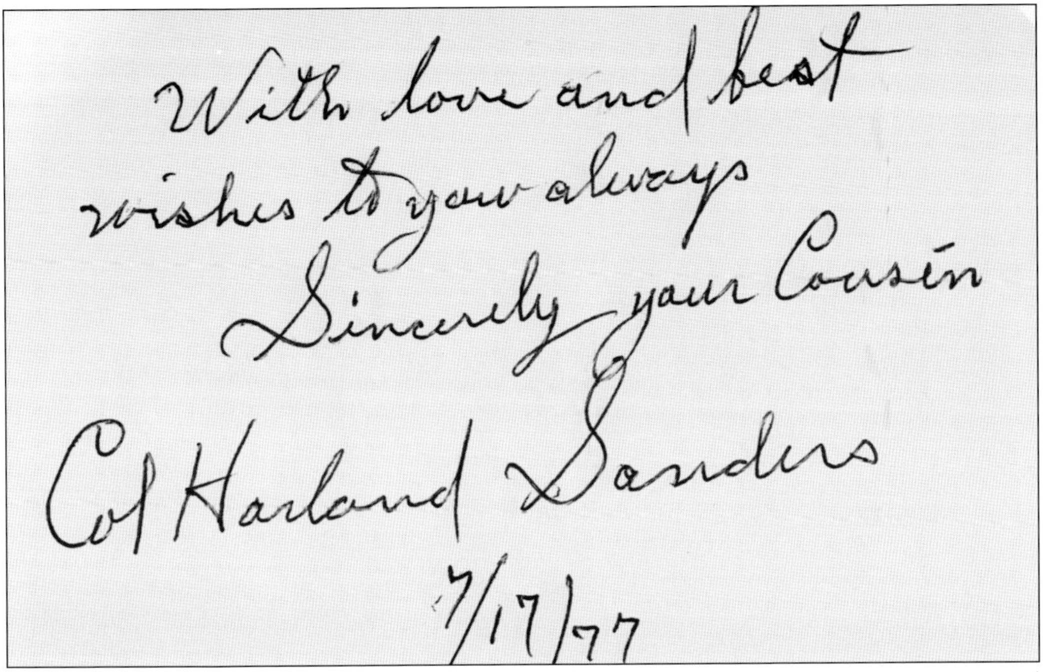
With love and best
wishes to you always
Sincerely your Cousin
Col Harland Sanders
7/17/77

CHICKEN KING VISITS. Col. Harland Sanders and Robert Cooper (see previous page) were second cousins. Sanders wrote the message seen above to the Cooper family in 1977. Sanders and his wife, Claudia, sometimes visited with the Coopers in Hanover. The Cooper's daughter Lynne snapped the picture below of Sanders and her mother, Ellie, during one of his visits while enjoying a meal in the Cooper's dining room. The colonel appears to be eating pie and drinking iced tea. When Robert Cooper died, Sanders drove up from Kentucky to attend the funeral in Hanover. Residents remember Sanders arrived to pay tribute to his cousin at the Hanover Presbyterian Church in a Rolls-Royce with 24-carat gold trim. They recall him walking right into the church just like everyone else. (Both, courtesy Lynne Cooper Abner family.)

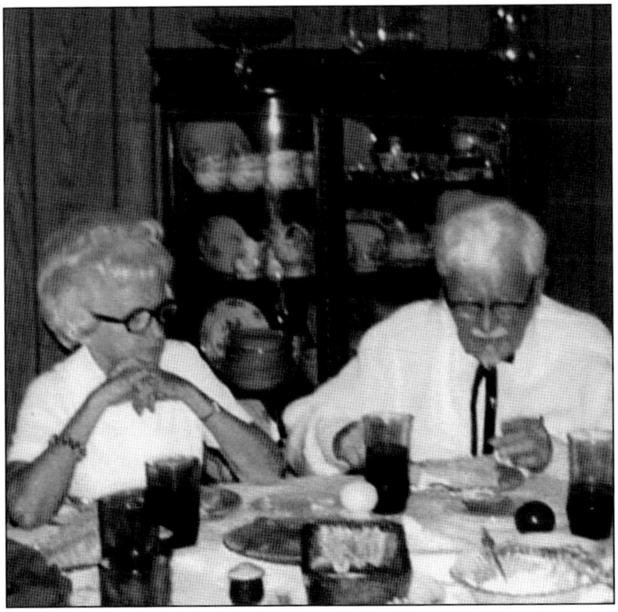

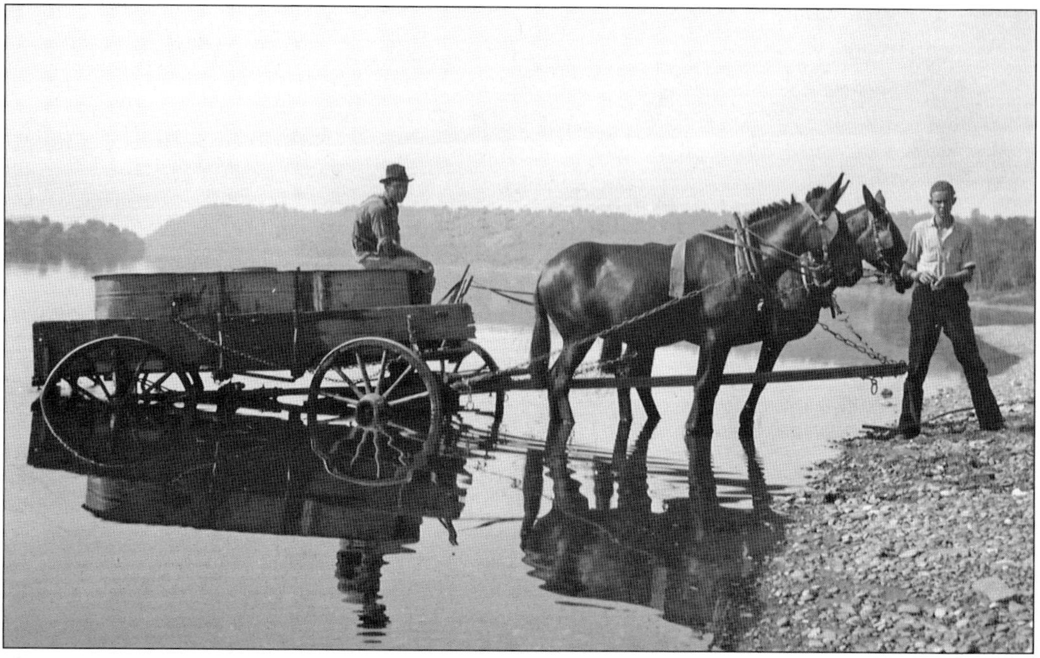

Wagon Pauses at Beach. The barrels in this wagon at Hanover Beach are thought to contain river mussels, which were used in a nearby button factory. Local historians point to the handles sticking up in the wagon, which would have been attached to tools used to rake the bottom of the river and separate out the mussels. At the factory, cleaned-out mussel shells were pierced with cutters to make pearl-like buttons. The young man on the right may be Johnny Mefford. (Courtesy LC.)

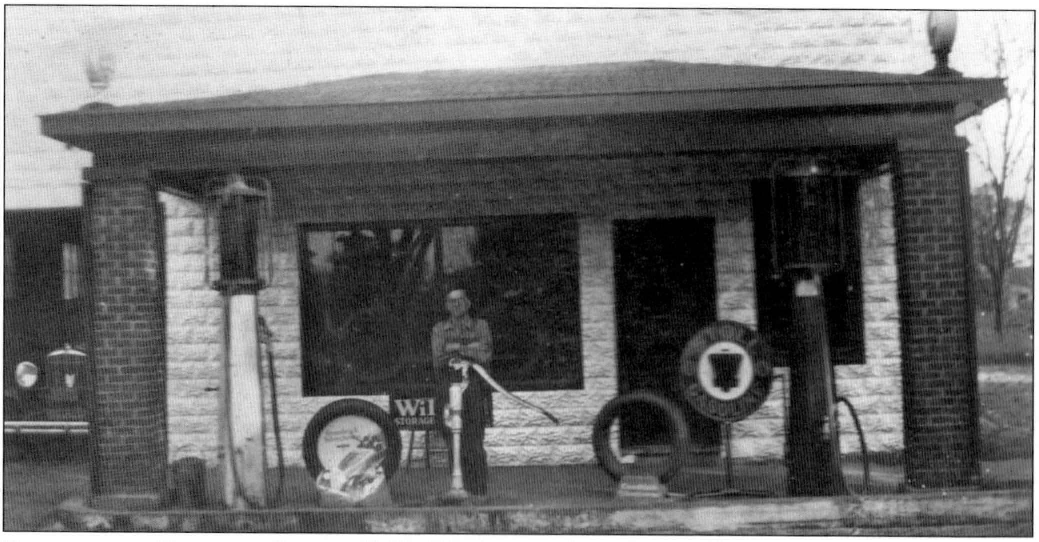

Repairs and Gasoline Given. Clifford Duke stands in front of his garage, which he built in 1918 at the corner of First and Main Cross Streets. Two gasoline pumps can be seen in this image as well as a bay where automobiles were repaired. Duke was a volunteer firefighter for 50 years and served as chief for at least 20 years. He also served as town marshal and street, water, and sewer superintendent from the 1930s until he retired in the mid-1960s. The post was then filled by Dewey Lee Marsh. (Courtesy D/M.)

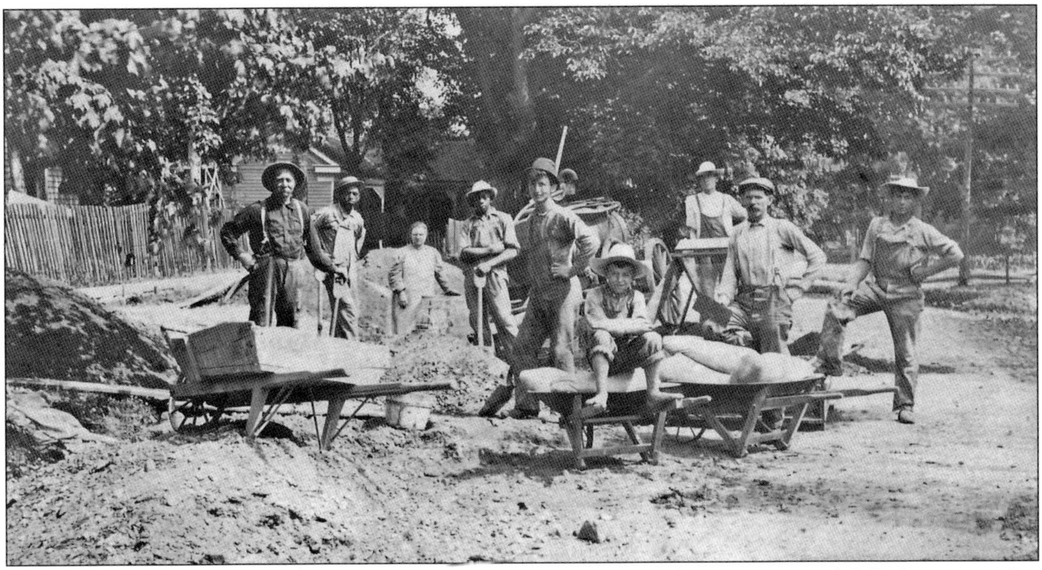

MEN POUR CONCRETE. John Duke ran a crew that worked with concrete and did plastering. On this day in the 1900s, they were building a sidewalk in Hanover. The man standing on the far right is probably Oran Sanders. John Duke is thought to be the man standing third from the right in the back of the photograph. Clifford Duke is sitting in the wheelbarrow with his shoes off. No one else is identified on the back of this rare photograph. (Courtesy D/M.)

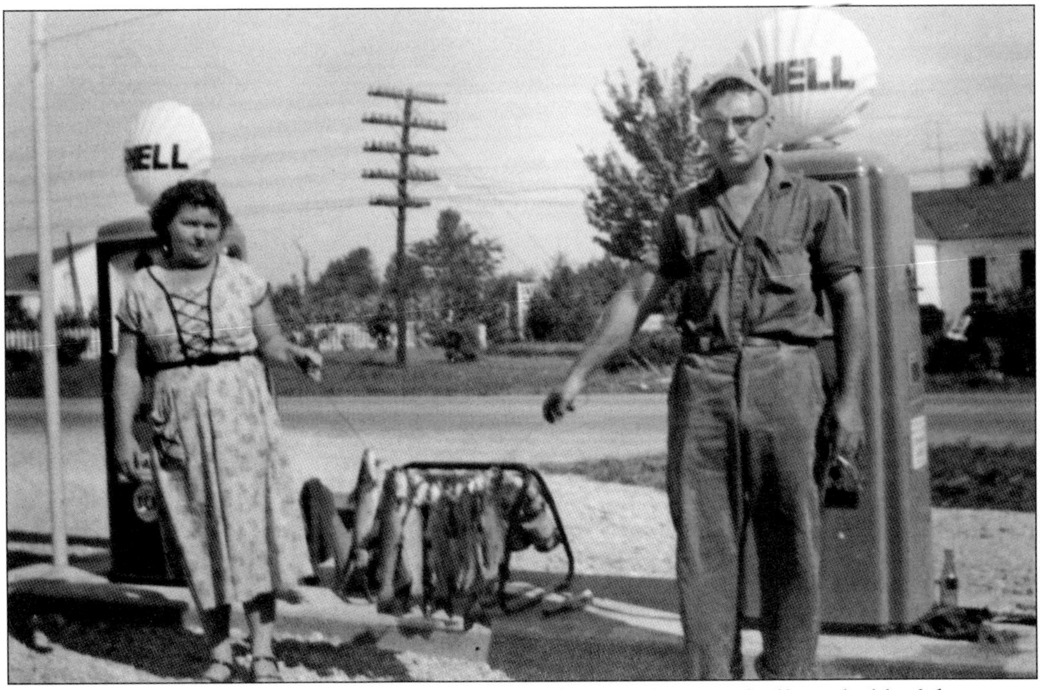

MESS OF FISH SHOWN OFF. Charles Henry Marsh and Naomi Larison Coffman hold a fish stringer with catfish and pike on it at Hanover's Shell station around 1954. Barney Coffman, Naomi's husband, and Charles had gone fishing. As Barney is pumping gas or welding (or maybe taking the picture), Naomi holds the stringer. (Courtesy Marsh family.)

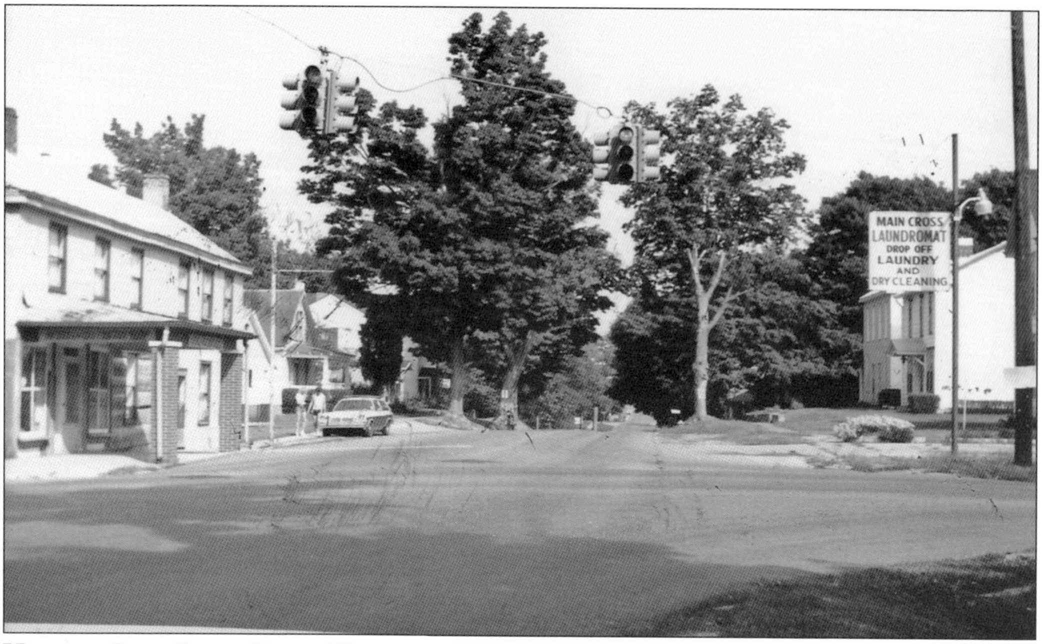

HISTORIC LOG CABIN GONE. This scene takes in several buildings at the corner of Main and Main Cross Streets looking east. The building on the left in the image dates back to the 1820s and was known as a Native American trading post. It was taken down around 2000. The land is used as a parking lot today. (Courtesy HC.)

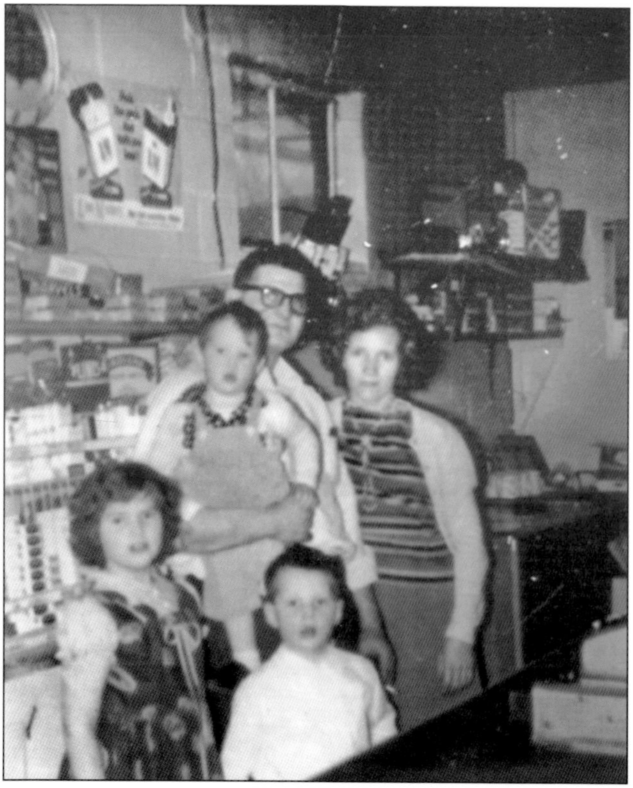

FAMILY RUNS GROCERY. Back in 1955, the business presently known as the Pride Family Market was called Cole's Grocery. William D. Cole and Lorine Callahan Cole pose with three of their children in this vintage photograph. Today John, Joe, Danette, and Tammy Bohman own the Pride Family Market. (Courtesy Cole family.)

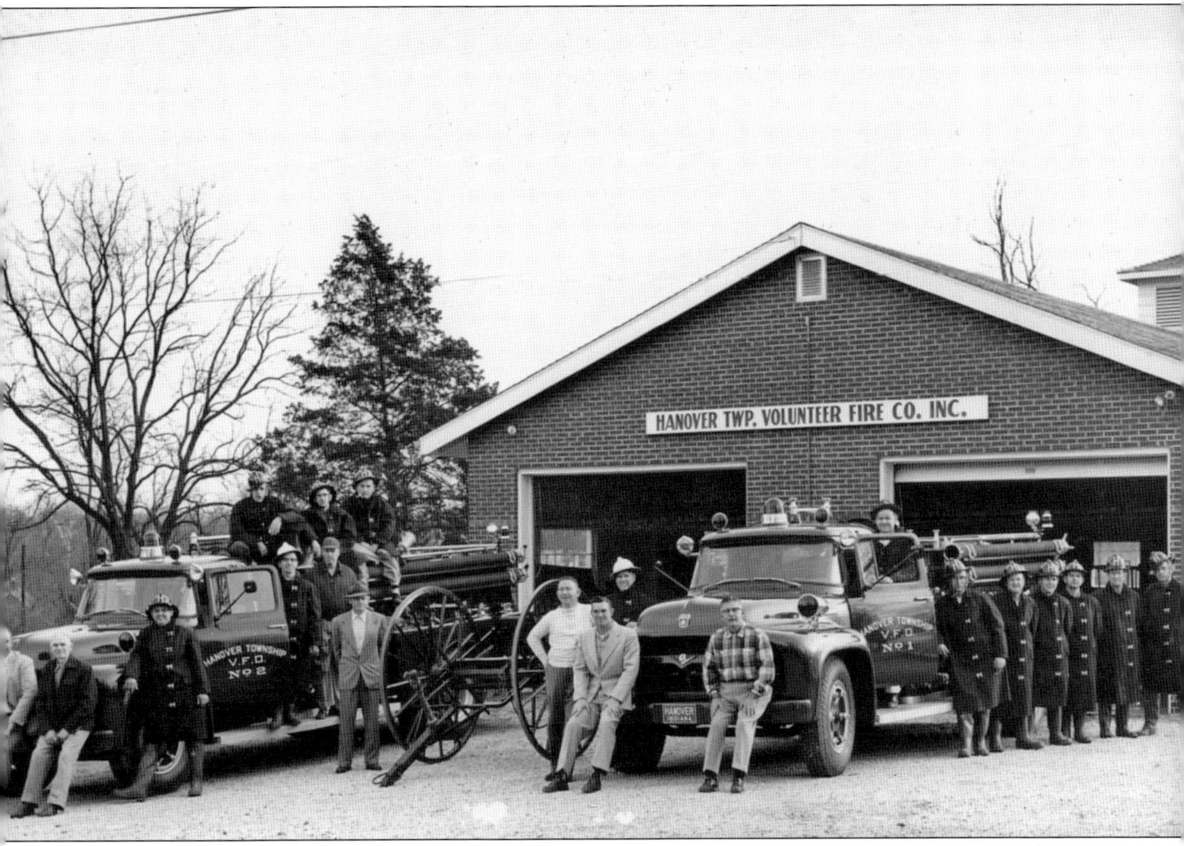

Prepared to Save. The Hanover Township Volunteer Fire Company was incorporated on December 28, 1954. The all-volunteer company grew out of a determined group of residents who worked together to help their neighbors with fires and other emergencies. Pictured in this 1956 photograph are, from left to right, Charles Hensler, Charles Schreiber, Dan Kreiger, Chief Clifford Duke, Harvey Ramsey, Fred Ryan, Kenny Land, Jim Foster, Pete Schuring, Bill Oldaker, Don Manaugh, Charles Marsh, Clyde Jobe, Carl Schnebelt, Bill Lindsey, Stanley May, and Gayle Manaugh. In the bed of the truck are, from left to right, Bill Bruther, Bill Faris, and Cecil Meier. The town benefits from the continued service of private citizens who serve as volunteers today. (Courtesy D/M.)

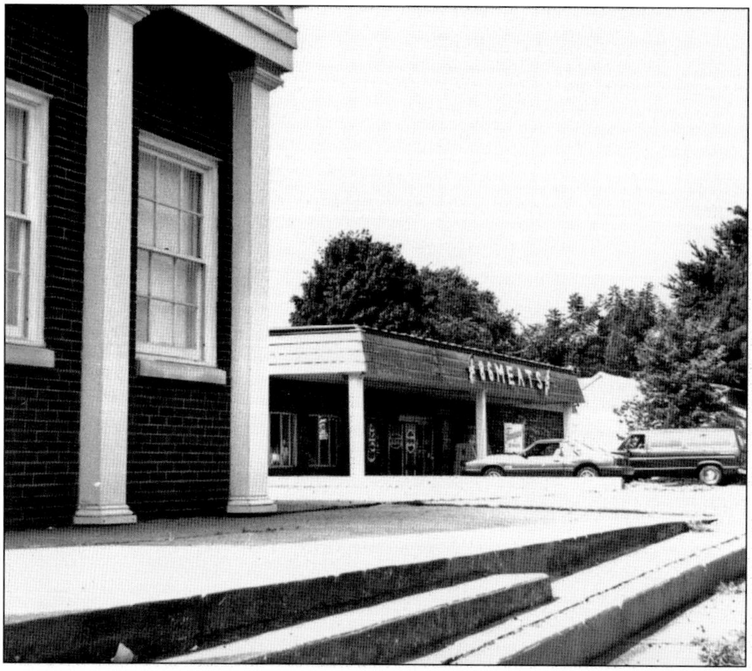

Tornado Leads to New Building. After a tornado roared through Hanover in 1974, Finnegan's store was rebuilt and housed B&G Meats. The meat market was later called Johnson's. Today it has been remodeled as an apartment building containing 16 apartments. The building on the left is presently owned by a telephone company. (Courtesy HC.)

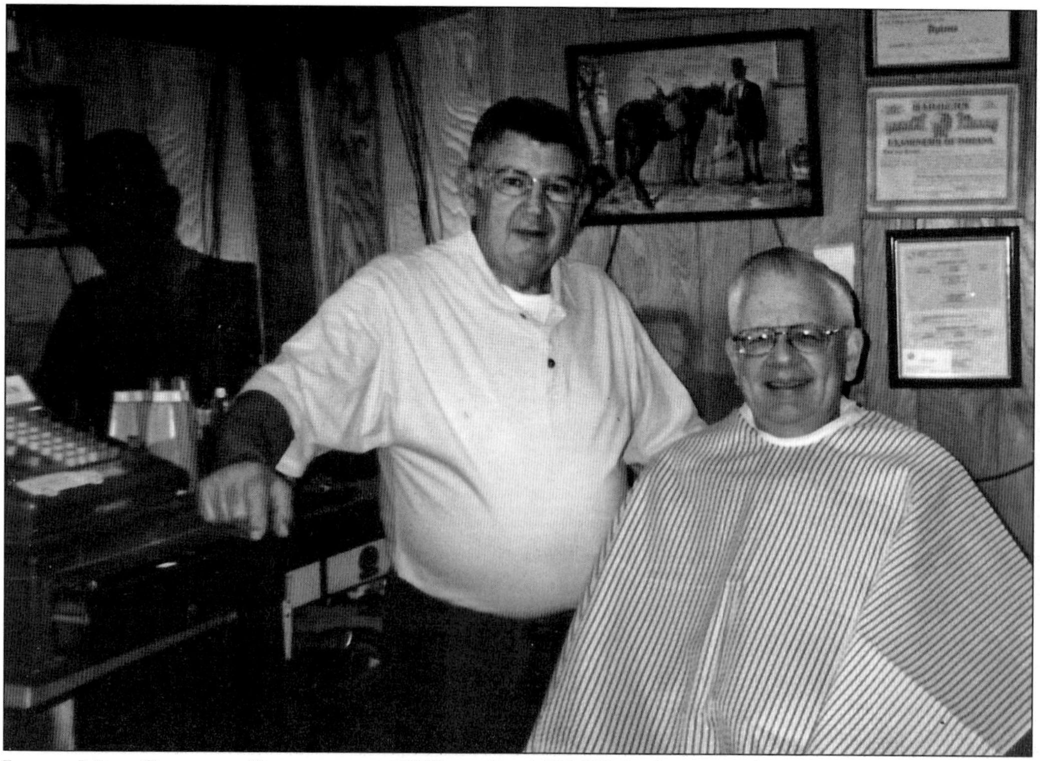

Local Man Operates Barbershop. William Paul ("Bill") Jackson graduated from Hanover High School in 1956. He has operated the Hanover Barber Shop since 1960. In this image he is cutting Ralph Seifert's hair. Seifert taught mathematics at Hanover College from 1979 until 2004 and served as town clerk-treasurer from 2004 to 2006. (Courtesy Bill Jackson family.)

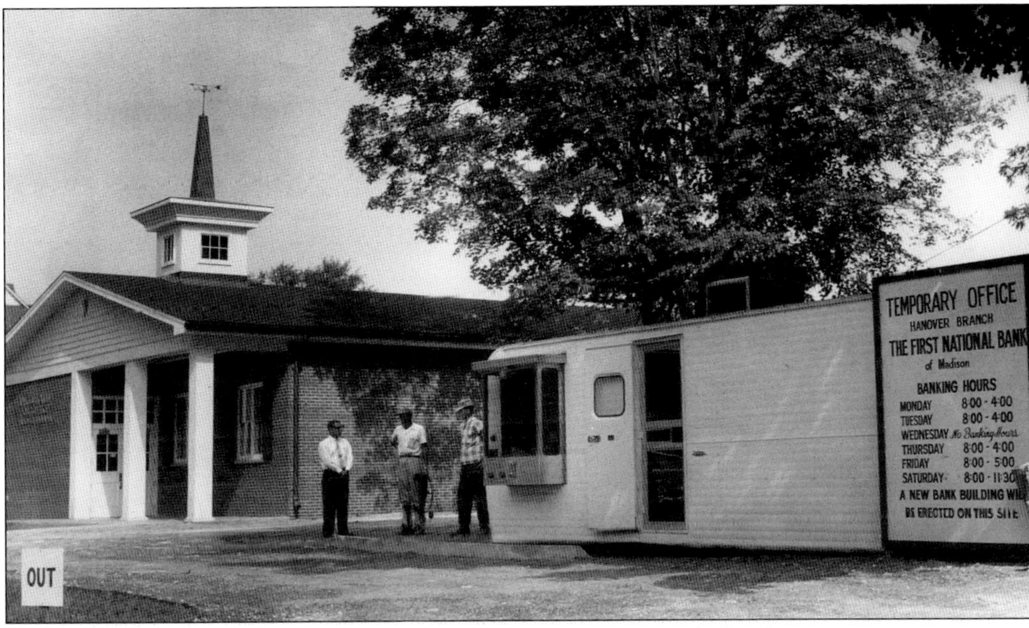

Post Office Unites Community. At the end of the 1800s, each family sent a representative to meet a bus or hack from Madison at 9:00 p.m. to collect the mail. The time together gave families the opportunity to gossip and catch up on what was going on. Later the mail arrived in the afternoon along with the delivery of the *Madison Courier*, an area newspaper still in production today. In the image with the unidentified people, the dog, and bicycle, the post office had moved to Main Street and Madison Avenue. The more recent image on Main Street with the present post office built in 1960 on the left also shows a trailer that housed the First National Bank for a while. Hanover's current postmaster is Brian DeCraene. (Both, courtesy HC.)

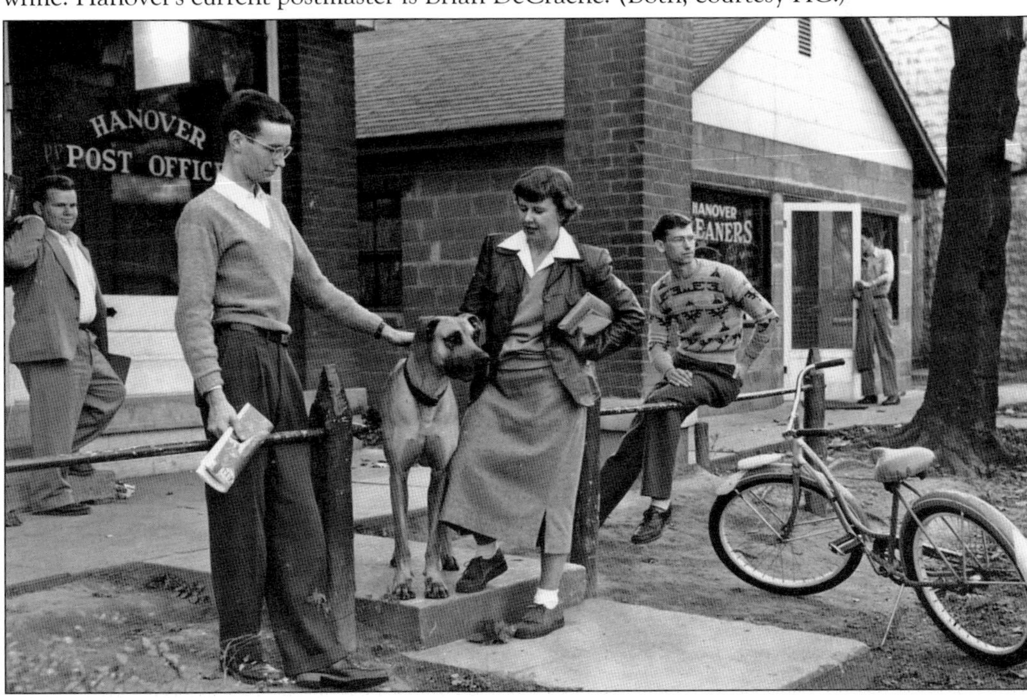

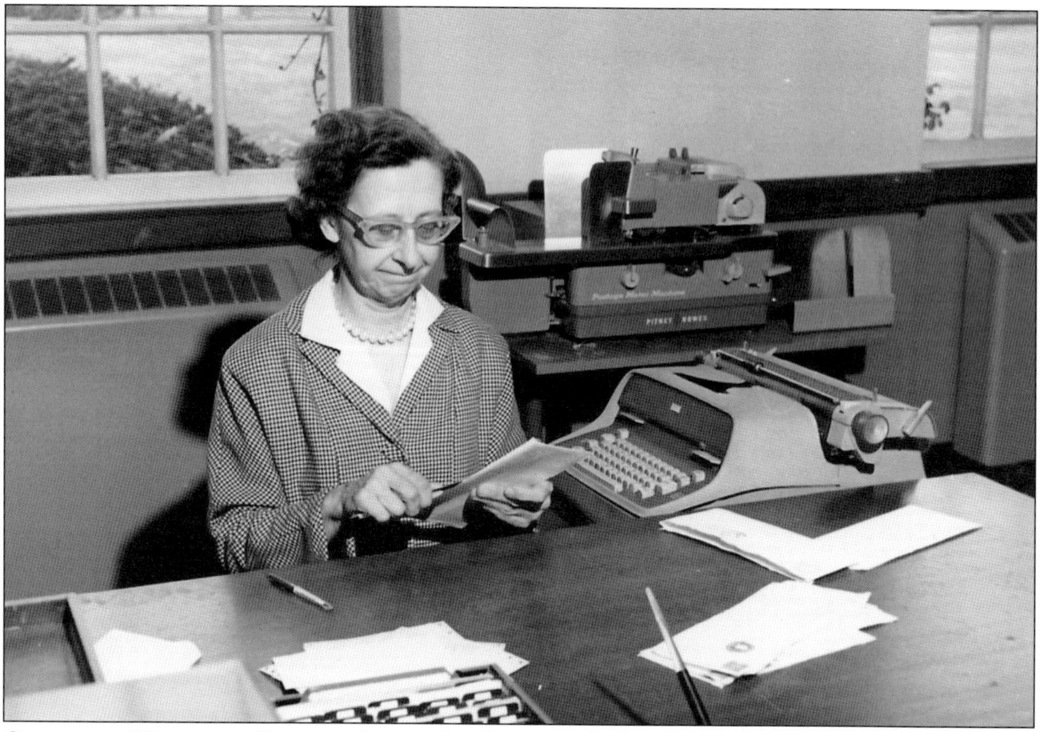

Graduate Works at College. Leona Snyder earned a bachelor of arts degree from Hanover College in 1931. She made a career working as an assistant for Hanover College presidents Dr. Albert Parker and Dr. John E. Horner. She retired in 1973. She was the sister-in-law of current Hanover resident Peg Snyder. (Courtesy HC.)

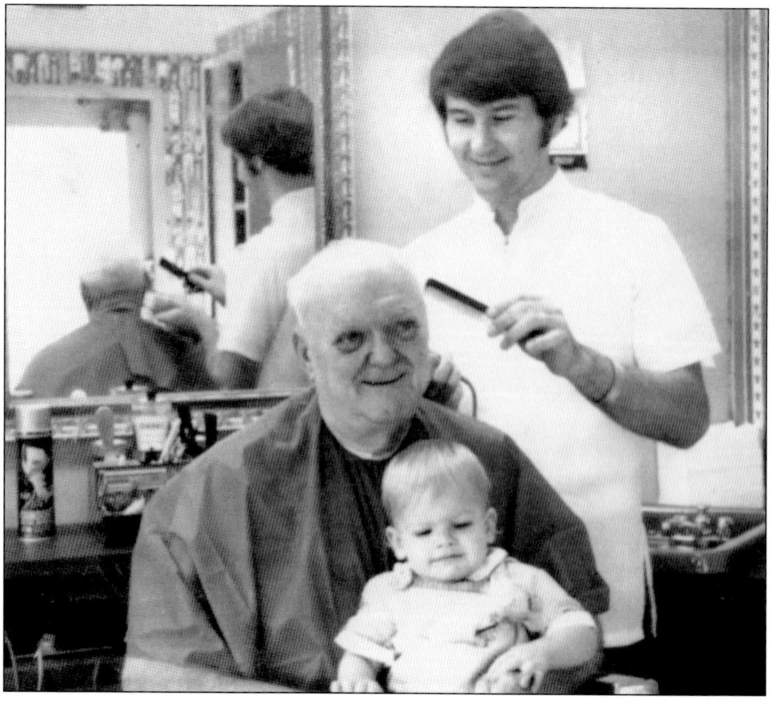

Barbershop Offers Cuts. Carl W. Risk gives Clyde Jobe a haircut while Clyde holds Carl's nephew Chuck Hensler. Chuck, now 38-years-old, works at Vehicle Service Group (VSG) in Madison. Risk has owned and operated Carl Risk's Men's Quarters since 1973. He studied at International Barber College in Indianapolis. (Courtesy Carl W. Risk Men's Quarters.)

Four

Landmark Events

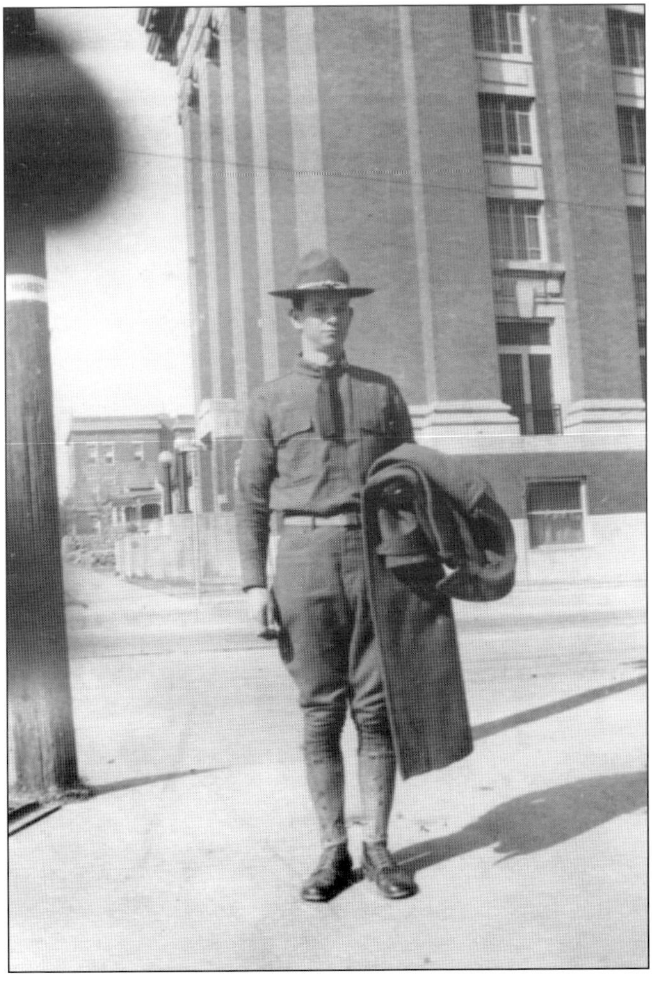

Hanover Man Serves in France. John Charles Craig was born in 1894. He served in the U.S. Army during World War I in France. When he returned from war, he farmed on a piece of property near Hanover College. Craig loved flowers. He never married. His image begins this chapter on landmark events, which includes wars, floods, tornados, new fire trucks, falling rocks, and freezes. (Courtesy HC.)

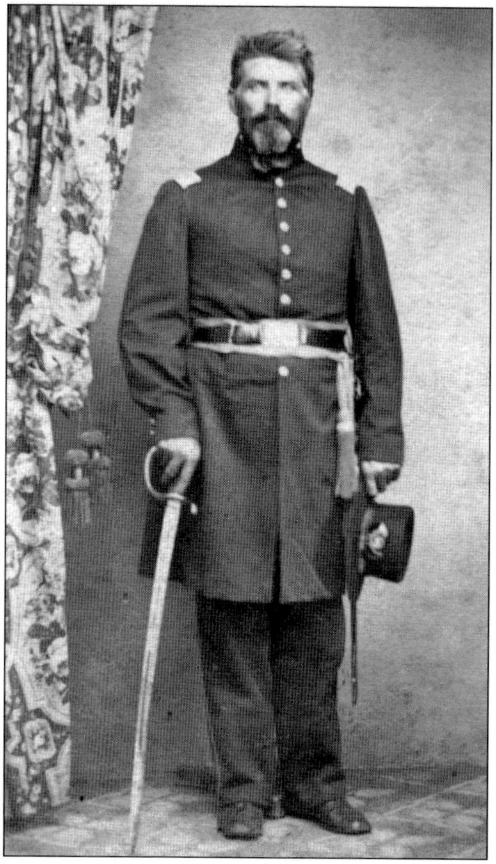

Civil War Touches Hanover. Gen. Samuel S. Crowe raised a company to fight in the Civil War. He served as a captain for three years in Company B in the 93rd Indiana Volunteer Infantry. He graduated from Hanover College in 1839 and was a son of Esther Alexander and John Finley Crowe, who founded Hanover College. (Courtesy HC.)

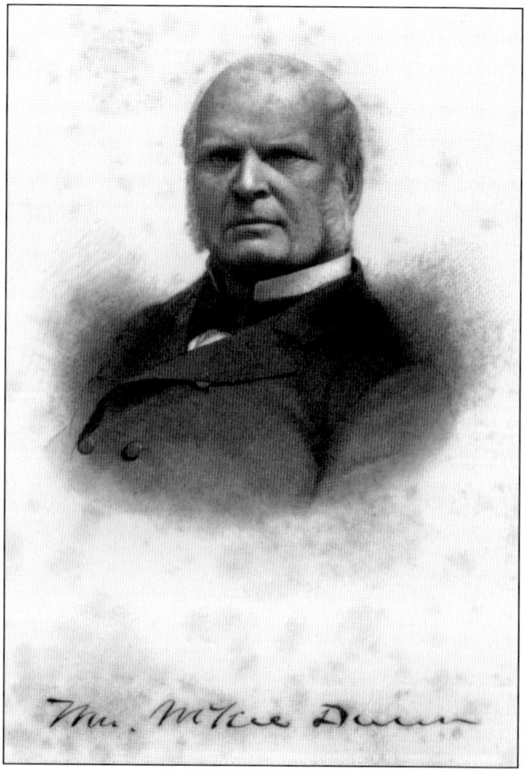

Local Man Serves. William McKee Dunn was born in Hanover and graduated from Hanover College in 1842. He practiced law in Madison and served in the U.S. House of Representatives from 1859 to 1863. He enlisted in the army during the Civil War. When the war ended, he was promoted to Judge Advocate General of the U.S. Army. (Courtesy Murray.)

Hanover Men and Women Serve. Hanover pioneers from Kentucky had barely unpacked their few possessions before they were off to the War of 1812. Most men of age in Hanover enlisted in either the Northern or Southern armies of the Civil War. Andy Means carried on the tradition of citizen soldier by serving as a "Rough Rider" with Teddy Roosevelt in the Spanish-American War. He is shown in 1899 wearing his uniform. (Courtesy D/M.)

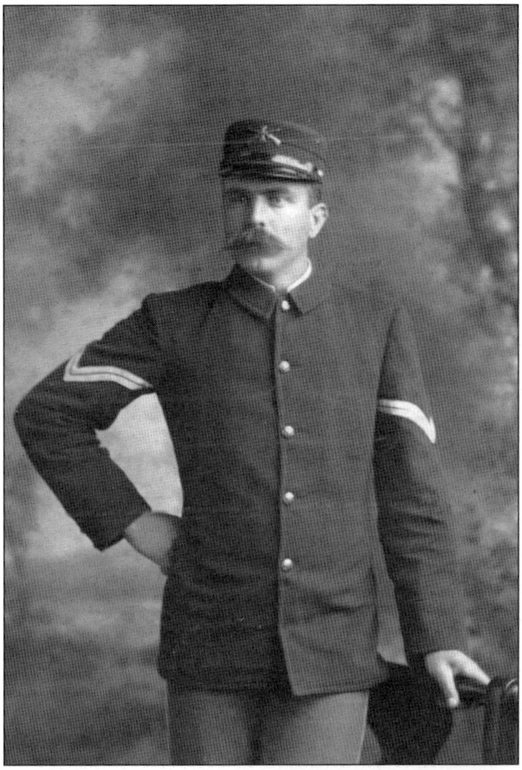

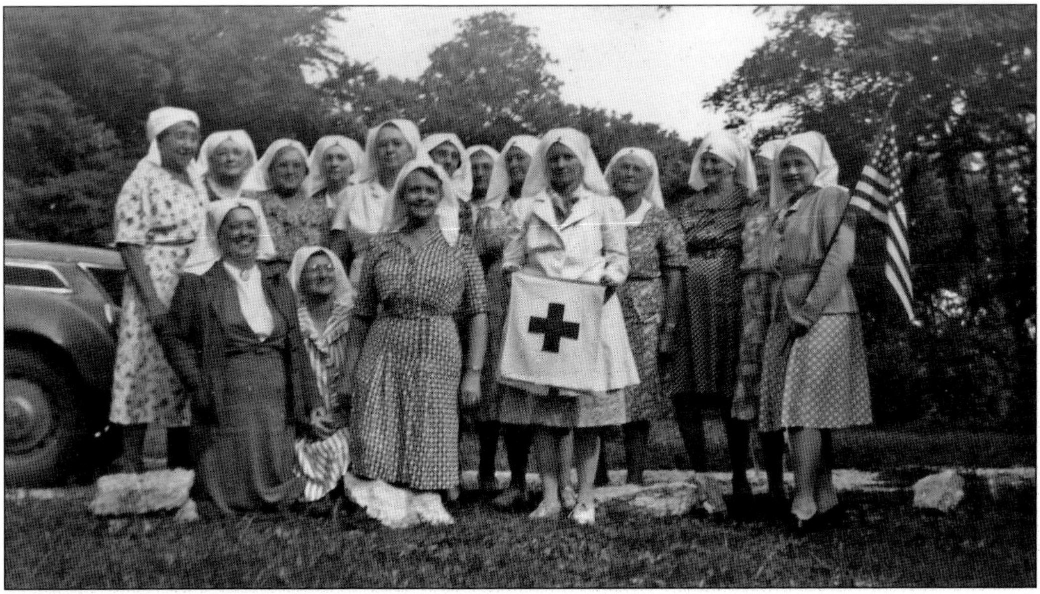

Women Roll Bandages. During World War II, Hanover women who were members of the Hanover Chapter of the American Red Cross got together to prepare materials for relief aid. Pictured are, from left to right, (first row) Rita Voltz, Patience Dryden, Irma Jones, and Mary Finnegan; (second row) Mrs. Smith and Mrs. Gable; (third row) Georgia Means, Mable Kyle, Gracie Bruther, Mrs. Guthrie, Mrs. D. C. Hill, Mrs. Tull, Mrs. Hart, Mrs. Dryden, Mrs. Taft, and Mrs. Hayes, who holds the American flag. (Courtesy D/M.)

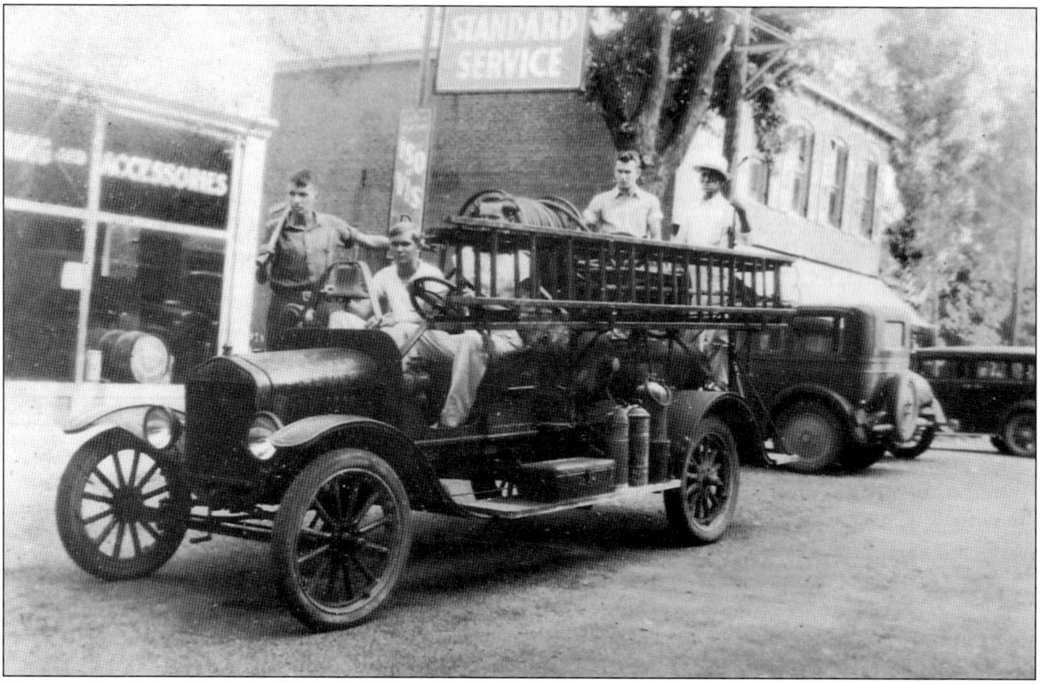

HANOVER BUYS FIRST FIRE ENGINE. Volunteer firefighters proudly show off Hanover's first fire engine, which is thought to have been bought in the 1940s. The engine is parked at Bovard's Garage in this photograph. Pictured are Jack Cozart on the running board holding an ax, Richard Orville Bolton in the front seat, and Bob Henning driving. Paul Tull, left, and Ed Judkins are standing at the back of the truck. (Courtesy Marsh family.)

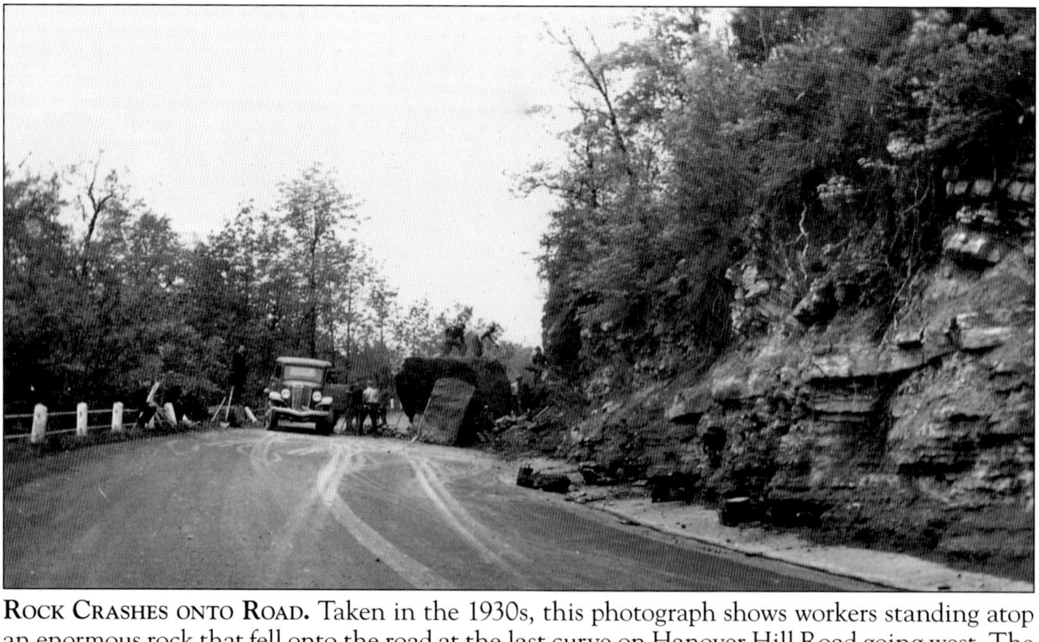

ROCK CRASHES ONTO ROAD. Taken in the 1930s, this photograph shows workers standing atop an enormous rock that fell onto the road at the last curve on Hanover Hill Road going west. The workers arrived in the truck and are figuring out how to clear the road. Signs in the area still indicate falling rocks, but few are ever this big. (Courtesy LC.)

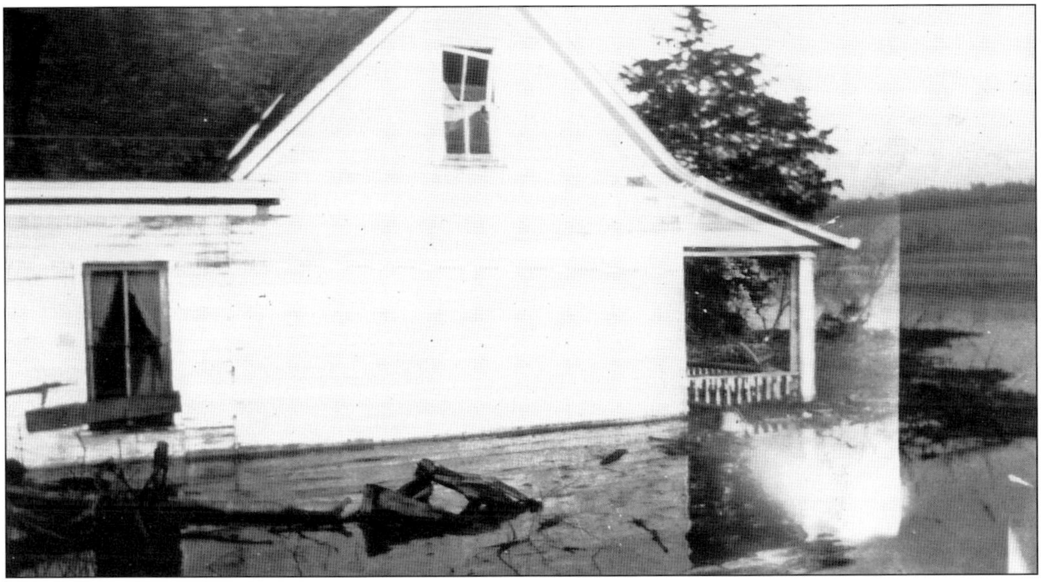

Flood Waters Devastate. In January 1937, the Ohio River flooded. Seen in this faded photograph is the second floor of the home at Sigmon's farm. The entire first floor was flooded. A harpsichord was carried above the high water line and was not damaged. The land near Sigmon's farm, off the present River Road, was a place where Native Americans fished and may have conducted tribal ceremonies according to local historians. (Courtesy D/M.)

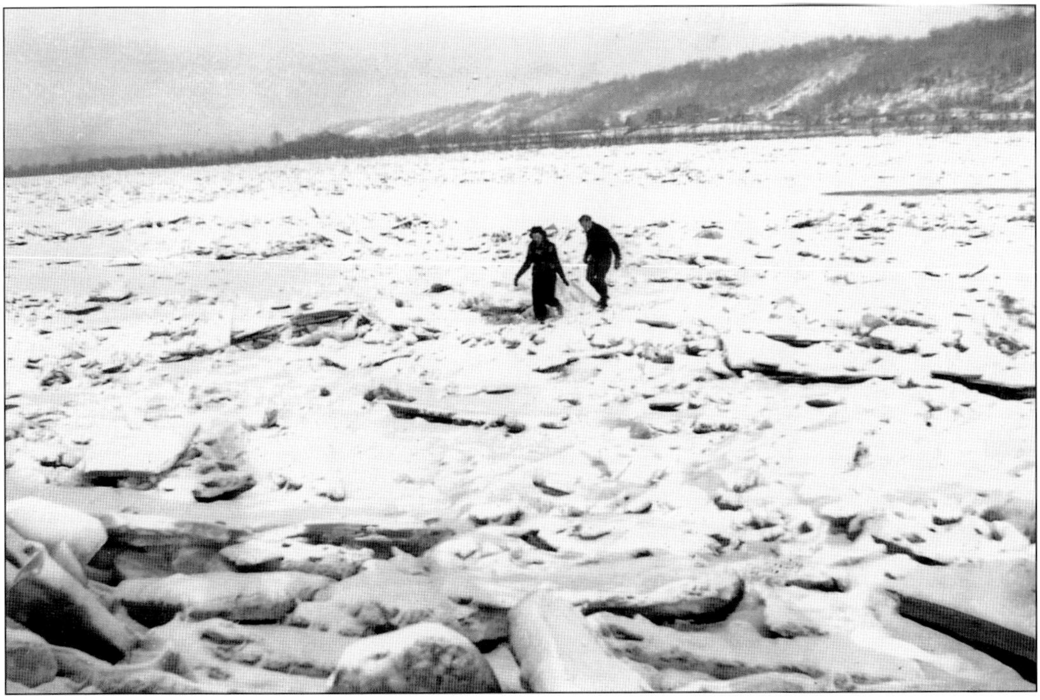

Freeze Follows Flood. Within a week of the 1937 devastating flood shown in the first picture on this page, the Ohio River froze. Two people walk on the ice with Kentucky in the background. Locals report a farmer drove his team and wagon from Indiana to Kentucky on top of the ice to help another farmer. (Courtesy HC.)

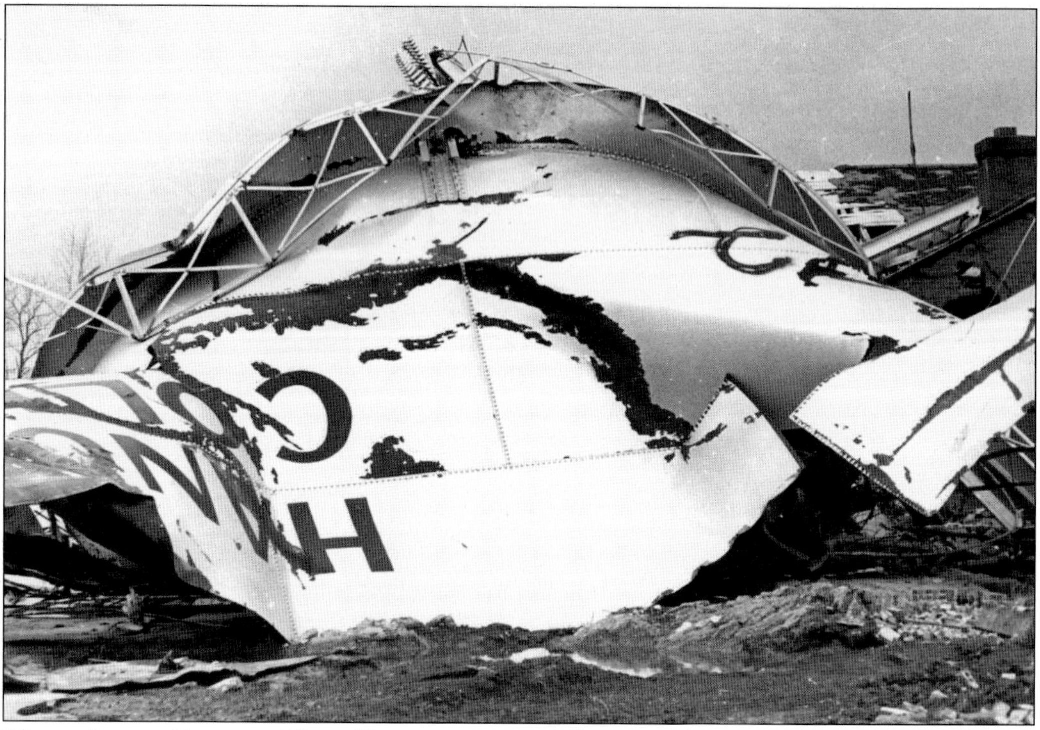

Water Tower Crashes. The college water tower fell on top of a maintenance building during a 1974 tornado, completely destroying it. A notation on the back of the photograph from the college archives says, "Miraculously no one was in the building at the time." However, four people elsewhere in Hanover died from the injuries they received. Some debris from Hanover was later found 137 miles away in Xenia, Ohio. (Courtesy HC.)

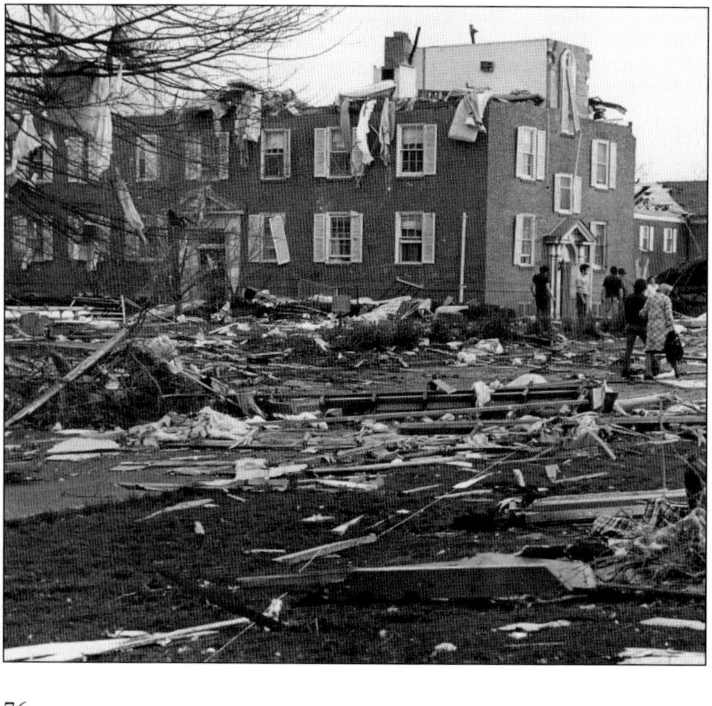

Storm Brings Devastation. The aftermath of a 1974 tornado stunned residents and college students. This image shows some of the widespread damage at the college. Similar devastation was inflicted in town, especially at Southwestern Elementary School, Southwestern Middle/Senior High School, and the surrounding neighborhood. Evacuating critically injured people was a challenge because roads were blocked by downed trees, parts of houses, and other enormous mounds of debris. (Courtesy HC.)

Five

Elementary and Secondary Education

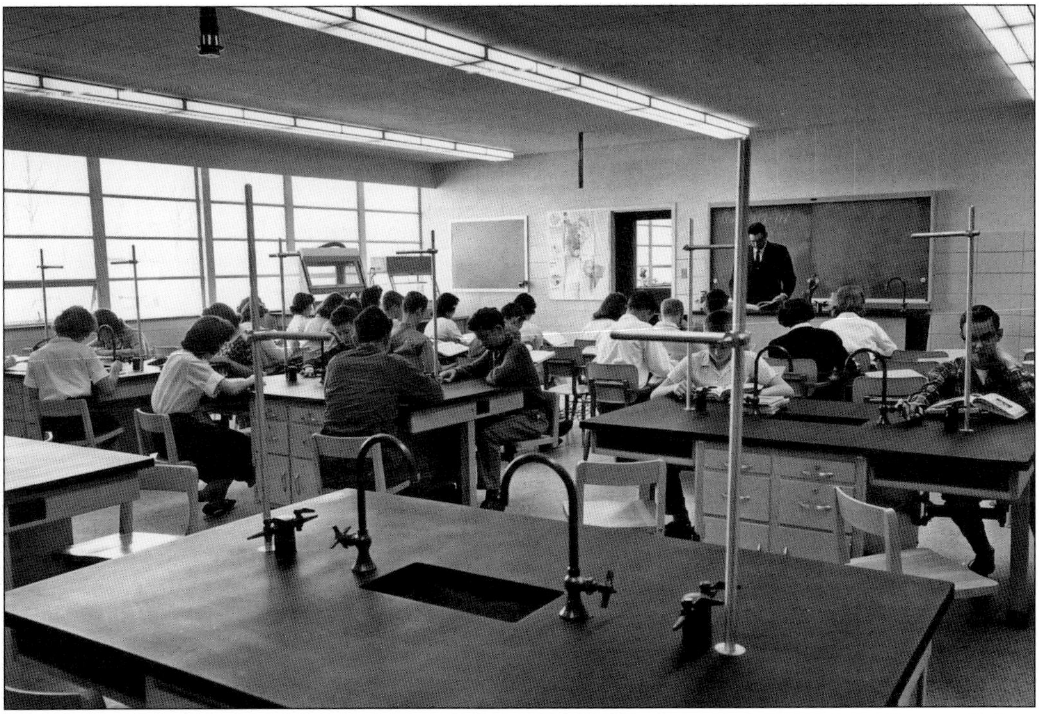

Students Concentrate. In 1960, Delmar Johnson's students prepare for a lab. Hanover's first school was, according to William McKee Dunn who attended it in the 1820s, "a rough cabin built of split logs slid edgewise, and an immense chimney at each end." An image of this building has not survived. The next school, called the Little Red Schoolhouse, and other school photographs can be seen on the following pages. (Courtesy Southwestern schools.)

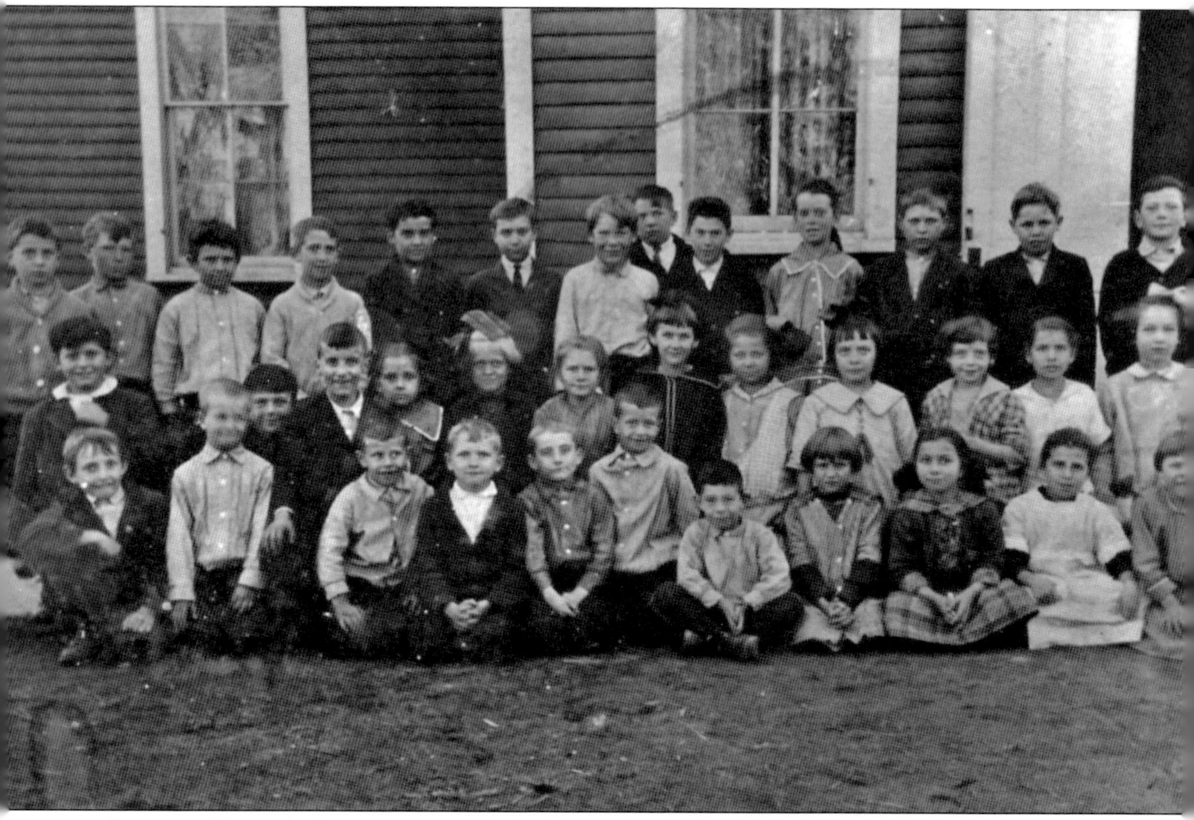

Bertha Watts's Class Poses. Third- and fourth-graders line up outside their schoolhouse in 1915. Pictured are, from left to right, (first row) ? Griffith, Paul Weiman, Ralph Snyder, two unidentified, Larry Sutherland, unidentified, Audrey Eses (or Elsea), Margaret Killian Wilson, Irene Kessler Goins, and Evelyn Davis; (second row) four unidentified, Bernice Mouser Oldaker, Georgia Sutherland, Opal Sparks Sauley, Laura Callamatta Ditzler Manaugh, Leona DeBurger, Grace Taft, ? Elsea, and Marjorie Scott; (third row) Tom Bruther, Paul Turner, John Warmen, Carl Bruther, Raymond Snyder, Paul Turner, Albert Ralph Manaugh, John Walker, Edith Wyne, unidentified, Arnie Johnson, and Lloyd Nieghbert. Laura Callamatta Ditzler (eighth from left in second row) and Albert Manaugh (tallest boy in back row) married in 1927. They had eight children: James Nelson, Albert Richard, Margaret Jean, Ada Marilyn, Linda Nan, Jack Norman, Karen Lea, and Robert Charles, who was named for his two grandfathers. Marilyn, Linda, and Karen still live in Hanover. (Courtesy Marsh family.)

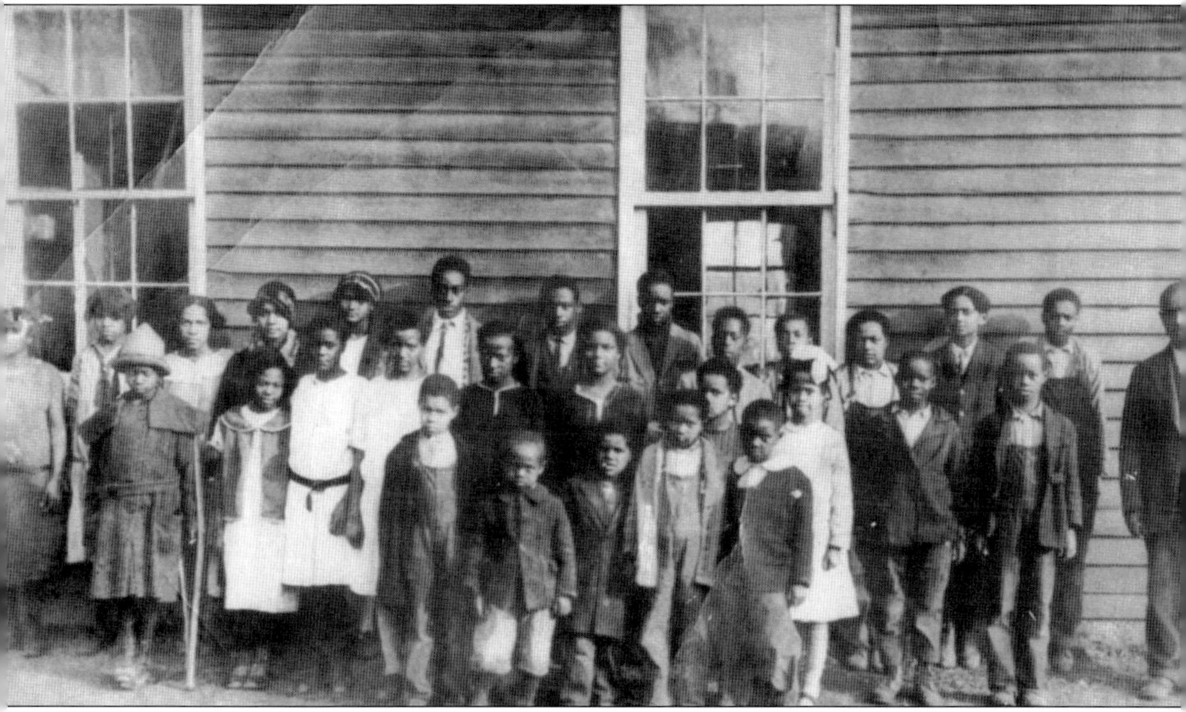

Classmates Become Husband and Wife. Helen Gradey is the girl in the second row, third from the right, in the white dress with the bow in her hair. Charles Smith stands in the back row, second from the far left. They have been happily married for "a good 50 or more years" and have four children—Jerry, Larry, Judith, and Charles Kendall—according to local historians. They attended school at what they called the "Hanover School." In the first row on the far left is Charles Cosby. Georgene Buckner stands at the far left of the second row and is wearing a hat. Two girls over is Josephine Smith Whittaker in the white dress with the slender belt. Nancy Jones Todd stands in the second row, two girls over from Josephine. Eva Cosby is in the back row, the third student from the left in the white blouse. Next to her, wearing a hat, is Virginia Beatty. Carl Johnson, sporting a slim necktie, stands two people to the right of Virginia. Carter Smith is in the back row, eighth from the left. Mr. Miles, the teacher, stands at the far right of the photograph, which was taken in the 1920s or 1930s. (Courtesy John D. and Freda Johnson Cosby family.)

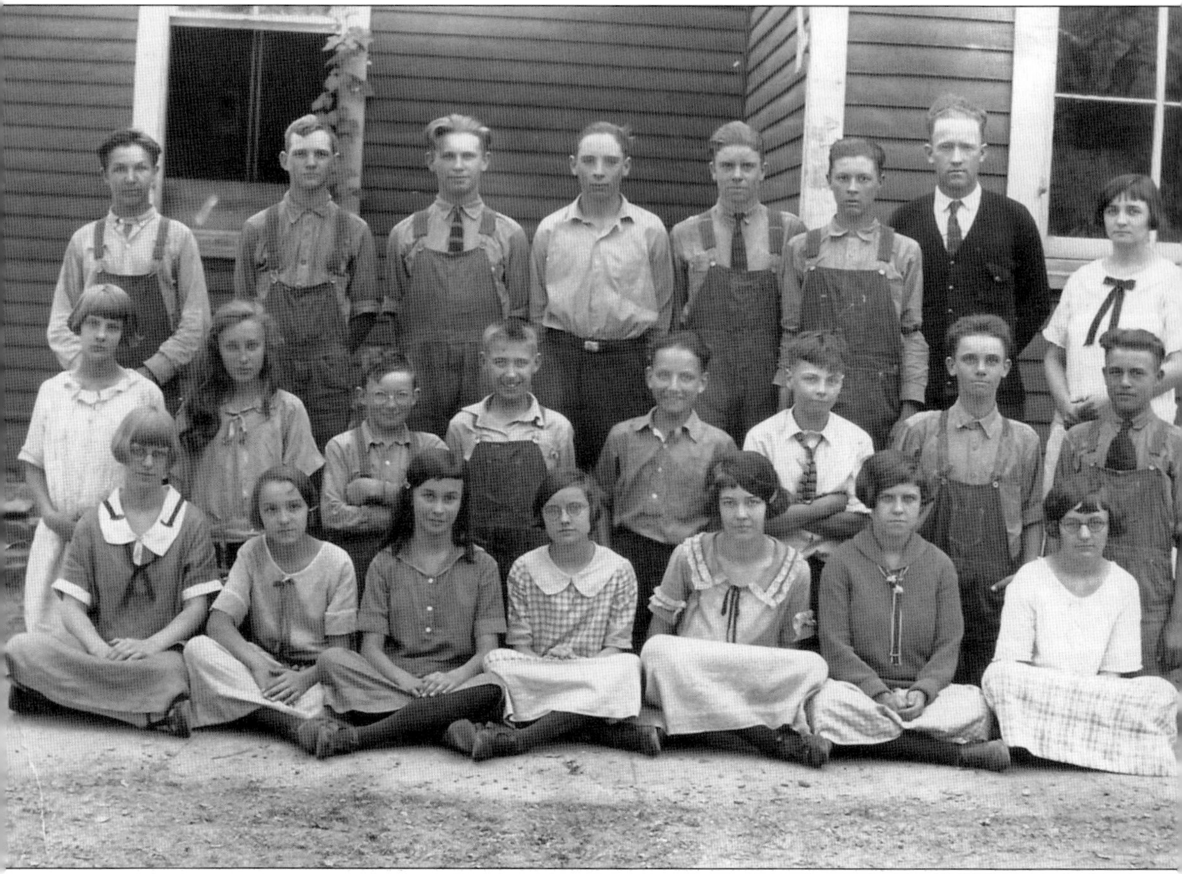

Students' Picture Taken. In 1925, these eighth graders pose with their teachers. Pictured are, from left to right, (first row) Ruth Smith, Hazel Clever, Helen Spry, Mary Blanche Jackson, Agnes Nighbert, Bessie Adams, and Clara Mae Nighbert; (second row) Datheryn Davis, Evangeline Farrell, Jimmy Rogers, Jennett Gray, George Millican, Harvea Rardt, unidentified, and Milton Rowlett; (third row) William Stillhammer, Melvin Frazier, Lewis Adams, Ralph Bruther, Ralph Sutherland, Edgar Richmond, teacher Eldo Lauderbaugh, and teacher Thelma Peters. Ruth Smith's father worked at a tack factory in Madison. (Courtesy Bob Ireland.)

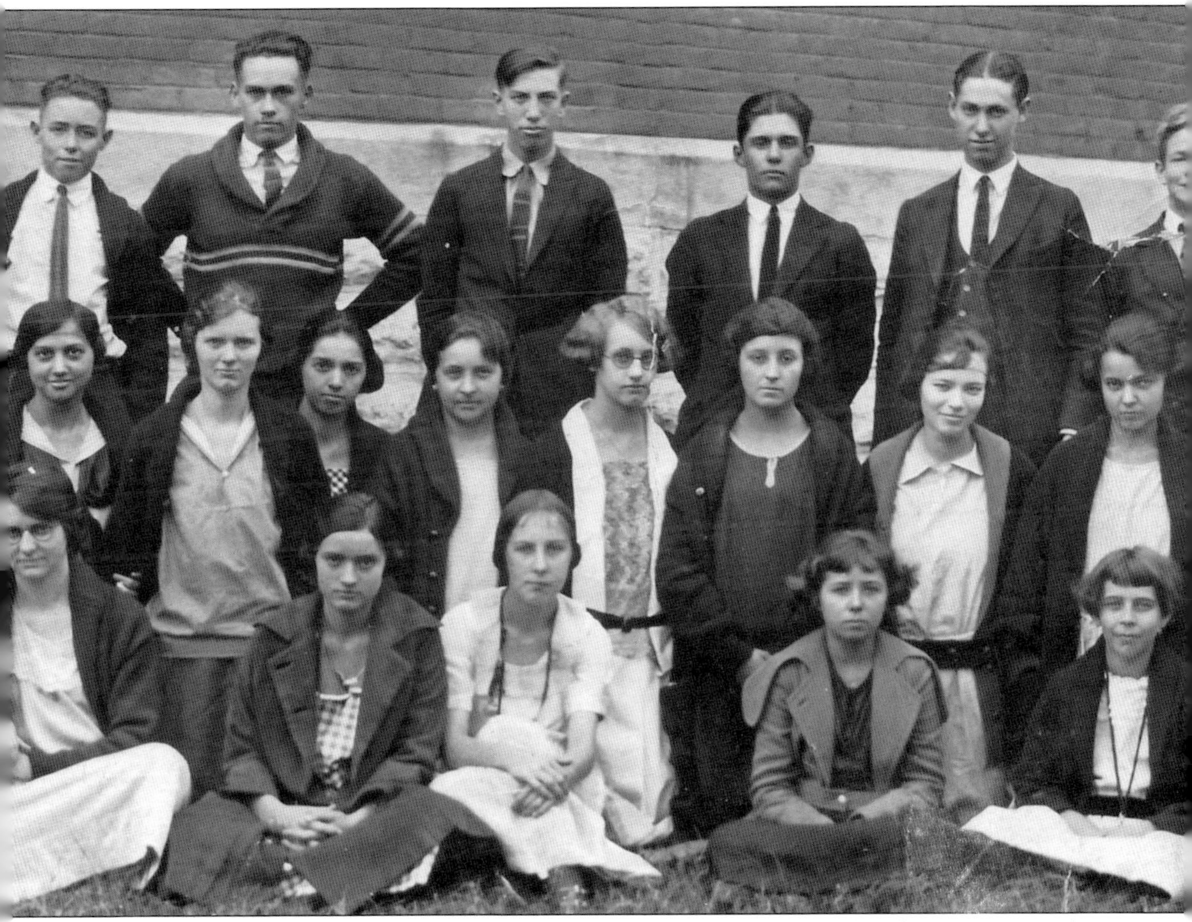

High Schoolers Assemble. Students from Hanover High School pose for their picture in the early 1920s. The second girl from the left in the second row is Mary Elizabeth Gray Kleopfer. The fifth girl from the left in the same row is Florence Uebel Bruner. The seventh girl from the left in the second row is Mona Simmons, whose sister Rita taught school in Hanover. The ninth girl from the left in the second row is Mary Rogers. (Courtesy Manaugh family.)

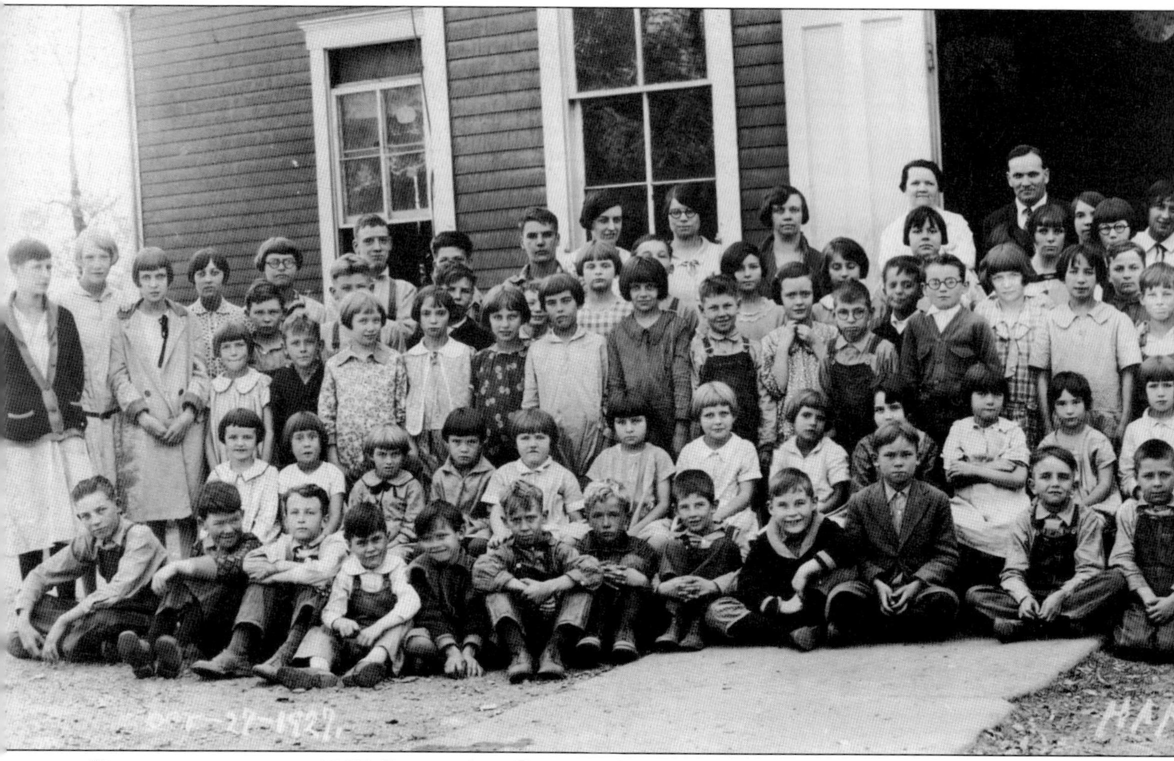

PHOTOGRAPH FROM 1927 SHOWS ALL GRADES. Hanover's Little Red Schoolhouse stood where the present-day fire station is located on Main Street. Children in grades one to eight attended it. The reader is asked to look at the names carefully, as several modern-day Hanover families are descended from these little ones. Pictured are, from left to right, (first row) unidentified, Lee Nighbert, Louis Huber, Victor Price, two unidentified, Thomas Harvey Adams, Shannon Matthews, Kenneth McKeand, Robert Mundt, Lester Hay, John Sutherland, Carolyn Clever, Dwight Lichliter, Jimmie Clemmons, unidentified, Kenneth McKay, two unidentified, Pascal Bell, Cecil Kelly, ? Duke, three unidentified, and Fulton ?; (second row, seated) Wilma Gabel, Evelyn Tull, unidentified, Martha Matthews, Norma Price, Anna Marjorie Kessler, Frances Aspinall, unidentified, Virginia Wooten, unidentified, Beth ?, Mary E. Wood, unidentified, Juanita Kelly, Ruth Keidel, Elizabeth Rowlett, Anna Margaret Pender, Norma Jean (or Jane) Kessler, Betty M. Gabel, Bernice Bell, Mildred Hostetler, Mary Edith Harris, unidentified, Catherine Gillespie, George Lee Bruther, and R. Fulton; (third row, standing) Isabelle ?, Kenneth Kyle, Dorcas Porter, Mildred Tudor, Florence Aspinall, Mildred Hay, Eloise Gassert, John Brooks, Virginia Morganson,

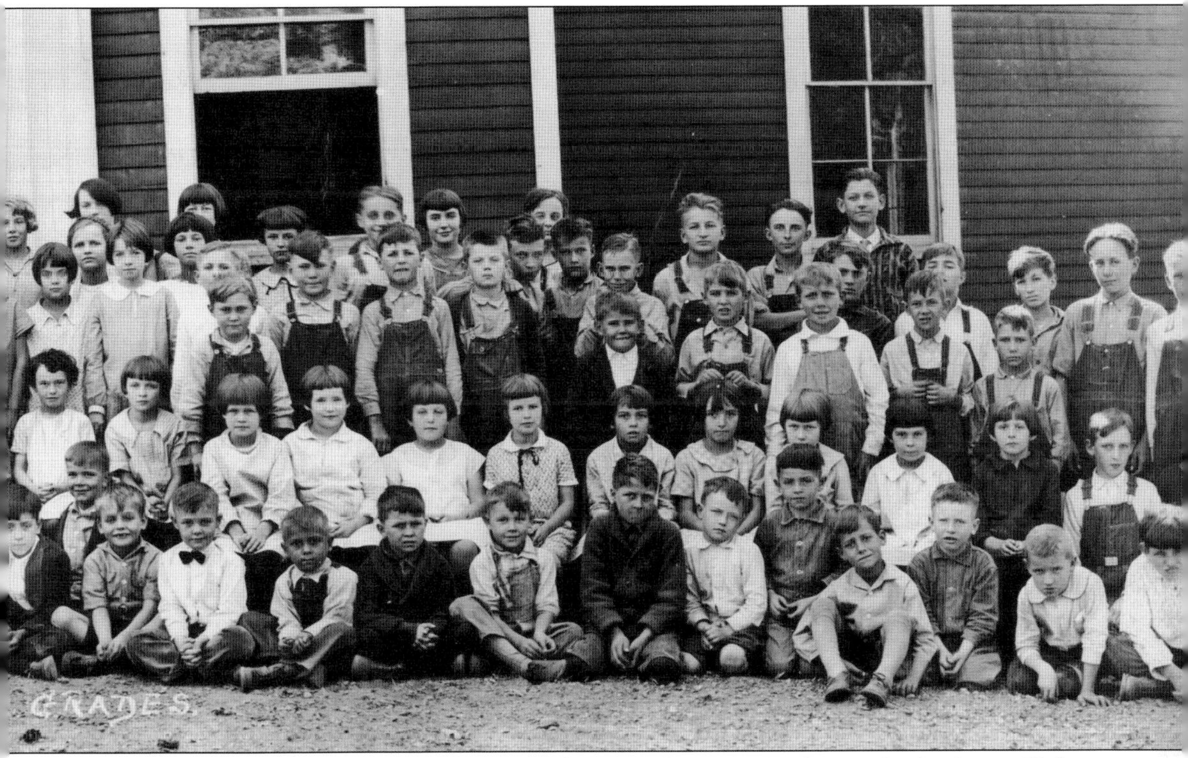

Billy Sutherland, John Crim, ? Hostetler, Opal H. Reed, Louise Catherine Lusby, Laura Huber, Ruby Manaugh, Janet Catherine Craig, Clarence Tull, Paul Tull, Paul Tull Duntz, William Brooks, Robert Park, Lester Hay, unidentified, Cecil J. Bruther, David McKeand, Robert Bolton, James Davis, and two unidentified; (fourth row) two unidentified, Frederick ?, James Stockdale, Margaret Gillespie, unidentified, Lucy Brook, Elizabeth Aspinall, Lanier McKeand, unidentified, Joe Rogers, Robert Ferguson, Eleanor Thornton, Edna Brooks, Frances Gabel, unidentified, Roberta Lee, Charles Judkins, unidentified, Robert Henning, ? Waggoner, Harold Gray, three unidentified, John Burdsal Young, and two unidentified; (fifth row) unidentified, Martha Dunn Adams, Beatrice Bruther, Rozena King, Clara Brooks, George Frazier, Elmo Richmond, Albert Lee, Jeanette Banta, ? McKeand, Grace Bolton, Lelia Rowlett, Dorothy Nighbert, Mary Catherine Truesdale, Mary Elizabeth Adams, ? Guion, and Stella Kelly; (sixth row) teachers Mrs. Percy, Rita Simmons, Mrs. Jones, Mrs. Henning, and principal Gar Rogers. Absent were Robert Craig Junior and Dorothy Porter, who was Dorcas Porter's twin sister. Both were home sick the day this picture was taken. (Courtesy Janet C. Cowen.)

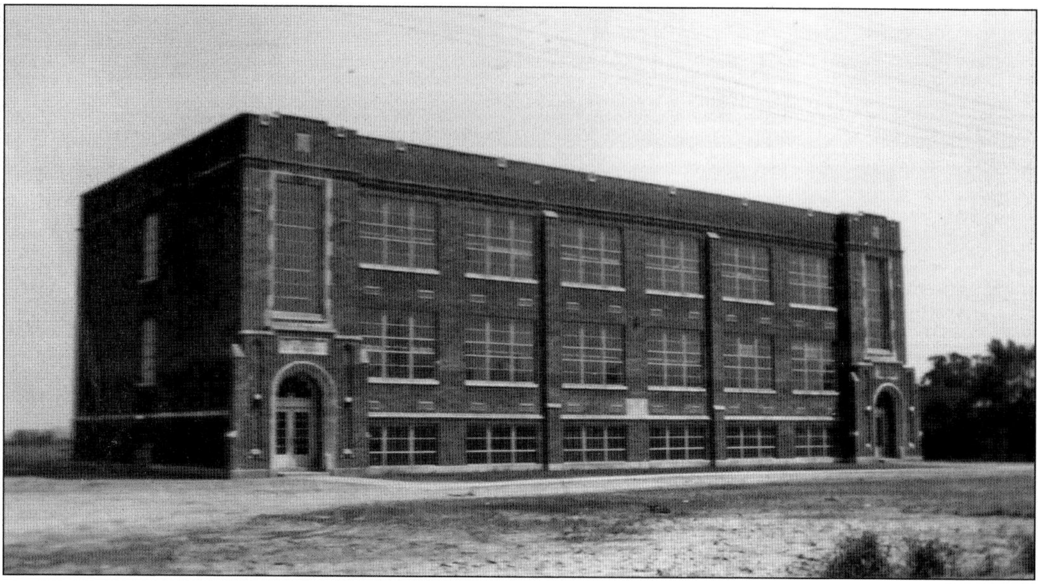

Hanover School Built. Students moved into a new school in 1928 from "the Little Red Schoolhouse," which housed elementary grades, and the Hanover College campus, used for a high school. A gymnasium was built in 1952 and a new elementary school in 1961. In 1960, Saluda school and Hanover consolidated to become Southwestern Jefferson County Consolidated School Corporation. A tornado in 1974 destroyed the high school and gymnasium. They were replaced with new junior and senior high schools. (Courtesy LC.)

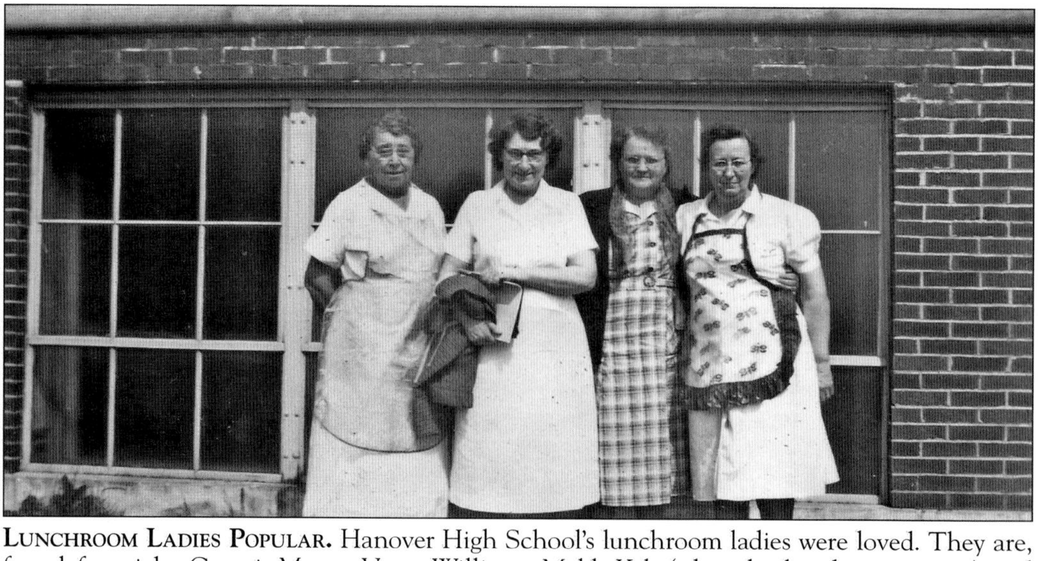

Lunchroom Ladies Popular. Hanover High School's lunchroom ladies were loved. They are, from left to right, Georgia Means, Verna Williams, Mable Kyle (whose husband was a grocer), and Mrs. Gable, who was the head lunchroom lady. Gable's husband was the school's principal and coach. Mothers of students sometimes went to the school to can tomatoes in the home economics laboratory to be used in school lunches. (Courtesy D/M.)

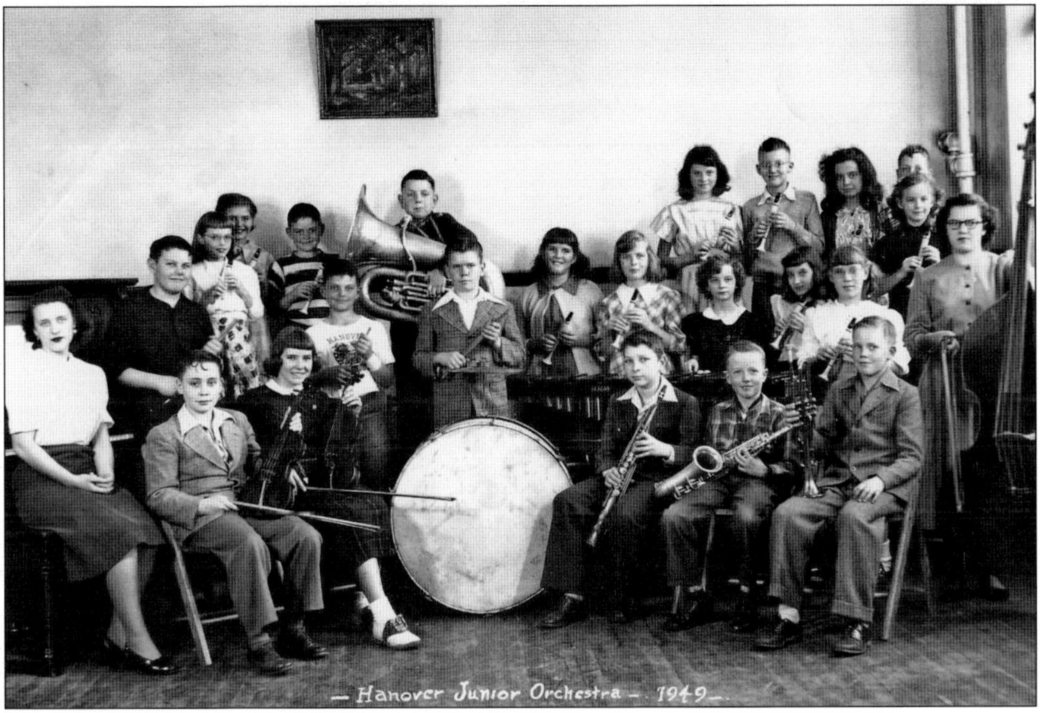

Instrumentalists Play. The Hanover Junior Orchestra members pose with their director in 1949. Fifteen of the students hold recorders, a wind instrument often played as an introduction to other instruments. Others hold a variety of stringed, wind, brass, and percussion instruments. (Courtesy Lynne Cooper Abner family.)

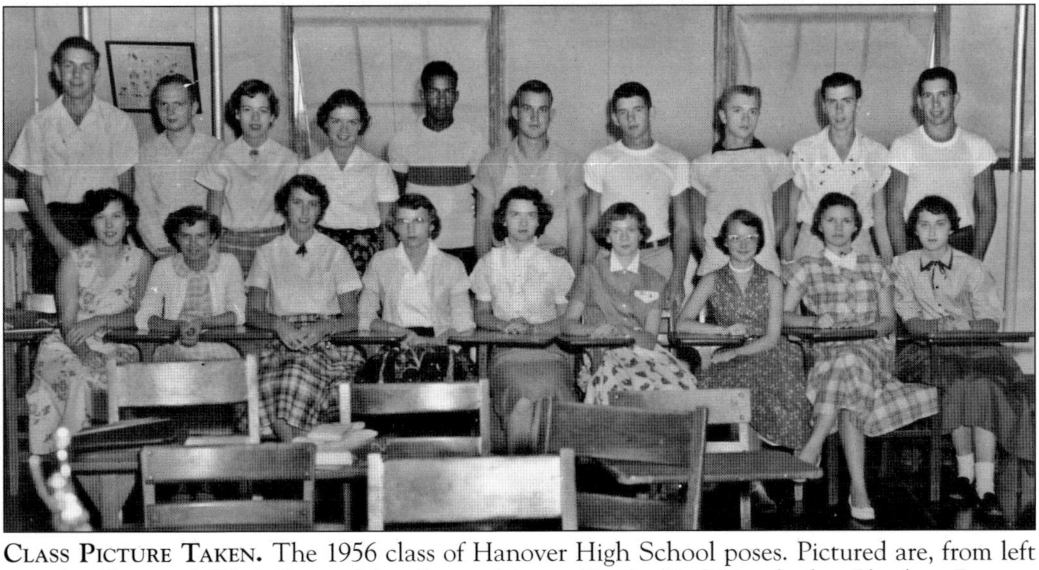

Class Picture Taken. The 1956 class of Hanover High School poses. Pictured are, from left to right, (first row) Edith Dunn, Mary Lynne Mason, Pat (or Dot) Hassfurder, Charlene Bagent, Patsy Watson, Pat Fields, Lynne Cooper, Agnes Smith, and Stella Singer; (second row) Dale Gwynn, Weir Baker, Shirley Sprong, Mille Zirkle, Melvin Humes, Earmel Eppley, Bill Jackson, Charles Rogers, Lanier Bibbs, and Clayton Bruner. Ann Anderson was absent. (Courtesy Lynne Cooper Abner family.)

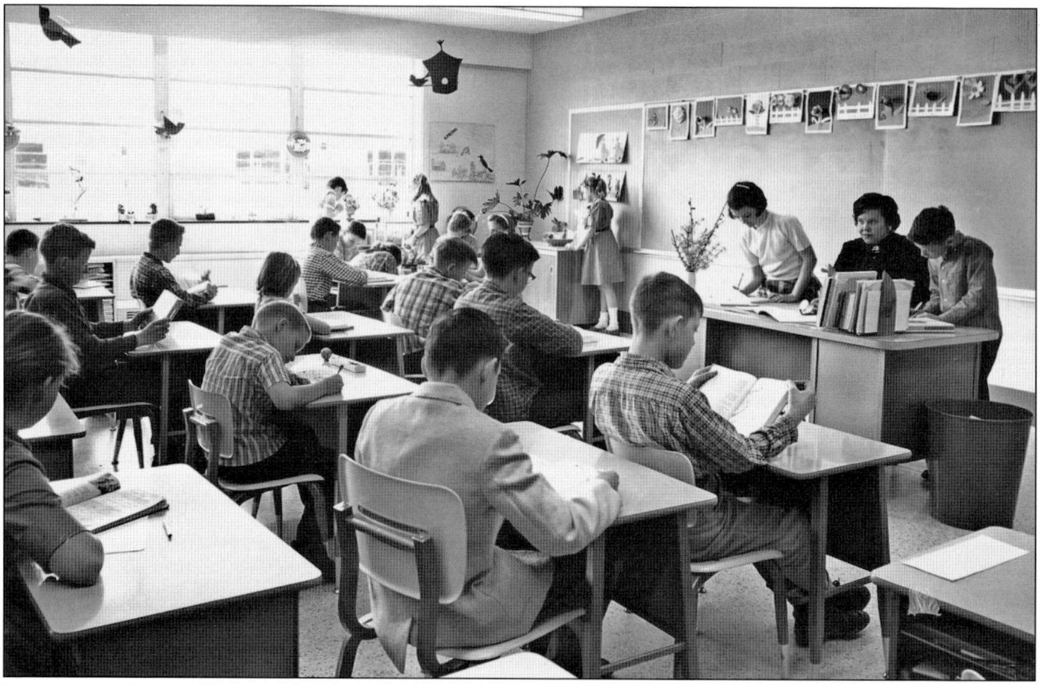

Boys and Girls Work. Children from the Southwestern schools read in the 1960s as teacher Neva Thompson Hill assists other children at her desk and supervises. Two girls are working in what appears to be a science corner. The class is doing a unit on birds complete with a hanging birdhouse. (Courtesy Southwestern schools.)

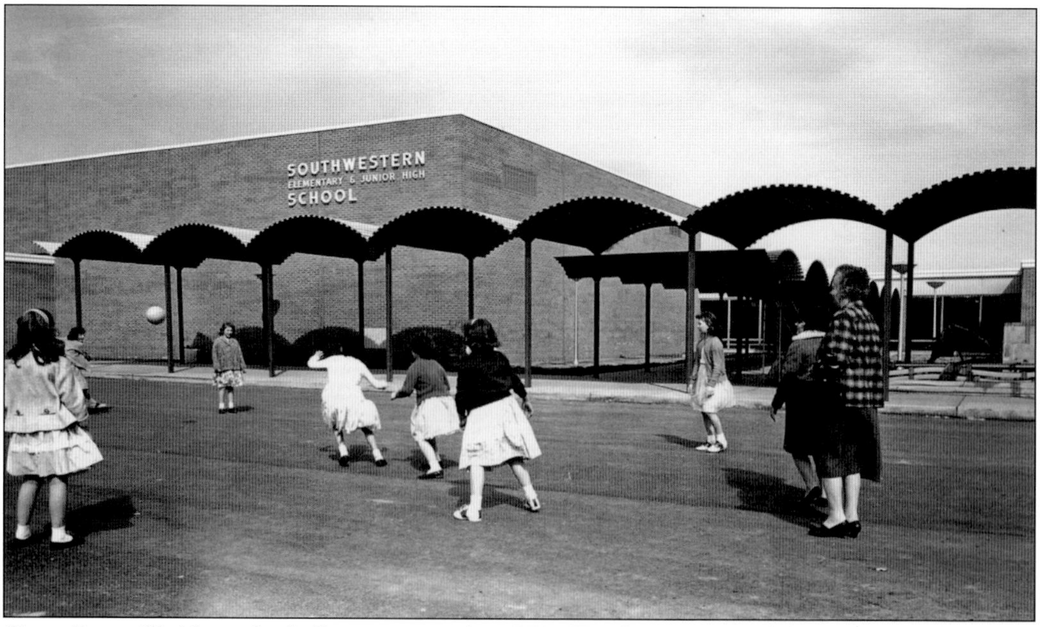

Girls Play. Children play ball at recess in the 1950s. Teacher Fern Stockdale, in the plaid jacket, watches from the right side of the picture. Note the saddle oxford shoes and dresses instead of physical education uniforms. The ball has been kicked and is getting ready to be kicked again! (Courtesy Southwestern schools.)

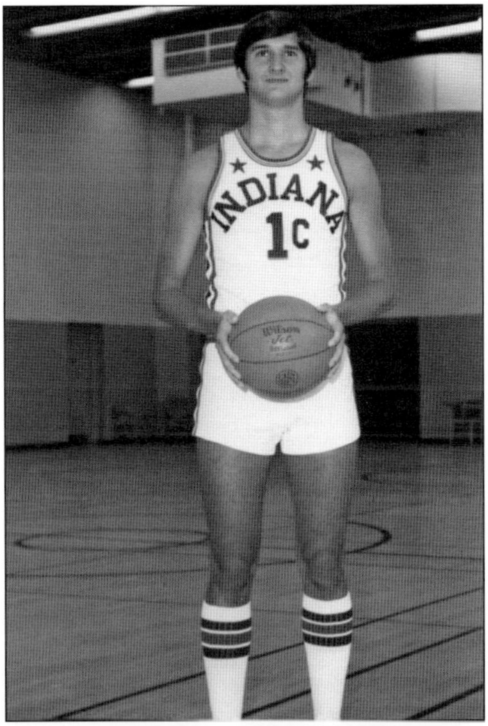

SOUTHWESTERN STUDENT WINS OVER LARRY BIRD. Steve Collier was selected "Mr. Basketball" in the state of Indiana instead of Larry Bird in 1974. Collier shared the honor with Roy Taylor of Anderson, Indiana. After graduating from Southwestern High School, Collier played ball at the University of Cincinnati and led his team to three appearances in NCAA tournaments. He went on to coach, become a school administrator, and a superintendent of schools. (Courtesy Collier family.)

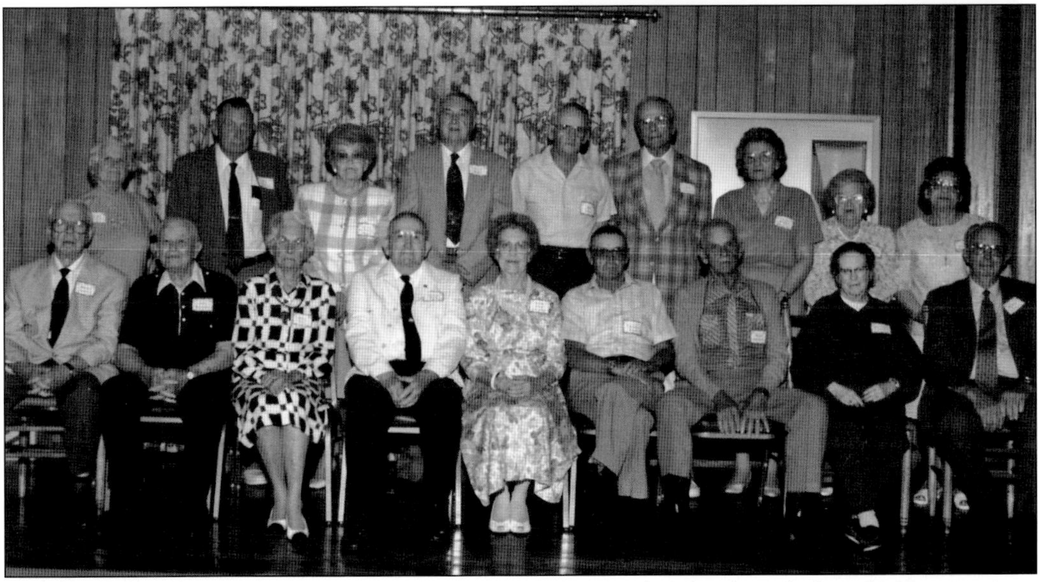

GOLDEN GRADS CELEBRATE. When graduates of Hanover High School reach their 50th anniversary of graduation, they become "Golden Grads." Shown at a 1992 reunion are, from left to right, (first row) Wallace Judkins, 1923; Dale Renschler, 1928; Helen Spry, 1929; Howard Banta, 1930; Edith Sever Christie, 1930; Thelbert Black, 1931; Wayne Jackson, 1931; Mary Helen Wells Schirmer, 1931; and Howard Gray, 1932; (second row) Eleanor Thornton Killin, 1932; Neil Manaugh, 1933; Wilma McDonald Moore, 1934; Louis Huber, 1934; Bob Craig, 1935; Carl Gray, 1935; Laura Huber Rankin, 1936; Betty Huffington Niccum, 1936; and Opal Hampton Humphreys, 1936. (Courtesy Don Wood Studio, retired.)

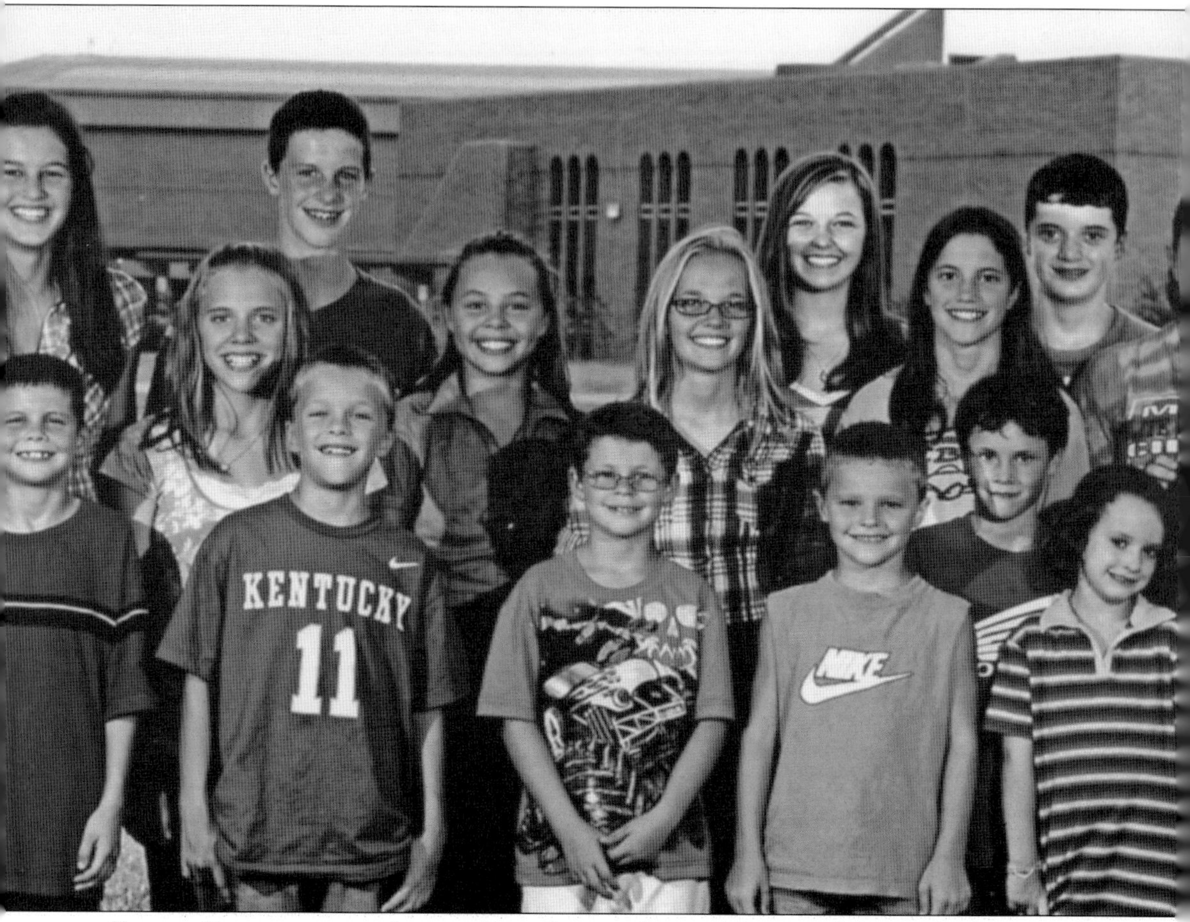

Fifteen Grandchildren Attend Same School. Loretta Martin and Grover Anderson graduated from Southwestern High School in 1970. They married and had five children: Grover David, Jon, Tonia, Joshua, and Jason. Grover David married Debbie Curry. Jon, Grover David's twin brother, married Lynette Marshall. Tonia married Joshua Cline. Joshua Anderson married Jenni Neace. Joshua's twin brother, Jason, married Susan Burgan. Every one of Loretta and Grover's 15 grandchildren attended Southwestern Elementary School and Southwestern Middle/Senior High School in 2010–2011. Pictured are, from left to right, (first row) Mitchell Cline, Adam Anderson, Thomas Anderson (the Anderson's youngest son, and uncle to all the rest), Jonathan Anderson, Clayton Anderson, Ashleigh Anderson, and Jacob Anderson; (second row) Camille Cline, Sarah Anderson, Greggory Cline, Rebekah Anderson, Elizabeth Anderson, Emily Anderson, Kaylan Anderson, Nathan Anderson, and Whitney Anderson. (Photograph by Ken Ritchie; courtesy the *Madison Courier*.)

Six

Hanover College

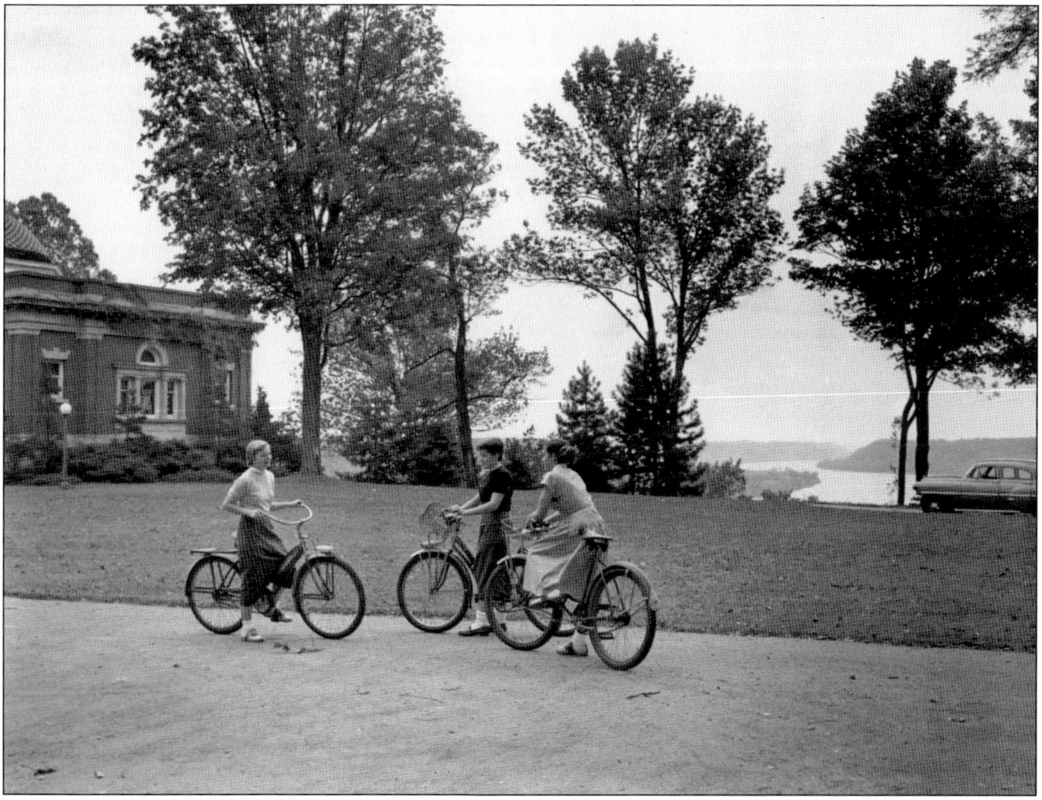

Students Enjoy Sunny Day. Women ride their bicycles on the college campus near Hendricks Hall with the Ohio River in the background. Carol Shields, on the far left, graduated in 1957, became an author, and later won a Pulitzer Prize. Hanover College was founded in 1827 with strong Scottish and Presbyterian traditions. Young men in the first class built their own classroom. Curriculum included religion, classics, manual labor, and the sciences. (Courtesy HC.)

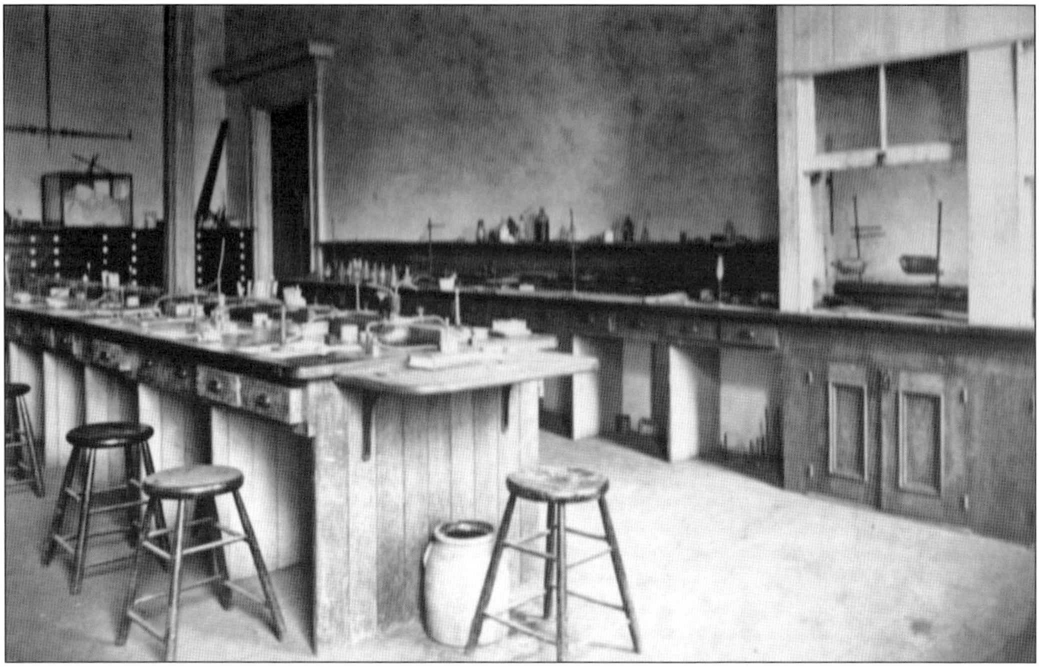

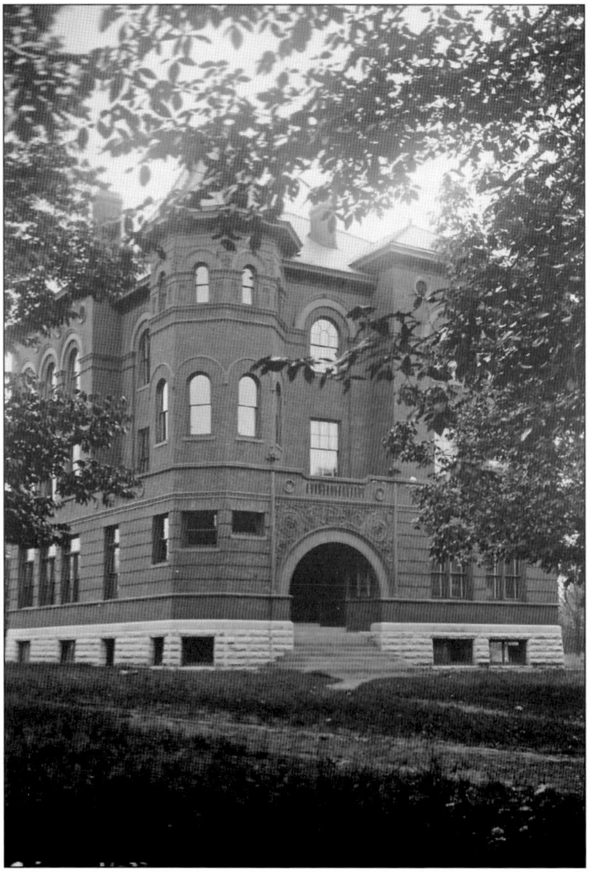

Faculty Revolutionizes. Hanover College's earliest science faculty members changed the way advanced science was taught. A laboratory component was added to lectures to enhance learning. The innovation was picked up by other colleges. Pictured here is a chemistry and geology laboratory in about 1890, where students could actually get their hands on what they were learning about. (Courtesy HC.)

Science Hall Opened in 1897. The scientific building pictured at left was built after Hanover College's president Daniel Webster Fisher visited the five top U.S. college campuses to get ideas for Hanover College's new building. Its cost of $29,000 was raised through donations. (Courtesy HC.)

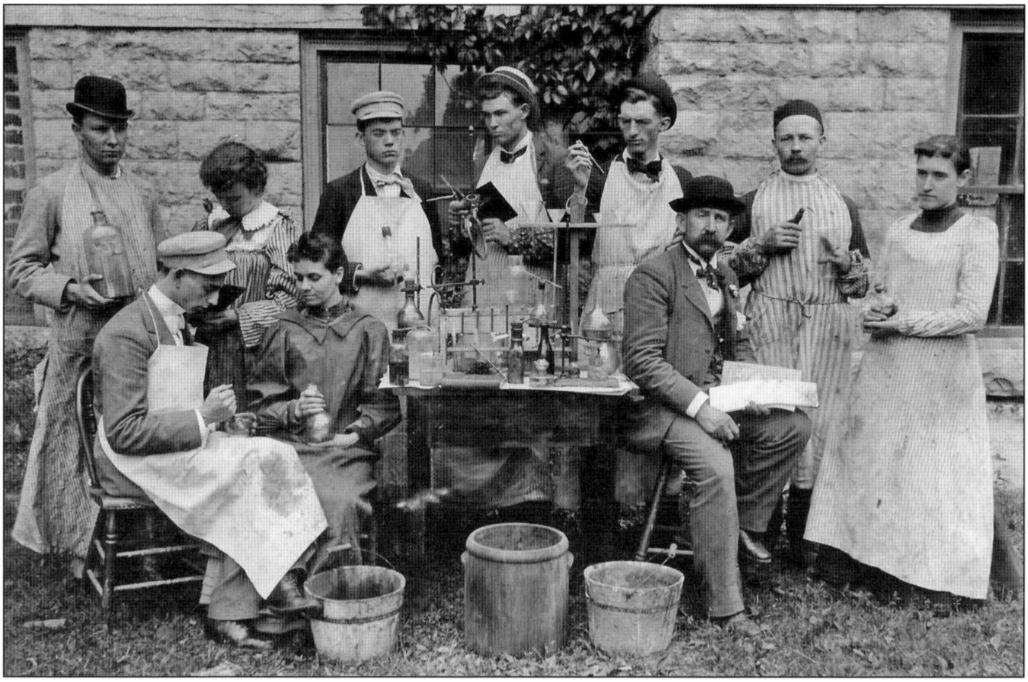

STUDENTS EXPERIMENT, 1893. Chemistry students pictured are, from left to right and by last name only, (first row) Burger, Sutherland, and Prof. Andrew Harvey Young; (second row) Bridges, Drayer, Peak, Shepherd, Jenkins, Harlow, Hall, and M. F. West. Young graduated from Hanover in 1871 and taught at the college for 49 years. He married Williamson Dunn's granddaughter Mary ("Molly") Agnes and passed up a lucrative chemistry career for his beloved Hanover. (Courtesy HC.)

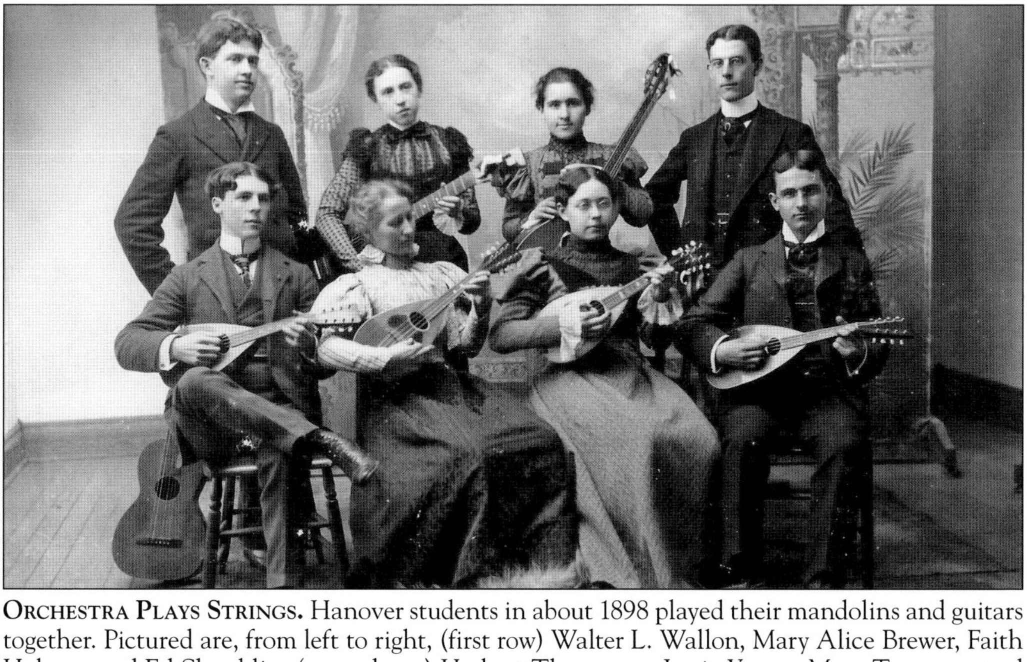

ORCHESTRA PLAYS STRINGS. Hanover students in about 1898 played their mandolins and guitars together. Pictured are, from left to right, (first row) Walter L. Wallon, Mary Alice Brewer, Faith Holmes, and Ed Shanklin; (second row) Herbert Thompson, Jessie Young, Mary Torrance, and Tom Whallon. (Courtesy HC.)

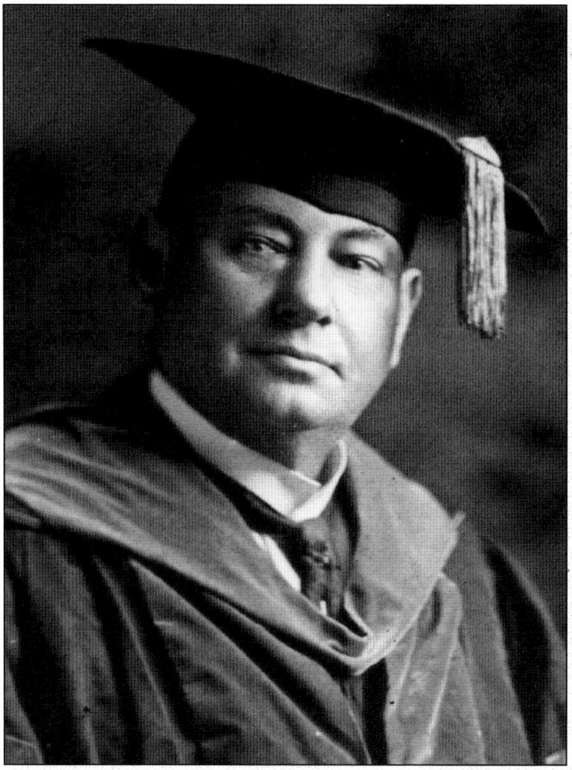

Chemist Leads Nation. Harvey Washington Wiley graduated from Hanover College in 1867. He worked as the chief chemist at the U.S. Department of Agriculture and is credited with writing most of the Pure Food and Drug Act of 1906. He is also thought to be the one who convinced Pres. Theodore Roosevelt and Congress to pass the act. (Courtesy HC.)

Hendricks Hall Honors Graduate. Thomas A. Hendricks graduated from Hanover College in 1841 and practiced law before entering politics. He served as U.S. vice president for nine months before he died in 1885. His wife, Eliza Morgan, gave funds to construct a library on campus, which is pictured below with the Old Well House in the foreground. Hendricks Hall was added to the National Register of Historic Places in 1982. (Courtesy HC.)

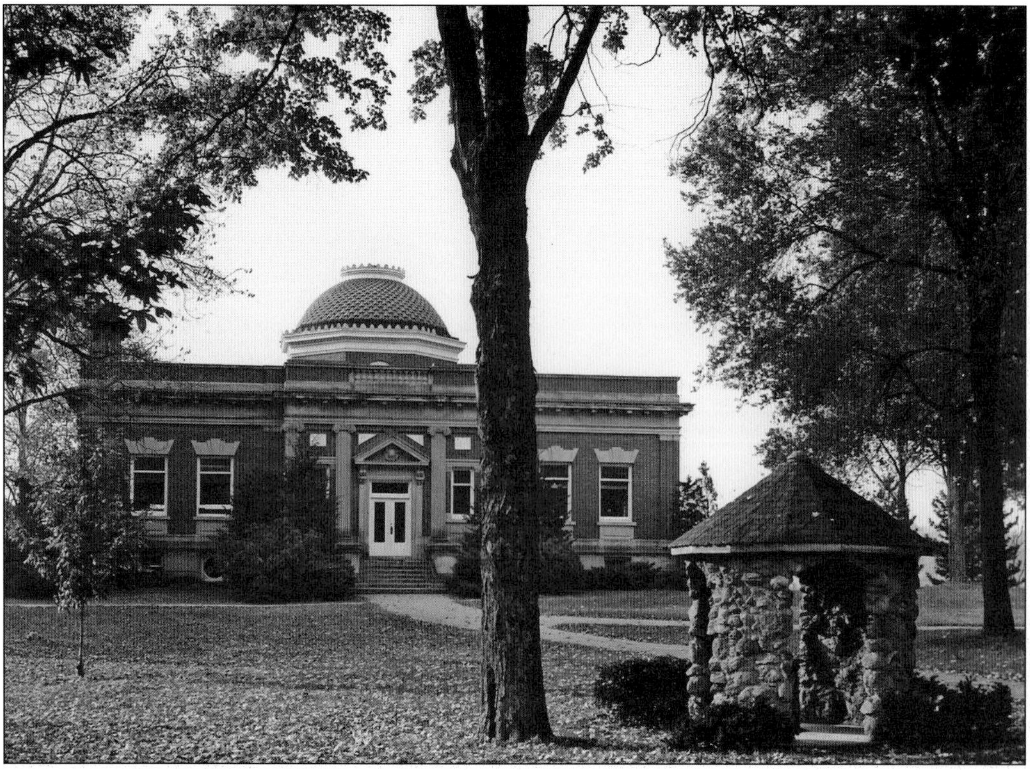

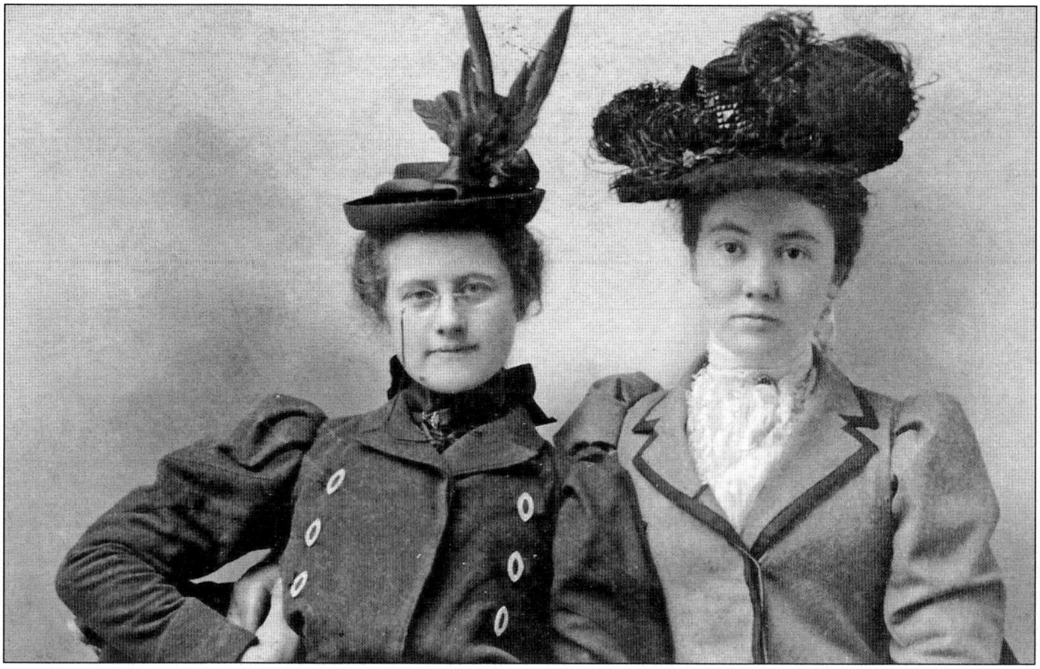

Five Represent Typical Students. Five Hanover College students pose around 1898. The women are Daisy Myrtle Dillon, left, and Gertrude S. Mason. The men are Halbert H. Britain (graduated in 1898), Frank Raymond Adams (graduated in 1899), and Virgil B. Scott (graduated in 1899). At Hanover College, these five would have engaged in a classical education infused with the latest scientific discoveries. They also would have been encouraged to read, both for reference and for the joy of enjoying poetry and popular literature. In addition, they would have been immersed in religious activities because of the college's deep Presbyterian roots. (Both, courtesy HC.)

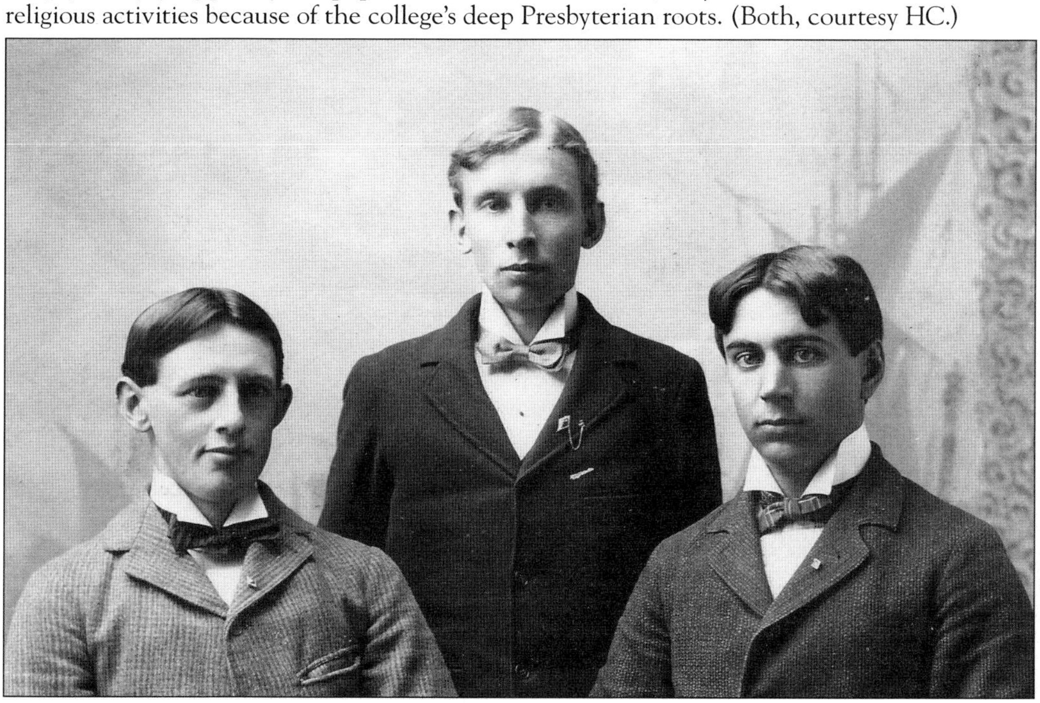

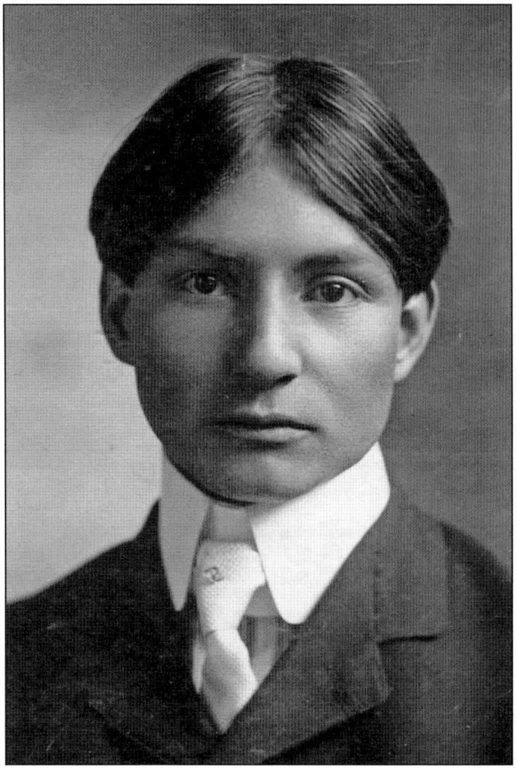

First Native American Plays Ball. Headright Moore was the first Native American to attend Hanover College. The back of this extremely rare photograph discovered in the college archives reads, "Muskogee, Indiana Territory now Oklahoma. Class of 1903—Phi Gamma Delta—football star." Headright came to Hanover to stay with his uncle Judge Napoleon Bonaparte Moore after his parents died. He was a star football fullback. (Courtesy HC.)

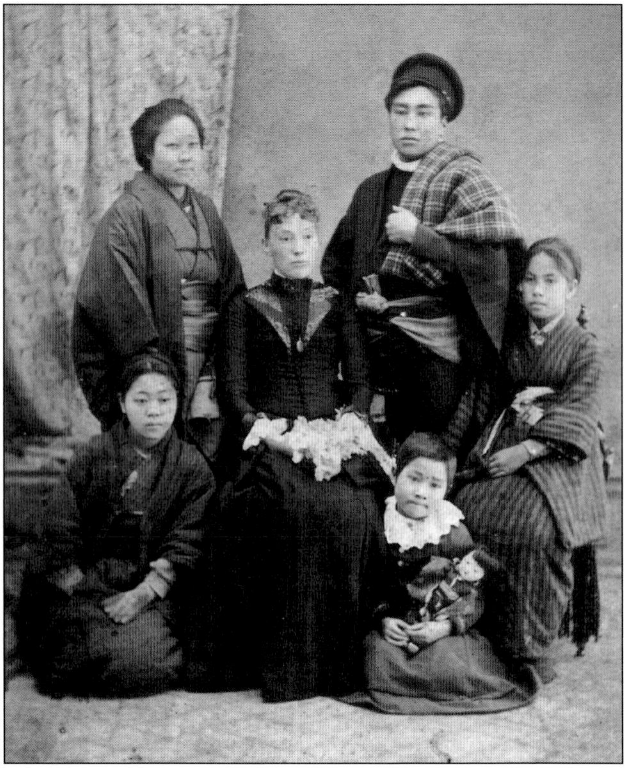

College Graduates First Female. Calla Harrison graduated from Hanover College in 1883. She poses at right in the middle of a group with what is inscribed on the back of this exceptional image as "college friends." Women had tried to enroll at Hanover College in 1869, but their requests were ignored. They enrolled anyway with special permission in classes not taught in their private school. By 1880, women were enrolled as regular students. (Courtesy HC.)

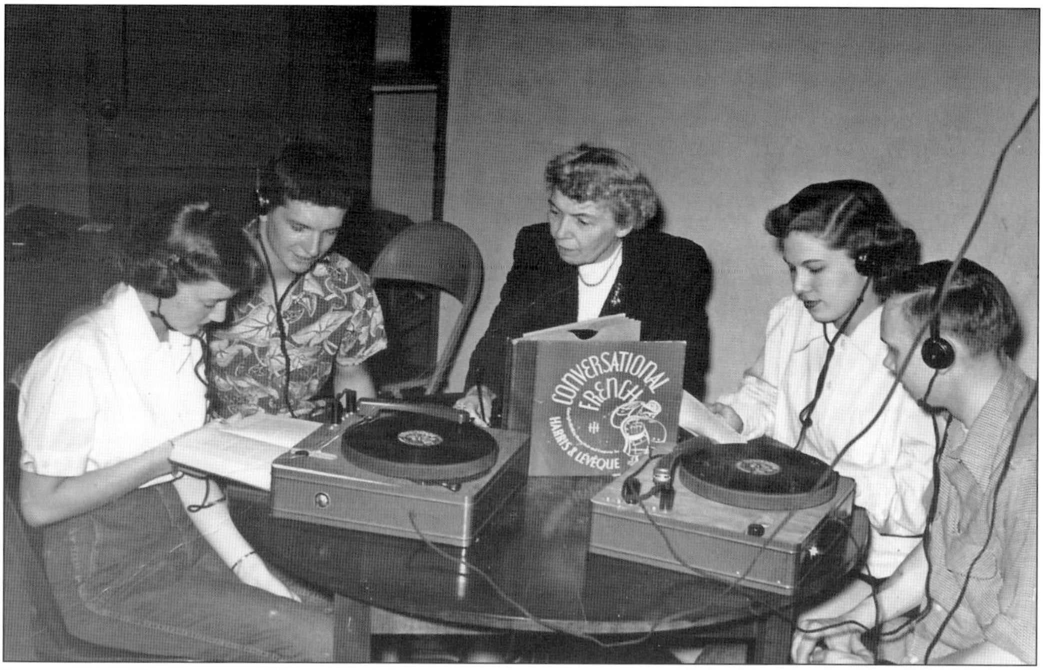

LANGUAGE TAUGHT BY HEARING, SPEAKING. Prof. Jean Anderson employed what was then a cutting-edge enhancement in teaching language: a listening center using record players and headphones. This image of her and four of her French students is thought to have been taken in the 1940s. Anderson served on Hanover's faculty from 1922 to 1952. (Courtesy HC.)

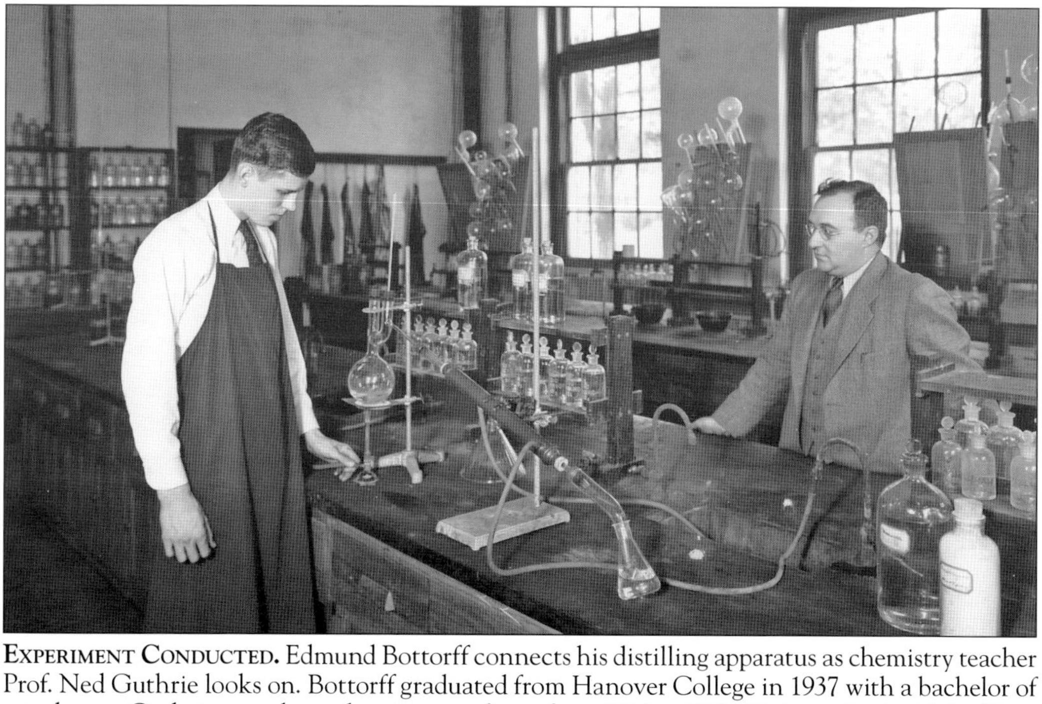

EXPERIMENT CONDUCTED. Edmund Bottorff connects his distilling apparatus as chemistry teacher Prof. Ned Guthrie looks on. Bottorff graduated from Hanover College in 1937 with a bachelor of arts degree. Guthrie served as a chemistry professor from 1926 to 1962. He is credited with building up the department after almost everything was destroyed in a 1919 fire. (Courtesy HC.)

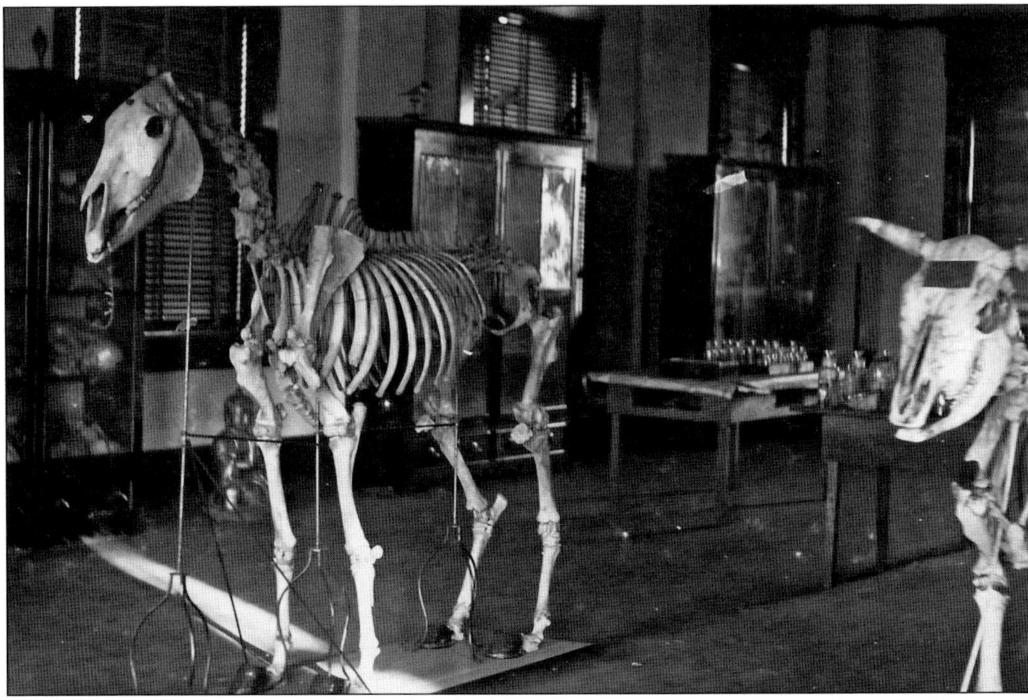

Skeleton Tricks Professor. Hanover College students were infamous from early on for Halloween stunts and tricks. One year, around 1910, students spirited the horse skeleton pictured above out of the college museum at night. They hitched the horse up to a buggy belonging to science professor Andrew Harvey Young. The horse of bones and buggy were left in front of the Presbyterian church. (Courtesy Lee Bruther.)

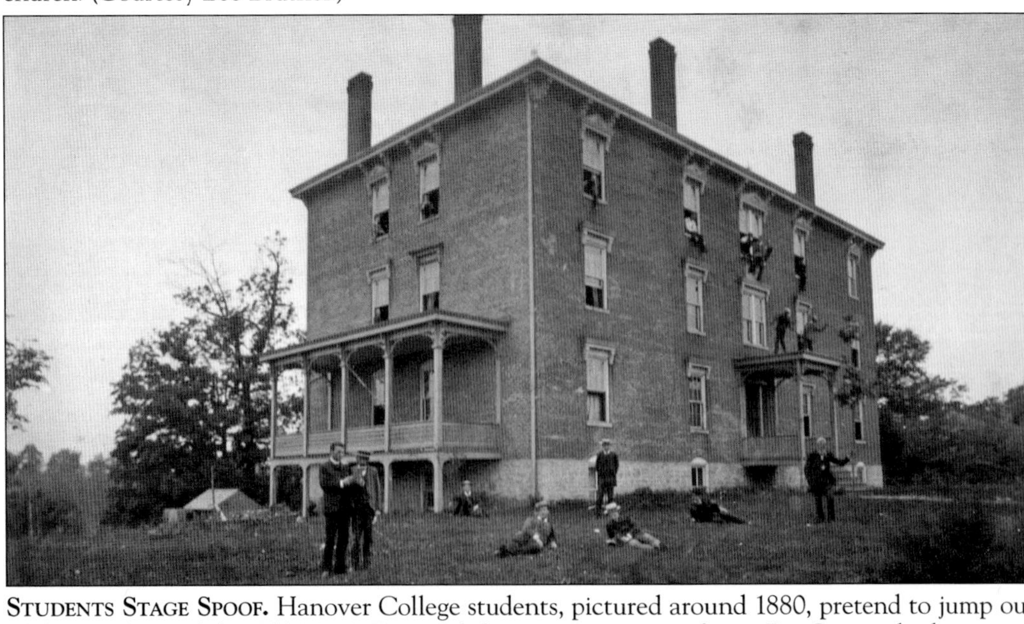

Students Stage Spoof. Hanover College students, pictured around 1880, pretend to jump out of the windows of the Old Men's Dorm while unsuspecting professor Dr. Garrett looks toward the camera from the lawn on the right. Two other professors consult with each other in the left foreground. (Courtesy HCHA.)

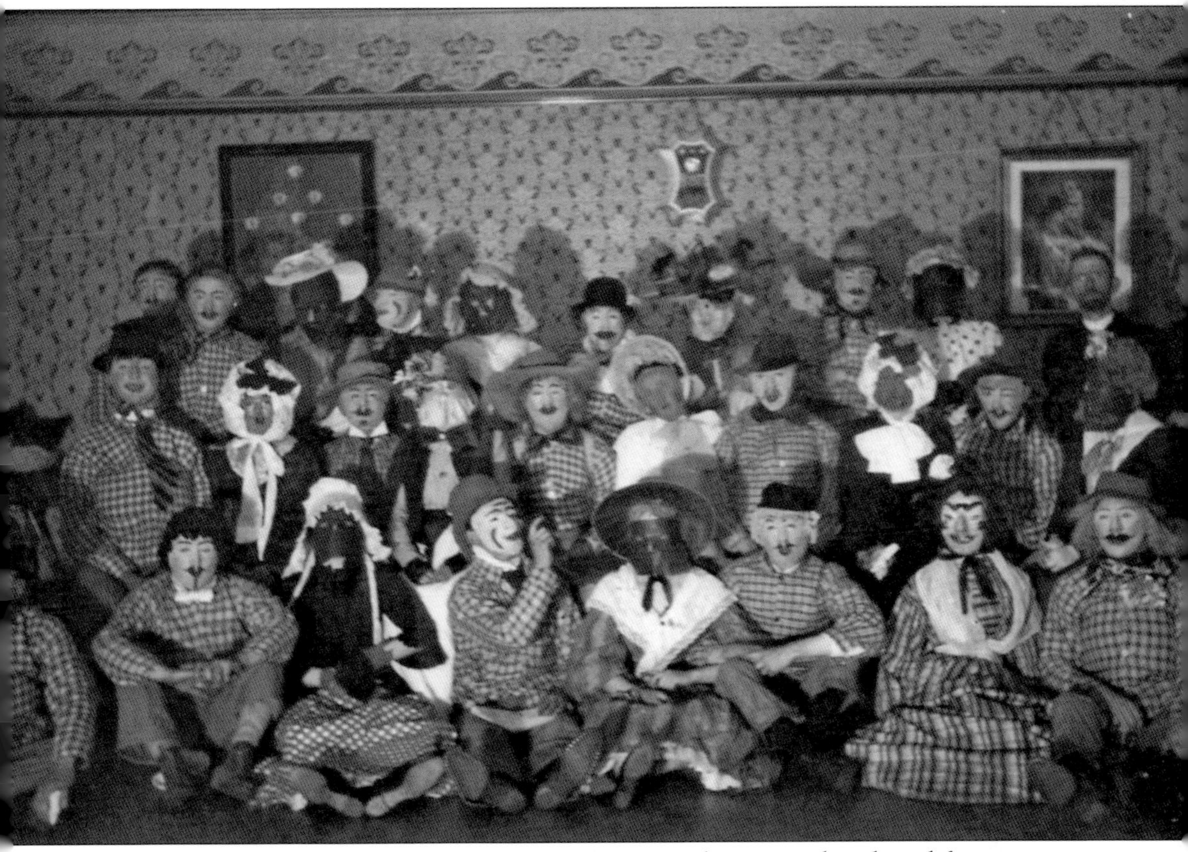

Betas Throw Halloween Party. Students' serious studies were abandoned for a time in 1900 to celebrate, according to this visual evidence. The students pictured above are shown in disguising face makeup and Halloween masks. A notation on the back of the image, which is from the college archives, says the students were enrolled in the 1901 to 1905 graduating classes. (Courtesy HC.)

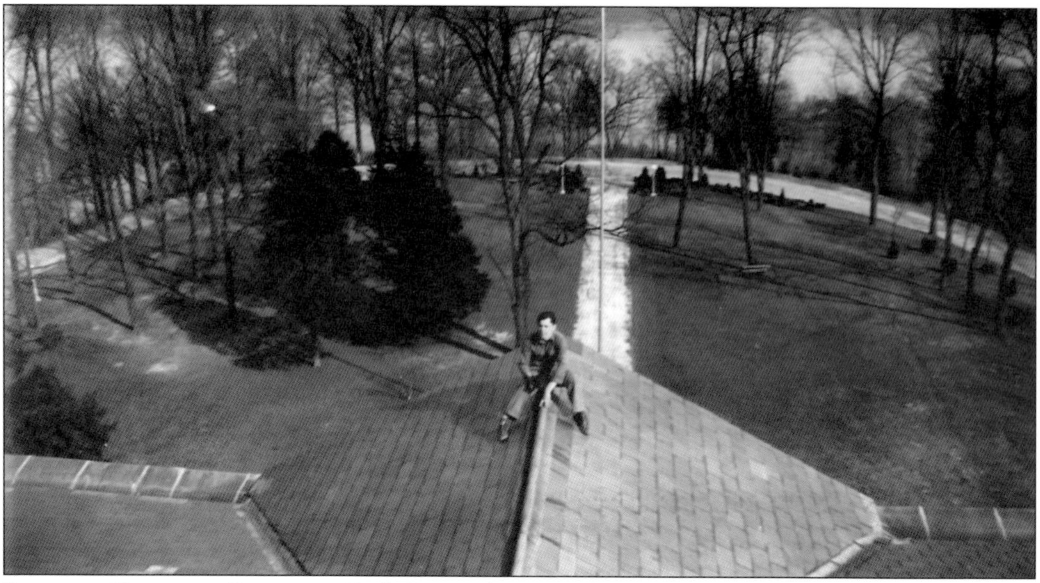

STUDENT CONQUERS BUILDING. Dick Sipe is shown in this rare view taken in 1940. He is perched on top of Classic Hall with a curving road and the Ohio River in the background. His classmate, Robert Craig, took this photograph from the belfry. (Courtesy HC.)

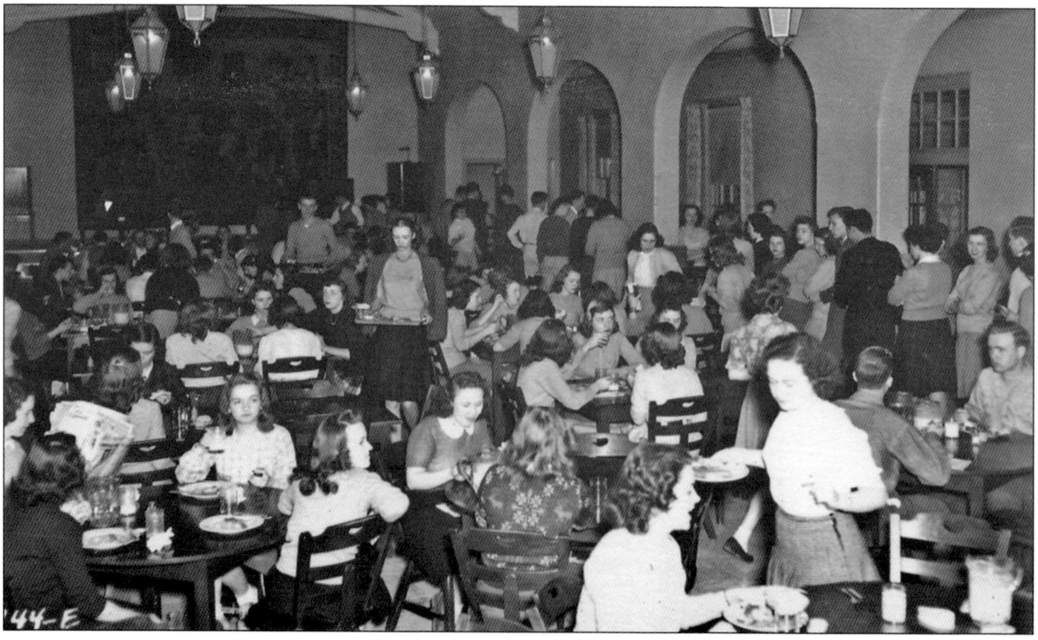

SOCIALIZING AT ITS MAX. Ask college students what they liked best about college and an often given response will probably be "the friendships." Here students are shown around 1947 in the ultimate friendship experience: eating together. This photograph was taken in Donner Hall, built in 1939, and shows students chatting, eating, and queuing up to get their meals. (Courtesy HC.)

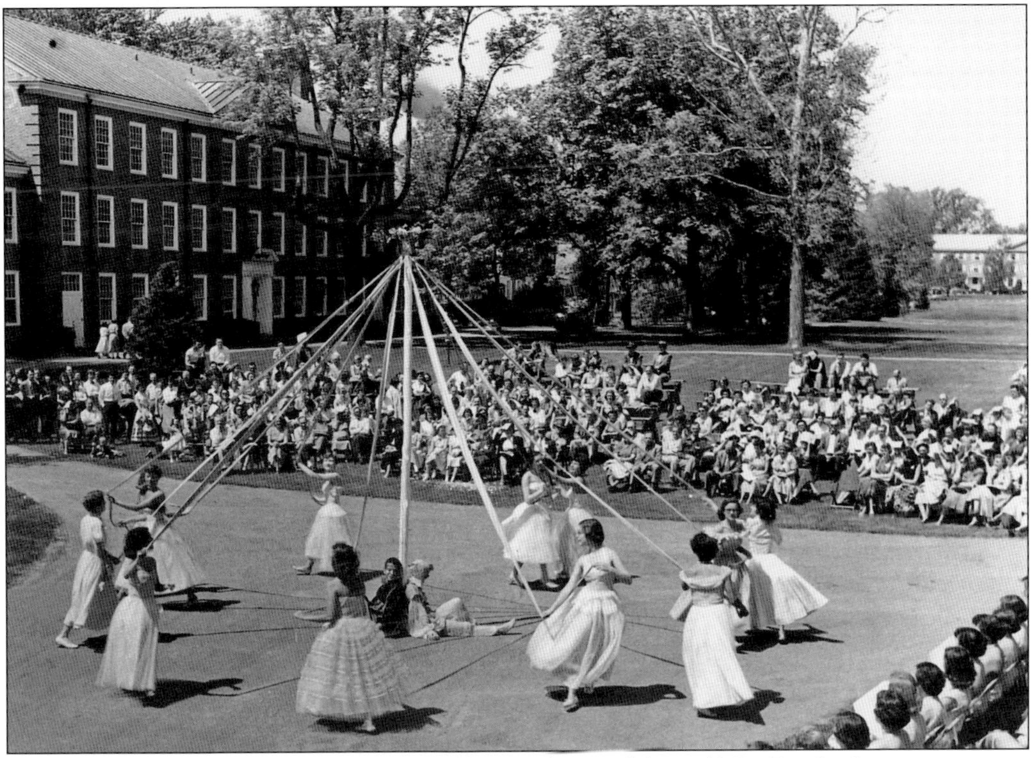

WOMEN DANCE ON MAY DAY. Hanover College students celebrated May Day by dancing, wearing white, and decorating with flowers. They also elected a king, queen, chancellor, maid of honor, and jester. In this photograph taken in 1953, Ruth Adair and John Hughes, who are sitting on the ground, hold up the pole. (Courtesy HC.)

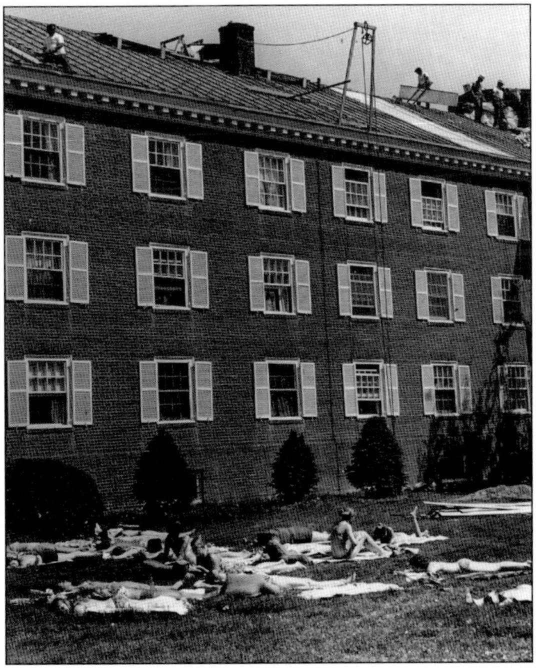

PHOTOGRAPH CAPTURES CONTRAST. A 1974 tornado almost wiped Hanover College off the map. More than $10 million was needed to rebuild the campus. In this photograph taken in May, just five weeks after the tornado struck, students are shown sunbathing on the lawn while workers repair the roof of Crowe Hall. (Courtesy HC.)

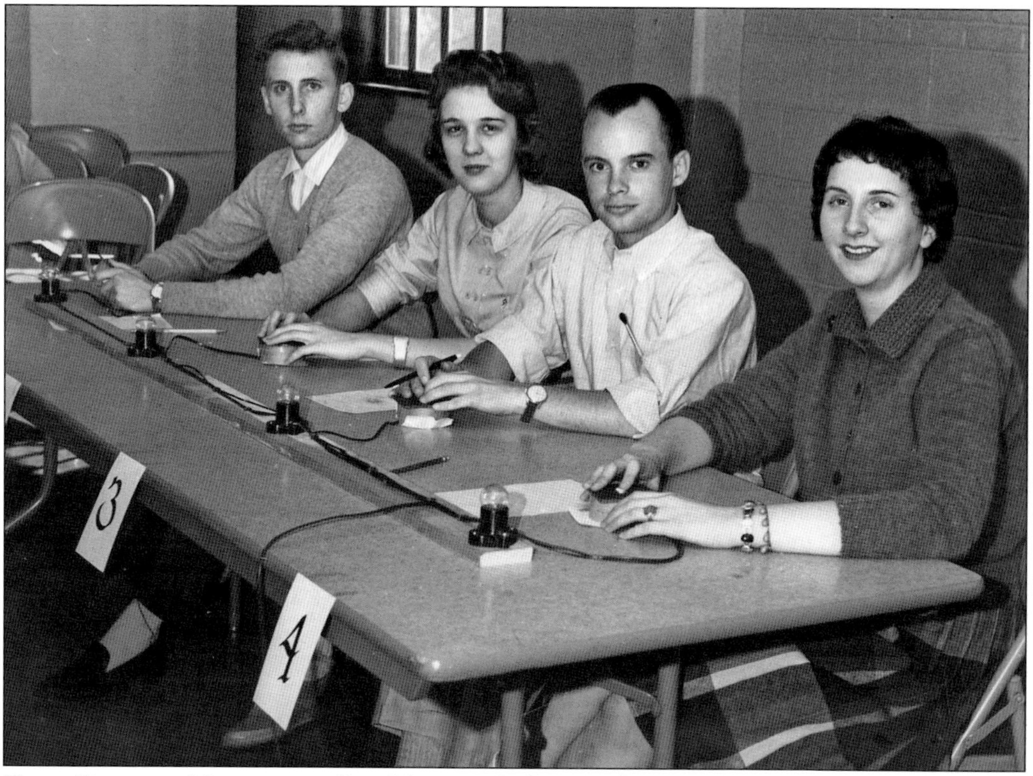

TEAM COMPETES NATIONALLY. Five Hanover College students traveled to New York in 1961 to compete in a network television show called *Brain Bowl*. Pictured are, from left to right, Doug Kurdys, Meredith Bubul, Bob Beckmann, and Liz Thurston. Alternate Bob Updike is not pictured. Their coach was mathematics professor Dr. John Yarnelle. Hanover won easily over Sweet Briar College in the warm-up round but lost during the actual competition 265-105. (Courtesy HC.)

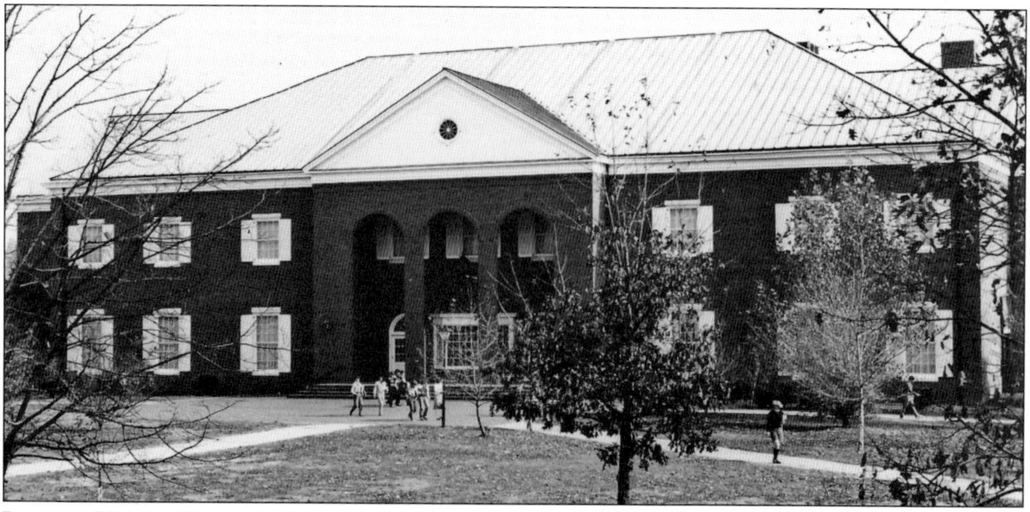

LIBRARY HOUSES DIVERSE COLLECTION. Hanover's newest library facility, the Agnes Brown Duggan Library, opened in 1973. In 1880, the library claimed 5,000 volumes. Today's library includes 316,000 volumes, periodical collections, an extensive archives department, and endless online access. Early librarians included Leila Garritt and Mary Louise Fitton. (Courtesy HC.)

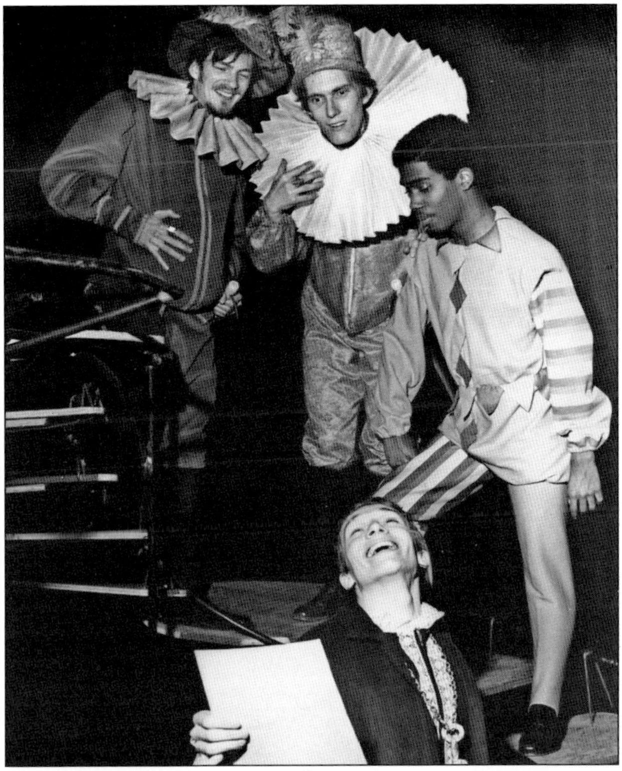

Shakespeare Performed. *Twelfth Night* was directed by Tom Evans in the 1967–1968 season. Pictured are, from left to right, unidentified, Roger Bulington, Clint Davis, and unidentified. Woody Harrelson continues to shine as Hanover's most famous theater student. He first made it big on the television show *Cheers.* He has since acted in 55 movies and was nominated twice for Academy Awards. (Courtesy HC.)

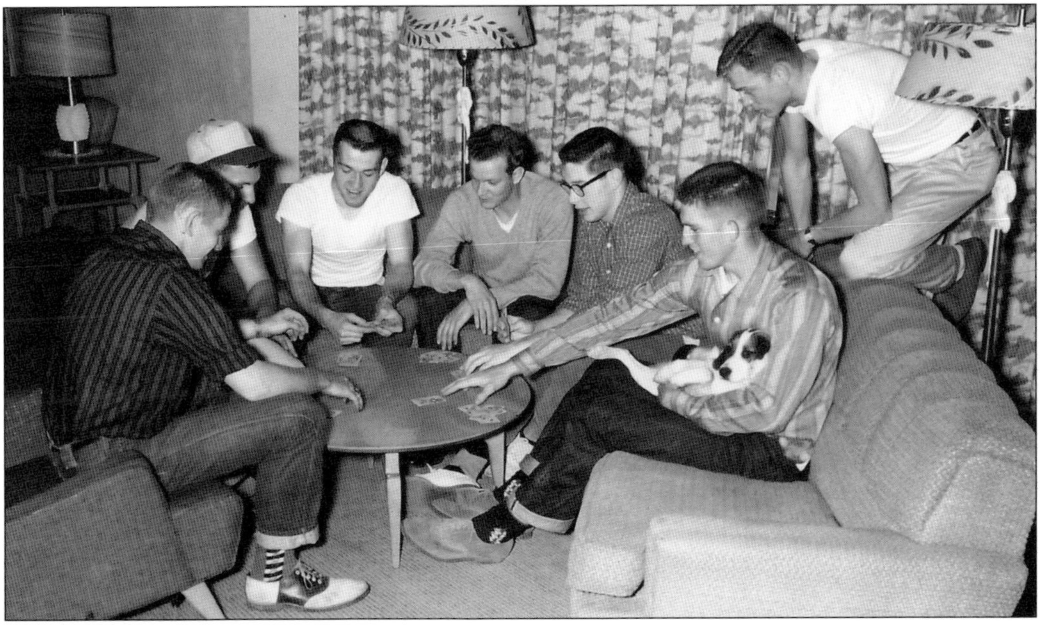

Fraternity Men Play Cards. Students gathered at the Lambda Chi Alpha house in 1958 to play cards. Fraternities, in addition to Lambda Chi Alpha, currently on campus include Phi Delta Theta, Phi Gamma Delta, and Sigma Chi. National sororities on campus include Alpha Delta Pi, Chi Omega, Kappa Alpha Theta, and Phi Mu. Today more than 50 percent of students are affiliated with a Greek organization. (Courtesy HC.)

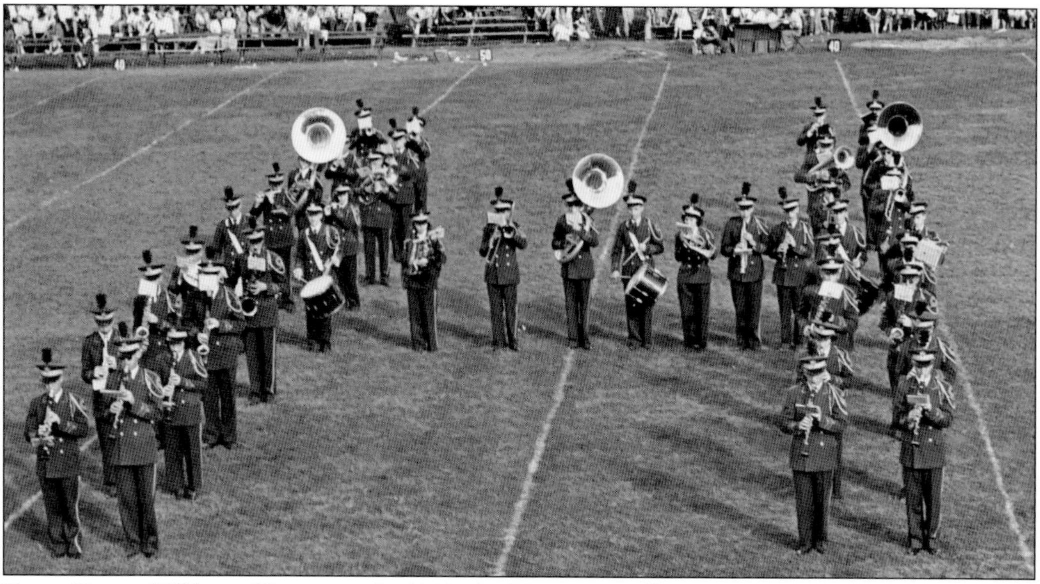

BAND FORMS "H" FOR HANOVER. In 1949, the Hanover College marching band members stood in formation on the football field. They entertained fans with a musical and marching routine, which included all 42 of them forming a traditional "H." Max Poland, the band director, served as a faculty member from 1929 to 1973. (Courtesy HC.)

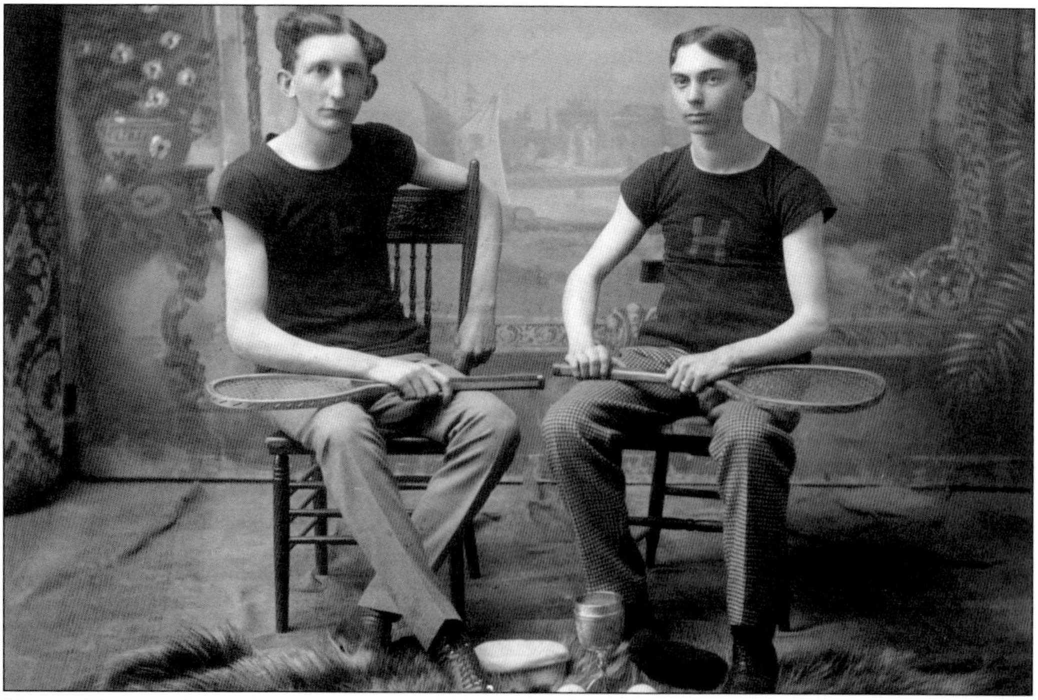

TENNIS PLAYERS SEIZE CHAMPIONSHIP. In 1894, a tradition of awarding a tennis cup to a winning fraternity doubles team began. Spirited matches were played during commencement week. The 1900 champions from Phi Gamma Delta are pictured above. John Harris Adams sits on the left with his partner, Frank Joseph Burger. Adams went on to win the state singles title in 1901. (Courtesy HC.)

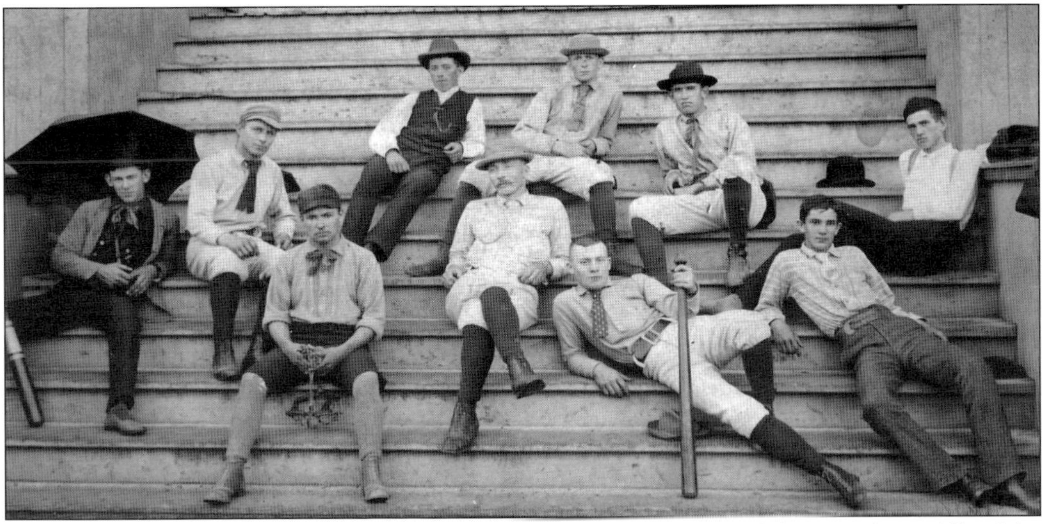

ATHLETES SHOW TOUGH SIDE, 1890S. Glenn Culbertson (with moustache) sits in the middle of the first row. Culbertson taught science at Hanover College from 1893 to 1927. Baseball was banned on campus for several decades after team members in 1870 engaged in a night of Halloween pranks. Their tricks had traditionally included writing on elderly ladies' windows with soap and pushing over outhouses. Hanover's professors were not amused, hence the ban. (Courtesy HC.)

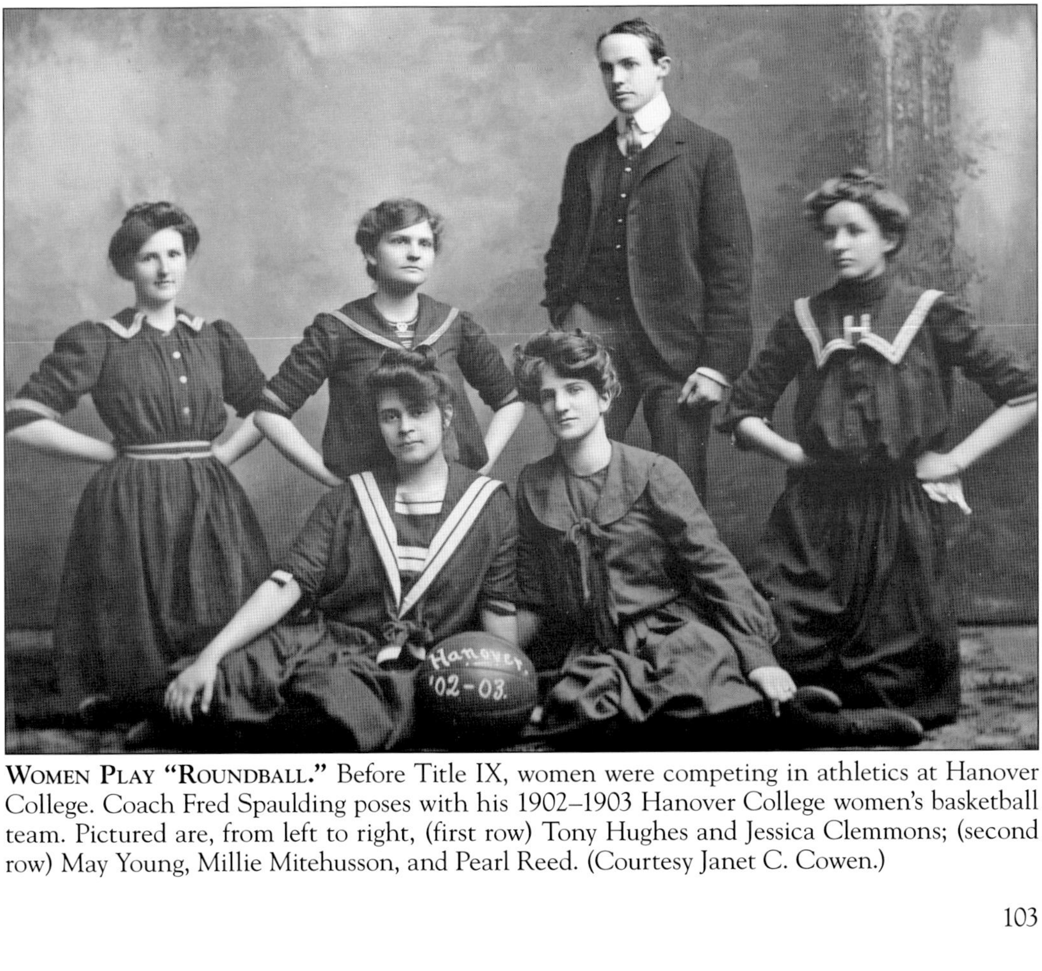

WOMEN PLAY "ROUNDBALL." Before Title IX, women were competing in athletics at Hanover College. Coach Fred Spaulding poses with his 1902–1903 Hanover College women's basketball team. Pictured are, from left to right, (first row) Tony Hughes and Jessica Clemmons; (second row) May Young, Millie Mitehusson, and Pearl Reed. (Courtesy Janet C. Cowen.)

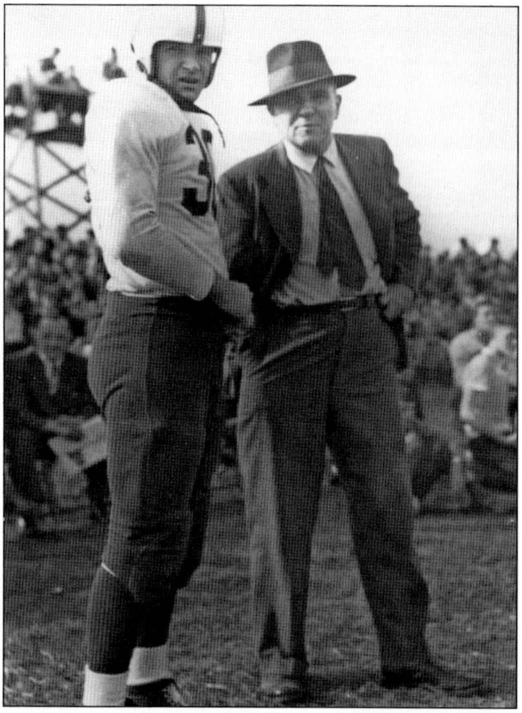

Two Giants Confer. Bill ("Turk") Klein, left, played football, basketball, and baseball and graduated in 1950. He was the first Hanover College athlete to be drafted by a professional team, the Los Angeles Rams. He also worked for the FBI and the Indiana State Police. Coach Raymond ("Dutch") Struck, right, served as a coach, men's athletic director, and chairman of physical education during his 1946–1968 career at Hanover College. He spoke fluent German and earned a chemistry degree from DePauw University with high honors. He also served in the U.S. Navy during World War II. (Courtesy HC.)

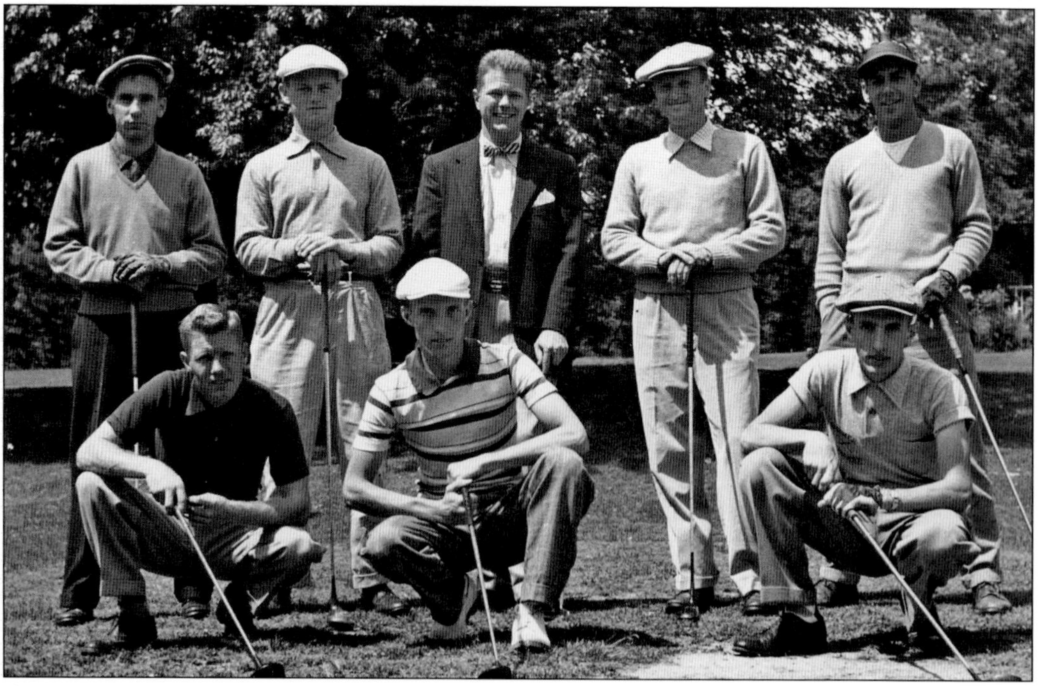

Golf Powerhouse Team Poses. Hanover College's 1952 golf team pictured above placed first in the Hoosier College Conference, as well as fifth in the National Association of Intercollegiate Athletics match in Abilene, Texas. Pictured are, from left to right, (first row) R. Brentlinger, Bob Kirkpatrick, and Dick Kirkpatrick; (second row) J. Sturgess, Darrell McFall, coach Valdimir Dupree, John Smith, and F. Terrell. (Courtesy HC.)

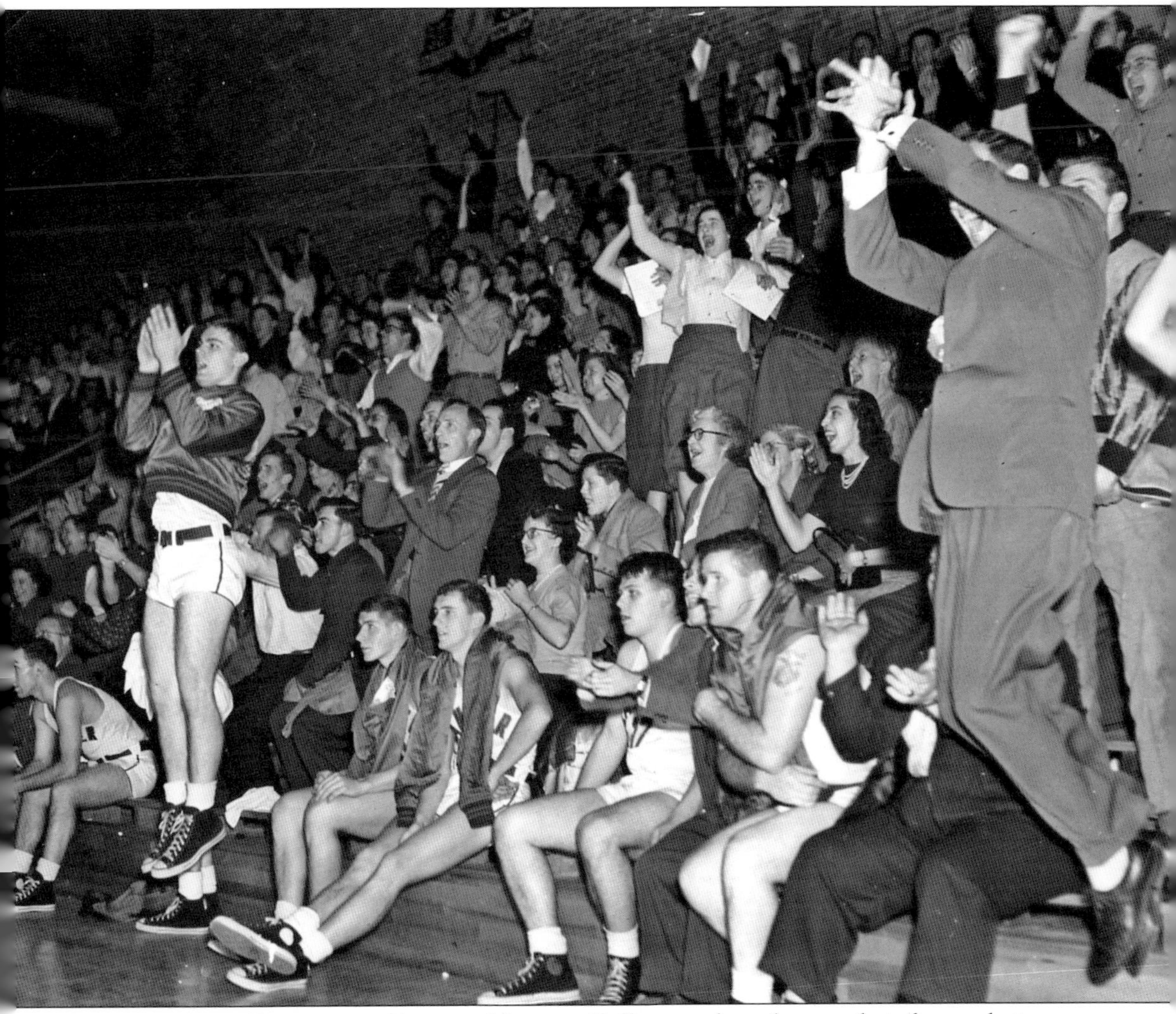

Students Show Basketball Passion. Hanover College students leap to their feet as their team scores its 100th point against Rose Poly in 1950. Hanover won 104-53. Guard John Collier, center Elmer Geisler, and forward Andy Taff were playing on the court. Pictured are, from left to right, (first row) Eddie Roth (sitting in uniform), Ray Green (in uniform jumping), Barney Scott, Bill "Gus" Moorehead, and Turk Klein; (second row) coach Jack Carl, Ralph Burris (in suit with tie), and Dottie Burris (in light-colored top and necklace); (third row) includes a woman named ? Kutz (in suit, wearing eyeglasses) and coach Carl's wife (wearing strands of pearls); (fourth row) Marlyn Duke Finnegan (standing, holding program) and Flora Waddle Rusk (standing with her arm extended in front of Marlyn's face). Directly behind Flora Waddle Rusk, Bill Shuck has his program in his right hand extended into the air. John Collier, one of the players on the court, later coached basketball at Hanover for 22 years. For 18 of those 22 years, he also served as athletic director. (Courtesy HC.)

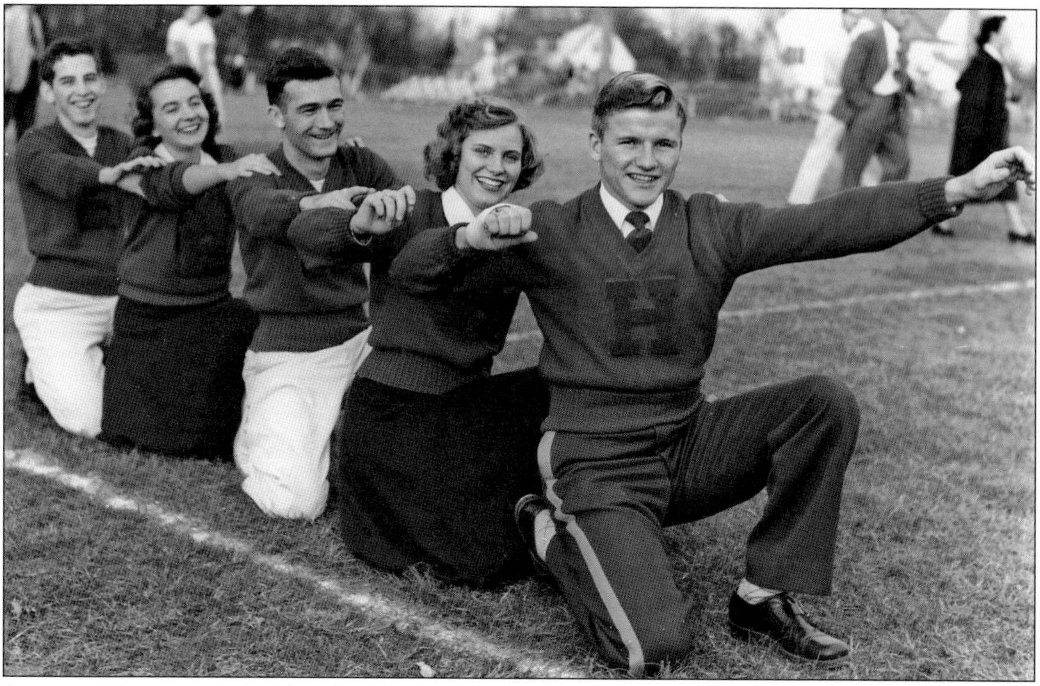

'Leaders Yell in 1949. Cheerleaders show spirit at a ball game. Cheerleading required athletic ability as well as the talent to connect with fans. Cheerleaders pictured are, from left to right, Dick Demaree, Mary Blackman, Andy Pelham, Natalie Virginia Frakes Cooper, and Skip Worland. (Courtesy HC.)

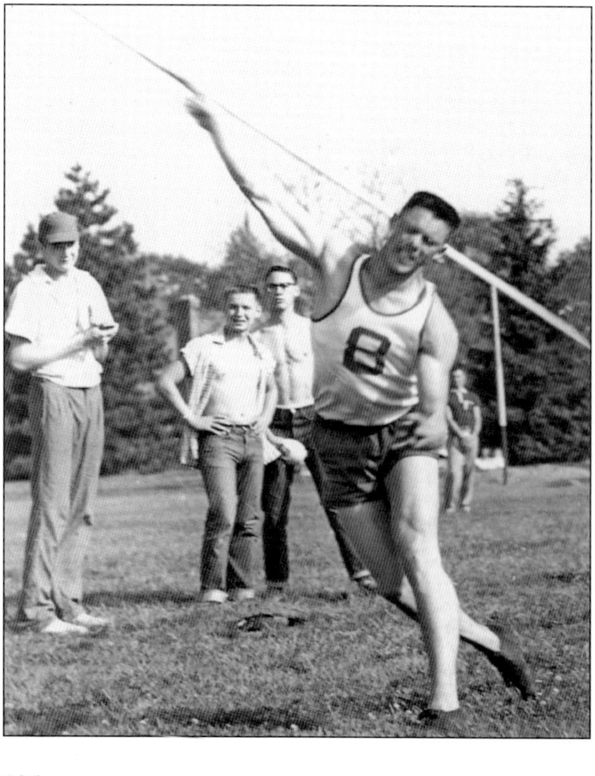

Catapulted to White House. Carroll (Tuffy) Hamilton competed in football, basketball, and track in college. He qualified for the 1956 Olympics in Melbourne, Australia, and could have been selected to fill a vacant spot in the broad jump, but the qualifying committee thought he was competing in another event at the same time. He joined the U.S. Marines and worked as a special agent in the U.S. Secret Service. He provided protection for three U.S. presidents and currently lives and works in Madison. (Courtesy HC.)

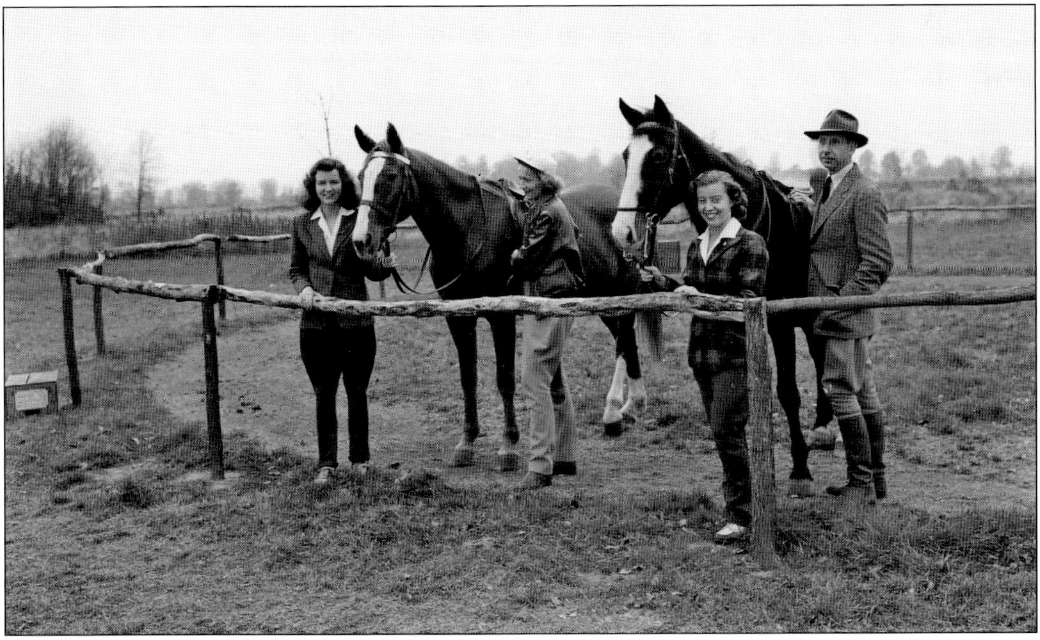

Women Go Horseback Riding. Women prepare for an equestrian class, which was added to Hanover College's sports curriculum in 1944. The women are identified as, from left to right, Frances Eickoff, 1945; Wilma Lindberg, 1945; and Jeanne Story, 1947. Their professor is Dr. Arthur Hogue, who served between 1935 and 1948 as a professor of history and as a dean. (Courtesy HC.)

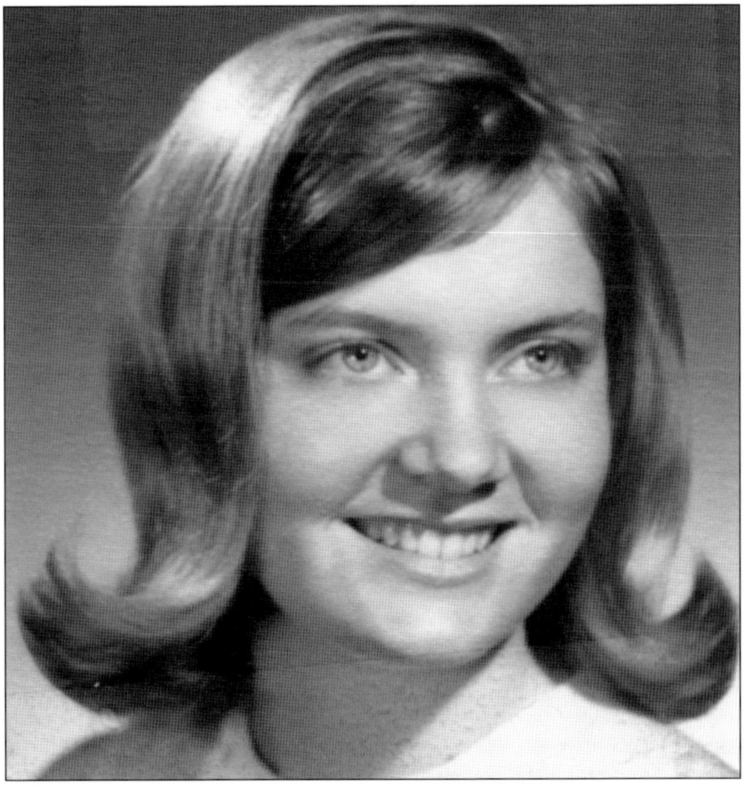

Woman Achieves. Marla Oberhausen held top honors in women's basketball, field hockey, softball, swimming, and volleyball. She graduated in 1971 and earned a doctoral degree from Ohio State University with emphases in sports psychology, consulting, and counseling. She worked at Ceiba Center first in Columbus, Ohio, and later in Bolder, Colorado. She also wrote professionally and served as a radio talk show host. She died in 2003 in Colorado. (Courtesy H/C.)

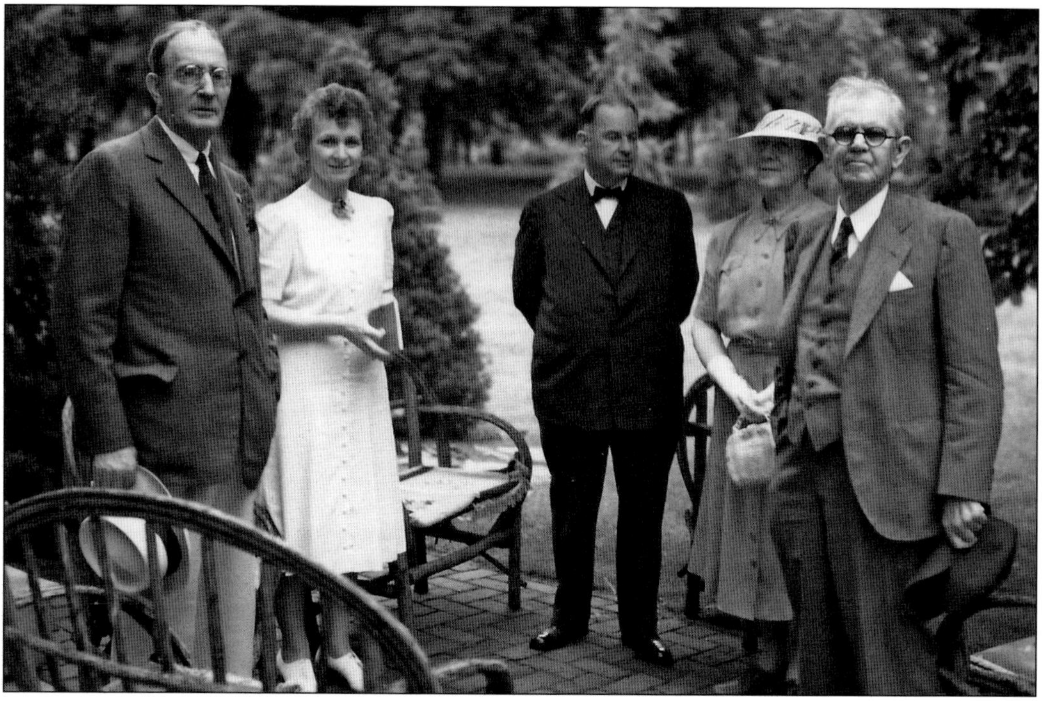

TRUSTEES MEET. In this undated photograph from college archives, Katharine Parker (second from left), who was the influential wife of Hanover College president Albert George Parker Jr. (1929–1958), socializes with trustees. Pictured are, from left to right, Albert Wiggam (1945–1946), Katharine Parker, Charles J. Lynn (1938–1958 and trustee president from 1948 to 1958), Mrs. Edgar H. Evens (1937–1965), and Stanley Coulter (1871 Hanover graduate and trustee from 1929 to 1944). Coulter served as a dean at Purdue University. (Courtesy HC.)

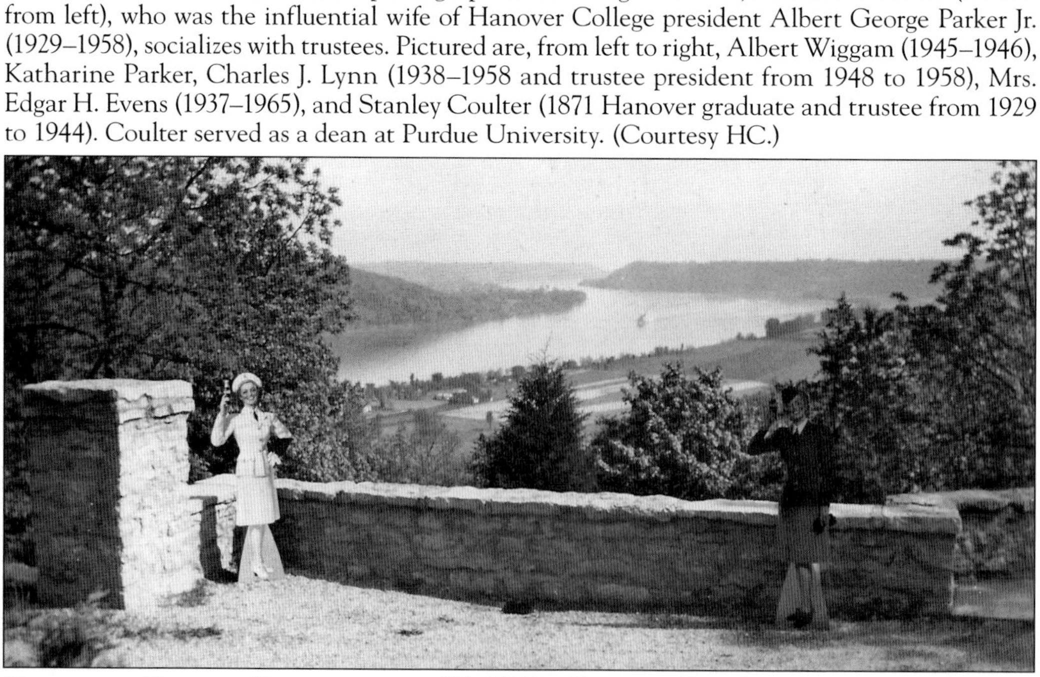

CARDBOARD CUTOUTS CLOWN AROUND. World War II–era cardboard women party on Hanover College's riverside campus. Locals know to take people on a walk or drive that hides the river most of the way. A turn in the road opens to this view, which usually makes the unsuspecting gasp or say, "Wow." Residents, students, and thousands of visitors have pictures in their scrapbooks snapped at this very place. (Courtesy LC.)

Seven

CHURCHES

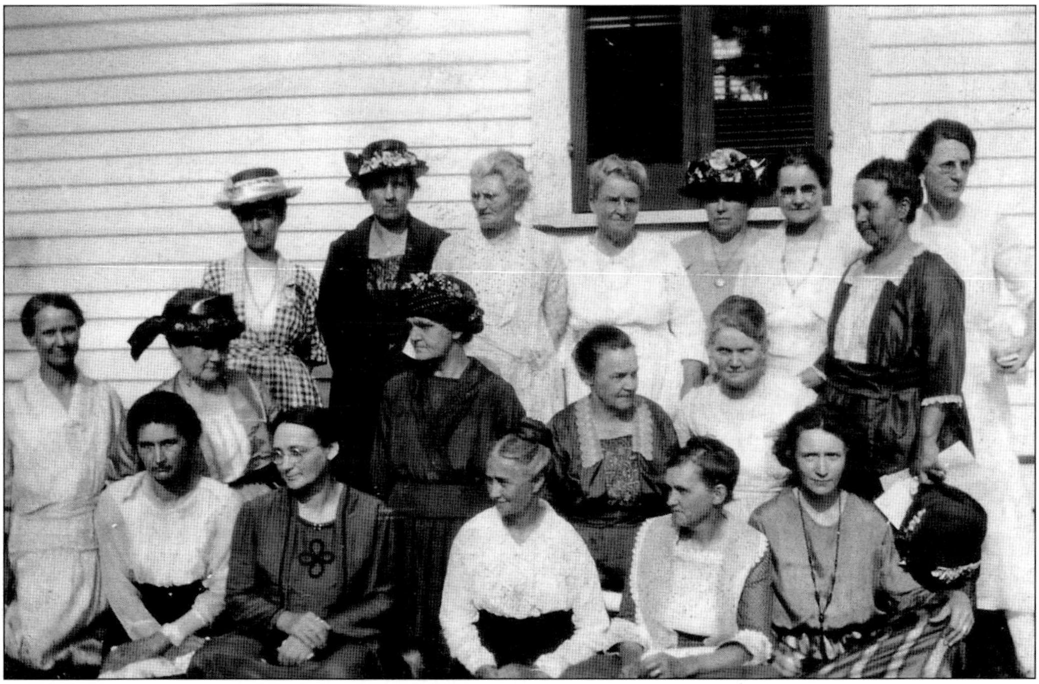

EARLIEST HISTORY CENTERED AROUND CHURCH. Hanover's European founders began as several loosely-knit Presbyterian antislavery groups that crossed the Ohio River into Southern Indiana. Those who settled in Hanover became very close and established the first Presbyterian church. Soon itinerant Methodists started showing up. Both forms of worship survived and flourished. The image above shows the Methodist Women's Aid in the 1920s. (Courtesy Linda M. Adams.)

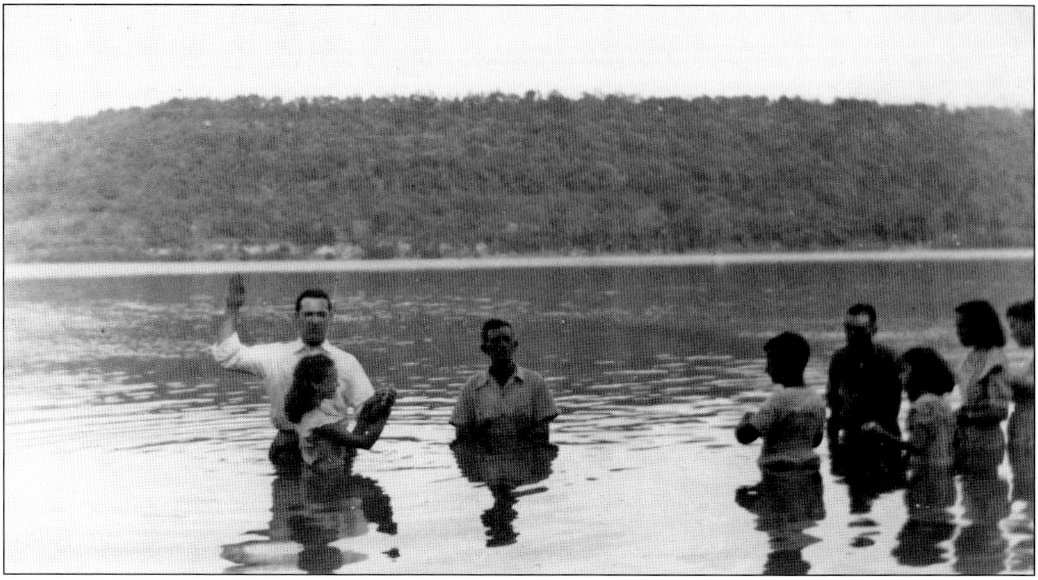

Converts Gather at the River. Betty Moore's family and friends from New Prospect Baptist Church in Saluda celebrate her baptism in the Ohio River around 1949. Rev. Bill Harlin holds his hand up in a blessing. Bill Gammons watches from his right. Bill Moore stands at the front of the group, which includes Bill King and Jimmy Taylor. (Courtesy William L. Moore family.)

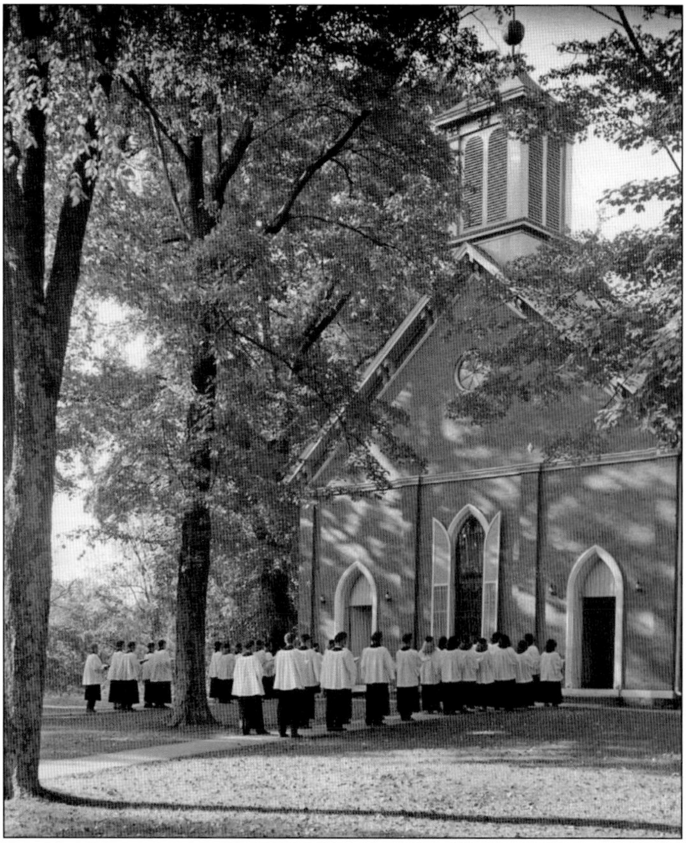

Town and Church Histories Intertwined. Hanover Presbyterian and the town of Hanover grew up together. At one time or another, they shared a common name, classrooms, worship space, offices, and staff members. The church was founded in 1820. A religious school was started in 1827. Both Hanover College and McCormick Theological Seminary in Chicago grew out of that 1827 school. (Courtesy HC.)

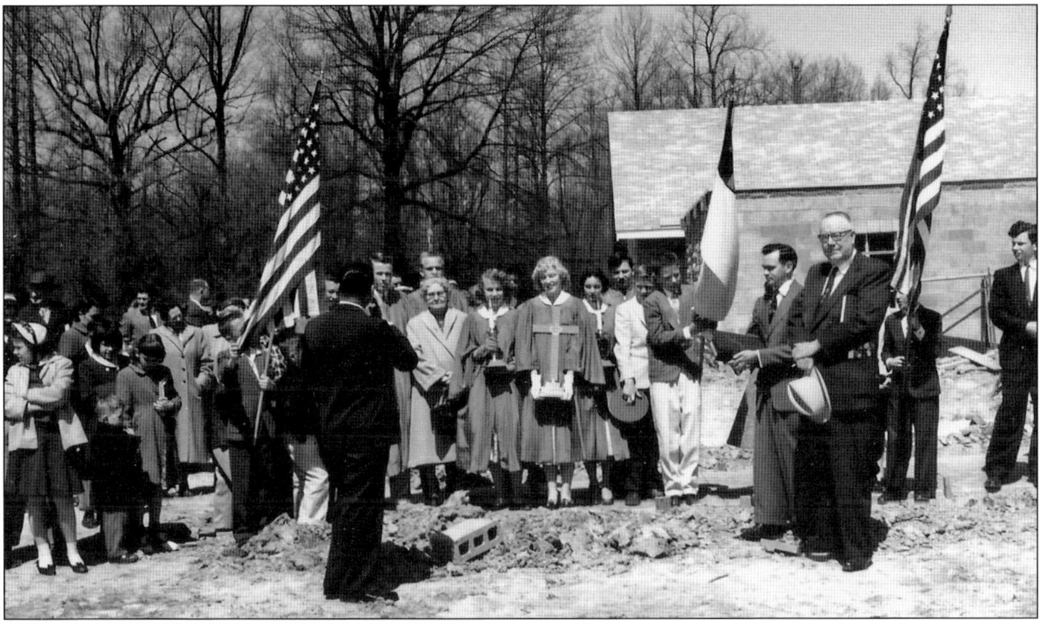

Methodists March to New Church. Hanover United Methodist Church moved to its current location on east LaGrange Road from Main Street on Palm Sunday, 1957. A procession made up of all members walked with some carrying cherished sanctuary appointments to the new site. As they went, they sang "Onward Christian Soldiers." (Courtesy Hanover United Methodist Church.)

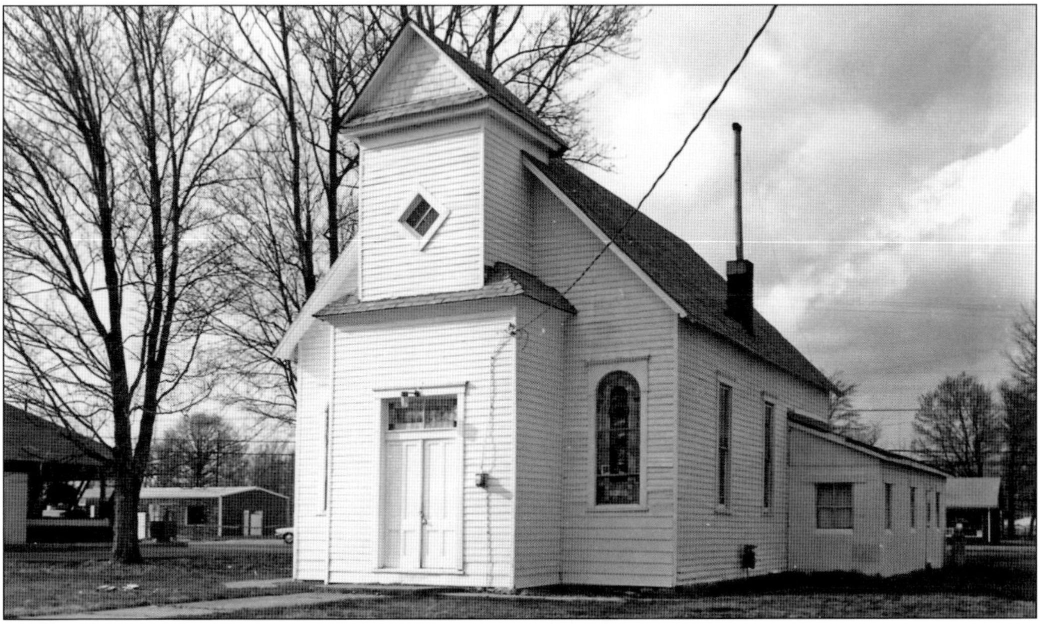

Church Tied to Underground Railroad. Jefferson County's oldest, continuously open, historically African American church is located in Hanover. St. Stephen's African Methodist Episcopal Church, founded in 1885, is partially constructed of wood salvaged from an African American church in Graysville after it closed. The first trustees of St. Stephen's were active in the Underground Railroad. The church was added to the National Register of Historic Places in 2000. (Courtesy HC.)

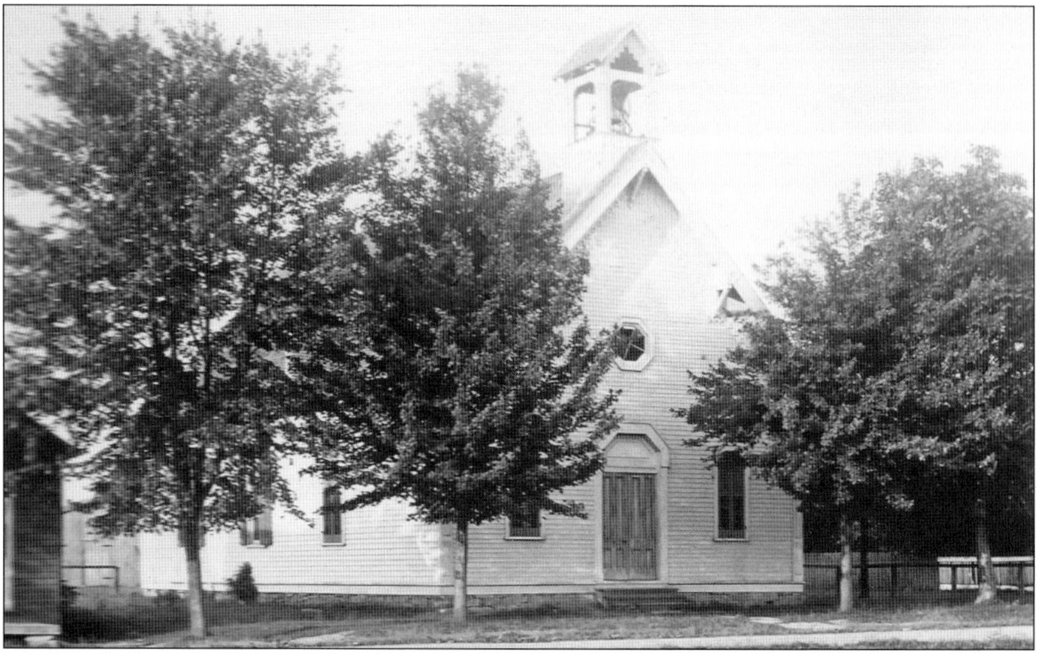

FIRST BAPTIST FIRST MEETS IN 1955. The above structure was built in 1898 and was purchased by Hanover's Baptist congregation in 1957 from the Methodists. The church burned down shortly after the purchase. A new building was constructed and dedicated in 1961. Other buildings were added in 1975, 1984, and 1997. (Courtesy Linda M. Adams.)

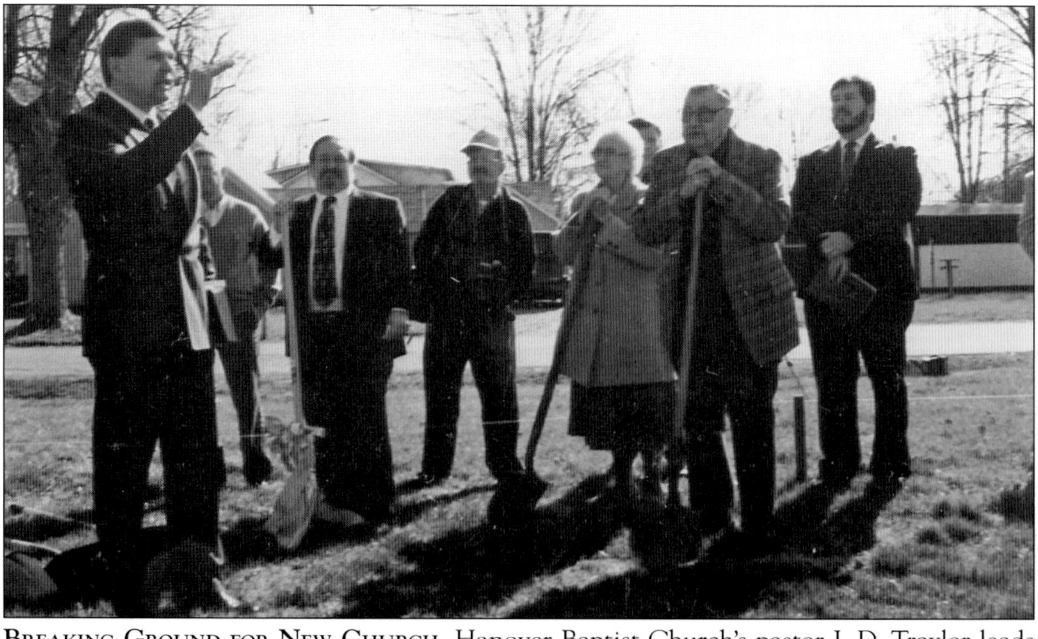

BREAKING GROUND FOR NEW CHURCH. Hanover Baptist Church's pastor J. D. Traylor leads members of his congregation as they break ground for the Godly Recreation And Christian Education Center (G.R.A.C.E.). Pictured are, from left to right, J. D. Traylor, Gene Sutton, Steve Bright, Don Wood, two unidentified, Bob Hunter, and Brad Dews. (Courtesy Hanover Baptist Church/J. D. Traylor.)

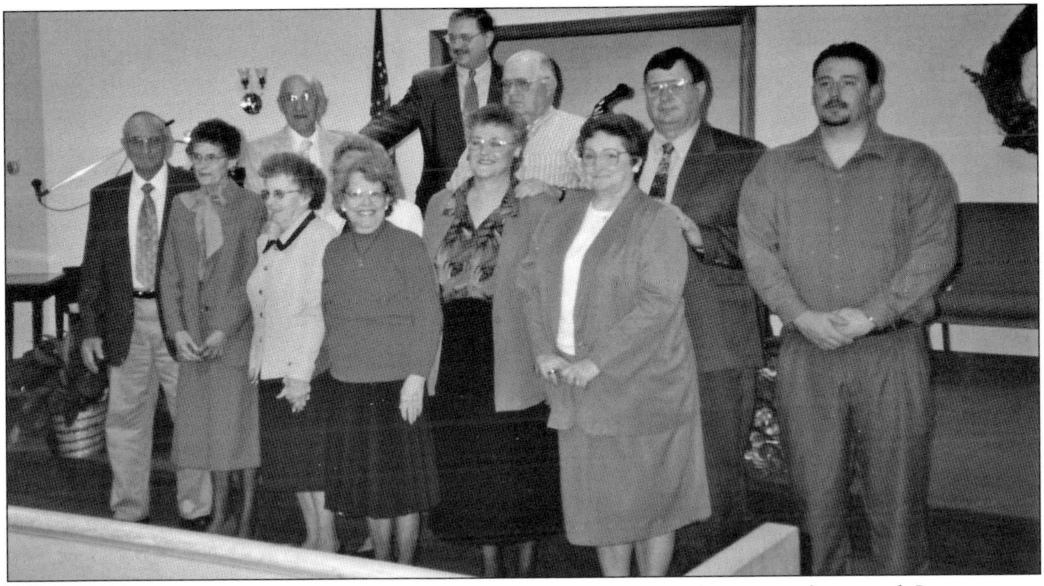

Cornerstone Baptist Charter Members Gather. About one dozen people started Cornerstone Baptist Church in 1982. The fledgling congregation bought out the Rusty Nail Lounge to renovate for worship and outreach ministries. Charter members pictured are, from left to right, (first row) Neal Meck, Marilyn Meck, Judy Rieman, Nell Wood, Janice Sanders, Pat Turner, and Dirk Turner; (second row) Bill Wood, Br. Jeff Jones, Bill Sanders, and Leon Turner, the first pastor. (Courtesy Cornerstone Baptist/Bill and Janice Sanders.)

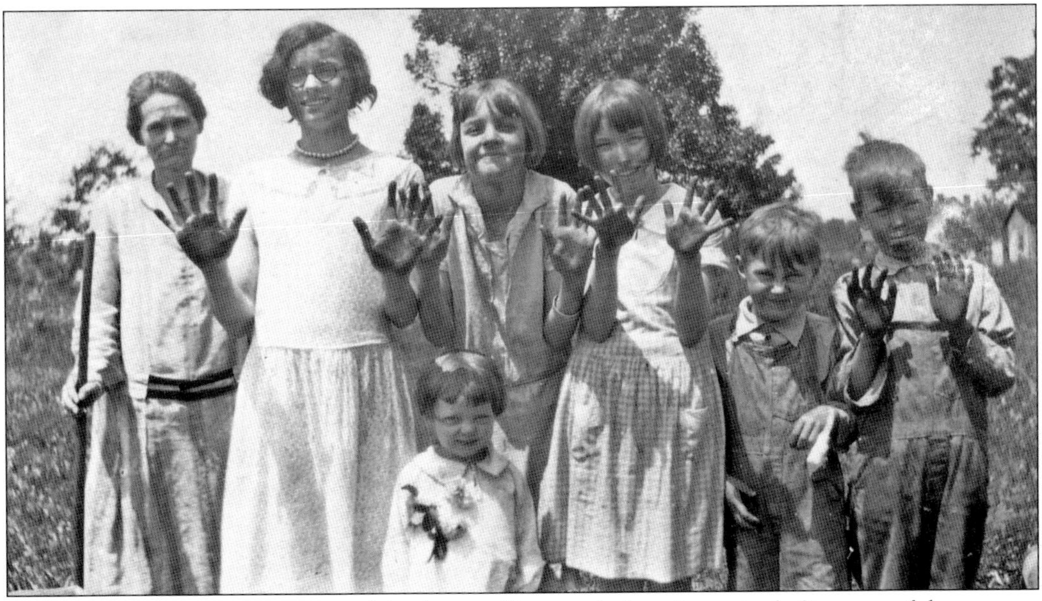

Church Work Can Get Dirty. Members in Hanover's churches—including one of the newest, First Christian Church of Hanover—historically hold regular, cooperative cleanup days. Shown in 1929 after they cleaned out the stovepipe in the kitchen at the Methodist church are, from left to right, Fannie Tull, Mary Blanche Jackson, Erma Kyle, Wilma Lowery, Thelma Jackson, Toots ("Clarence") Tull, and Paul Tull. (Courtesy Wilma Lowry Harrell.)

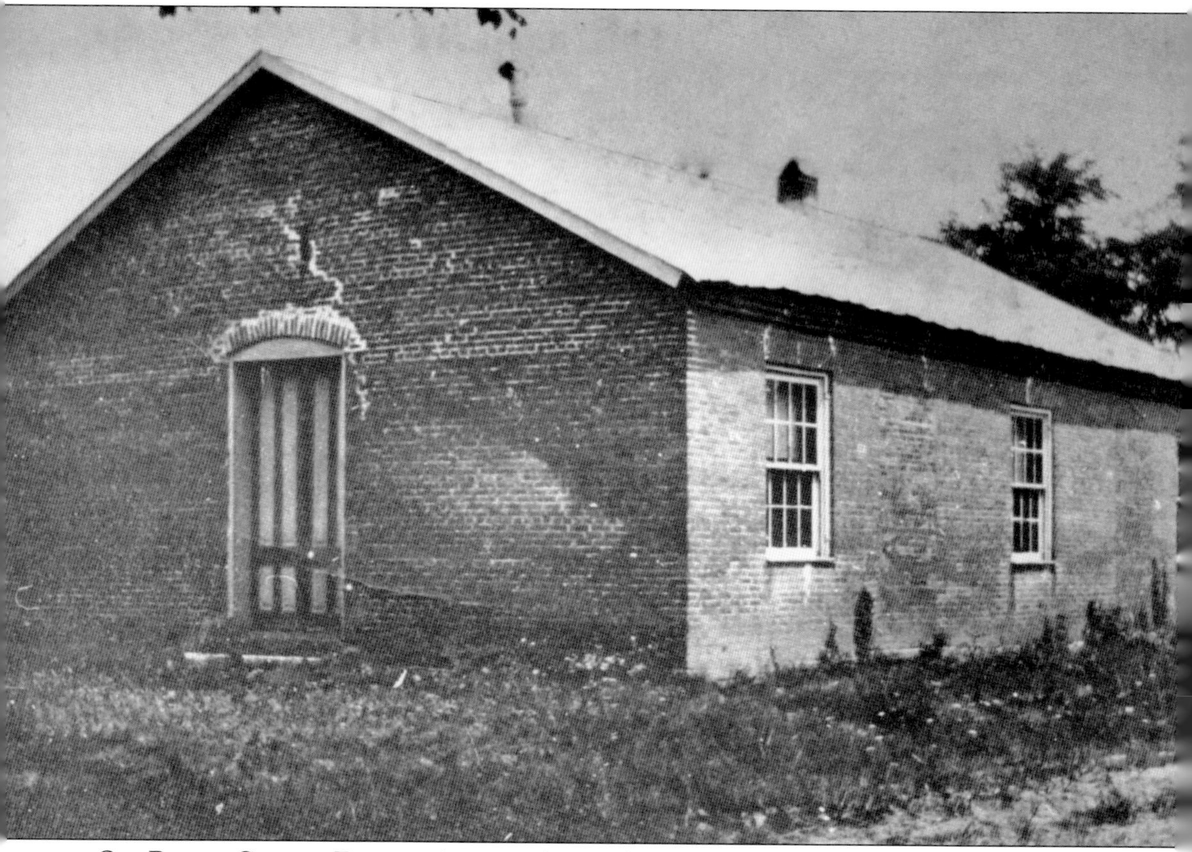

OLD BETHEL CHURCH FORMED. A group of Scottish-Presbyterians with ties to a synod in Scotland obtained ordained ministers who began their service in Lexington, Kentucky. These clergy and their congregations were antislavery. The going was slow in Kentucky on the slavery issue in the late 1700s, so these Presbyterians moved to Ohio and Indiana. One of their churches was established near Hanover. It was called Carmel, and the people were known as seceders because of a separation in Scotland about 80 years before. A minister, straight from Scotland, became the minister of Carmel church in the early 1820s. He did not adapt to American customs, and a significant number of parishioners left the church to build what became the Old Bethel Church. At a later time the churches reunited, and eventually both were razed. In this extremely rare photograph taken in 1915, the repairs made above the door assisted church historians in identifying the structure as the Old Bethel Church. (Courtesy HC.)

Eight

Hanover's Neighbors

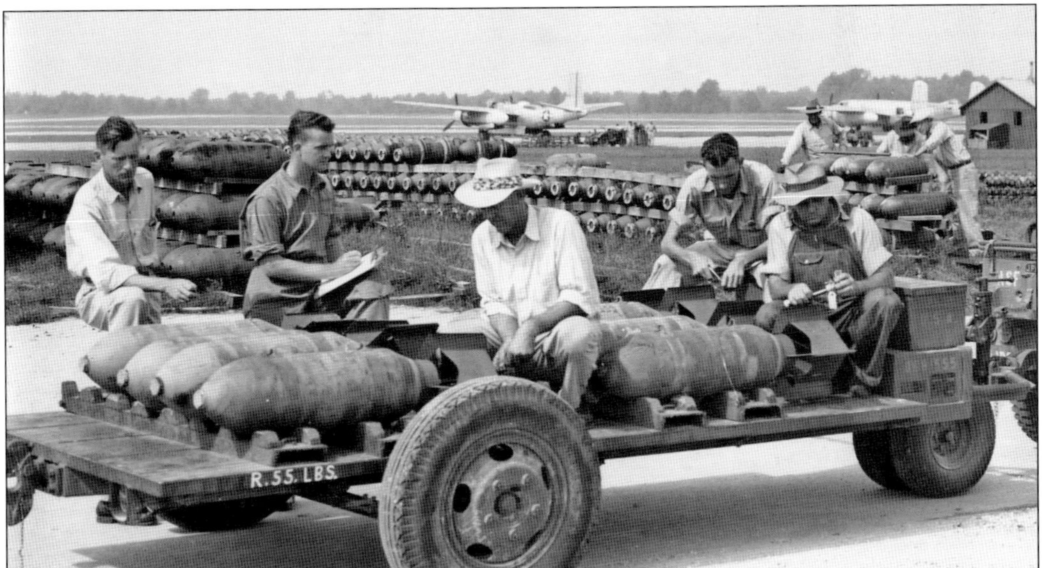

Men Test Munitions. The Jefferson Proving Ground (JPG) tested munitions 11 miles northwest of Hanover. Several farmers with Hanover connections were displaced when 56,000 acres were secured in 1941 for the facility. Hanover residents worked at the JPG, some for decades. The army ordnance testing area closed in 1995. The JPG image above introduces this chapter about some of Hanover's closest neighbors. (Courtesy JC.)

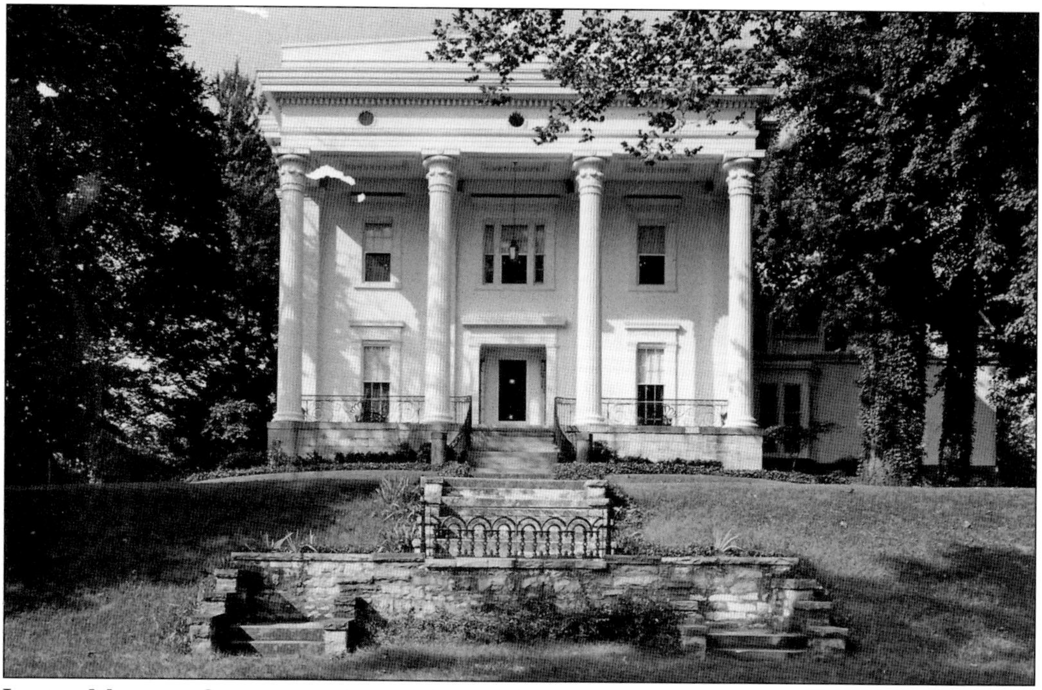

LANIER MANSION CONNECTED. Gen. William McKee Dunn, who was born in Hanover, married Madison's Elizabeth Lanier in 1841. She was a daughter of James F. D. Lanier, who in 1844 built the Greek Revival mansion pictured above. Located in Madison, the property is on the National Register of Historic Places. Dunn taught at Hanover College, served in the U.S. House of Representatives, and held the rank of general in the U.S. Army. (Courtesy JC.)

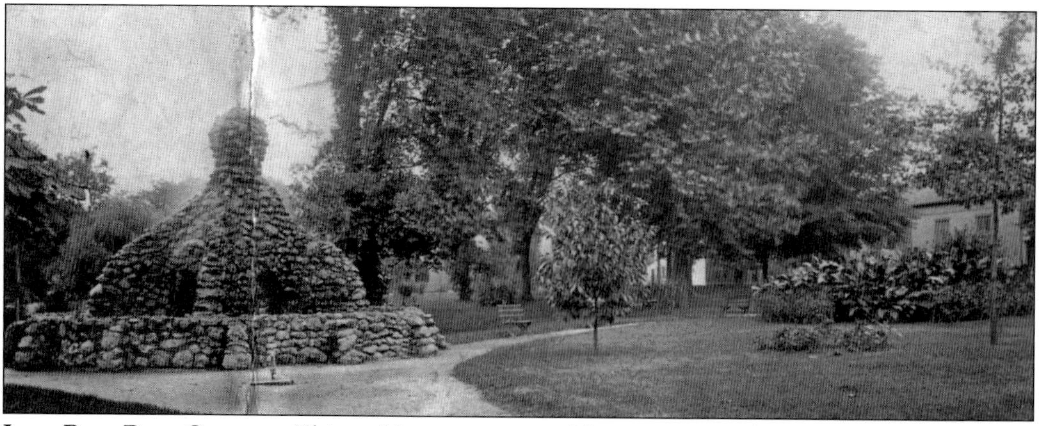

JOHN PAUL PARK CREATED. This park's connection to Hanover comes through Madison's founder, John Paul, and Hanover's founder, Williamson Dunn. They were contemporaries, and both purchased land at the Jeffersonville Land Office in 1809. The park was created in 1904 and is partially supported by the City of Madison, the John Paul Park Conservancy, and the local Daughters of the American Revolution (DAR) chapter. (Courtesy JC.)

Chimney among World's Tallest. The Clifty Creek plant of the Indiana-Kentucky Electric Corporation opened in 1955, five miles from Hanover. The coal-fired power station currently employs 365 workers and recently announced a $460 million plan to improve emission controls. One of the plant's chimneys is among the tallest in the world at 980 feet. (JC.)

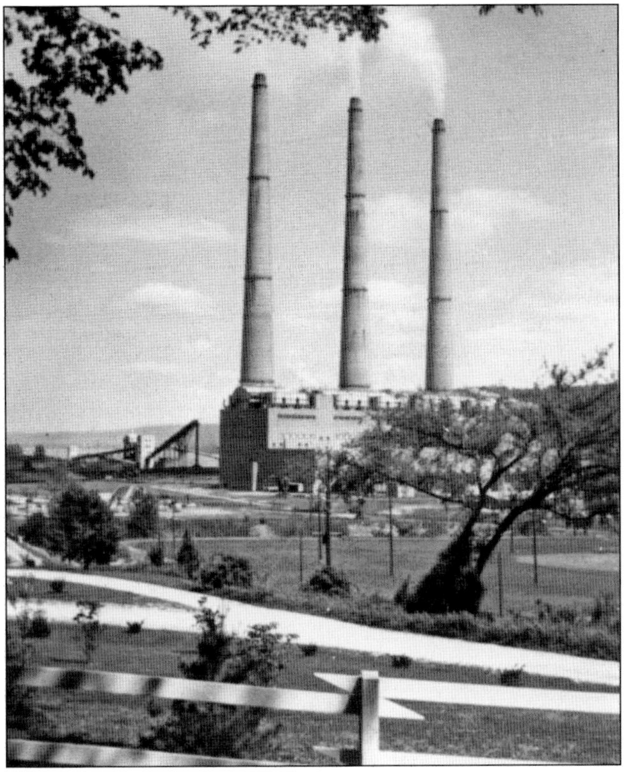

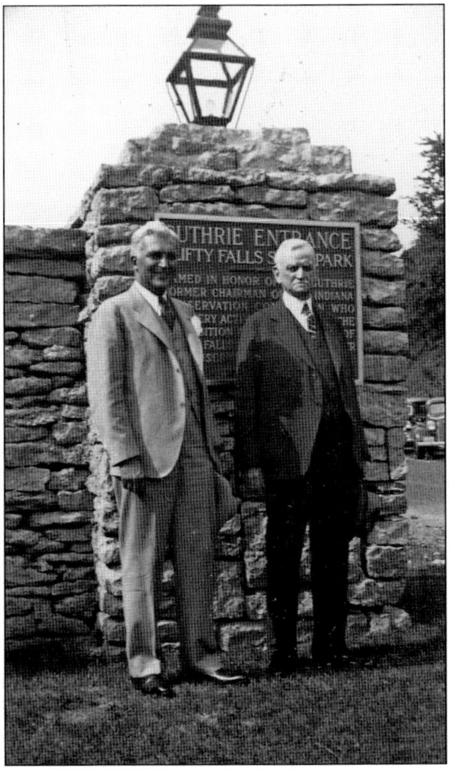

Park Entrance Dedicated. People from Hanover have worked at, studied in, and enjoyed nature at Clifty Falls State Park since before it officially opened in 1920. A second entrance to the 1,416-acre park was dedicated in the late 1930s. Indiana governor Paul V. McNutt, right, honors W. A. Guthrie, chair of Indiana's first conservation department, after whom the new park entrance was named. (Courtesy LC.)

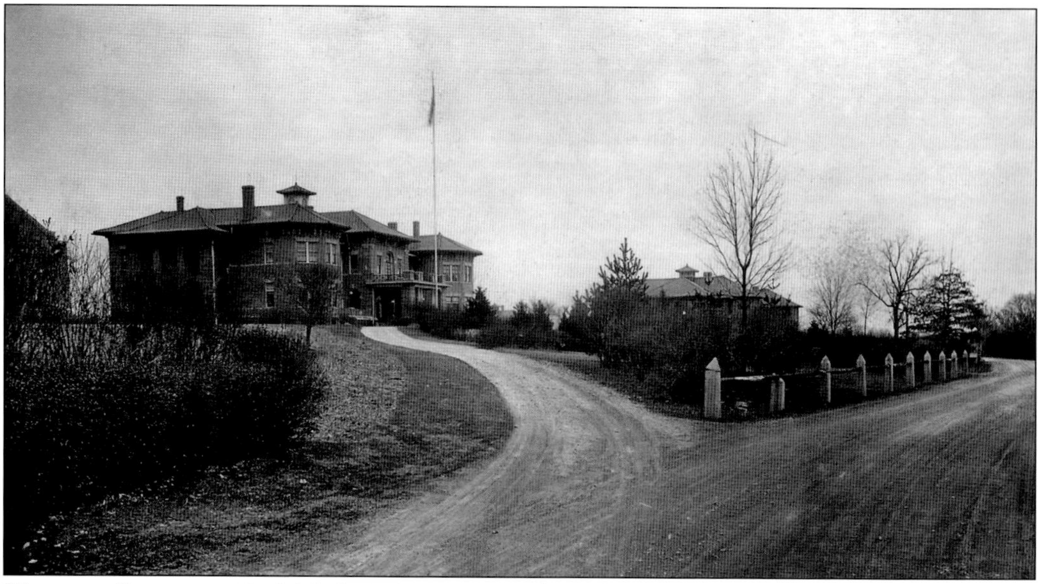

Hospital Opened in 1915. Madison State Hospital was first called the Southern Indiana Hospital for the Insane when it opened in 1910. At the facility near Hanover, patients lived in cottages and received what were called humane treatments, which included appreciation of the beauty of the Ohio River. The hospital has employed health care professionals and treated patients who live in Hanover as well as the surrounding area from its beginning. (Courtesy JC.)

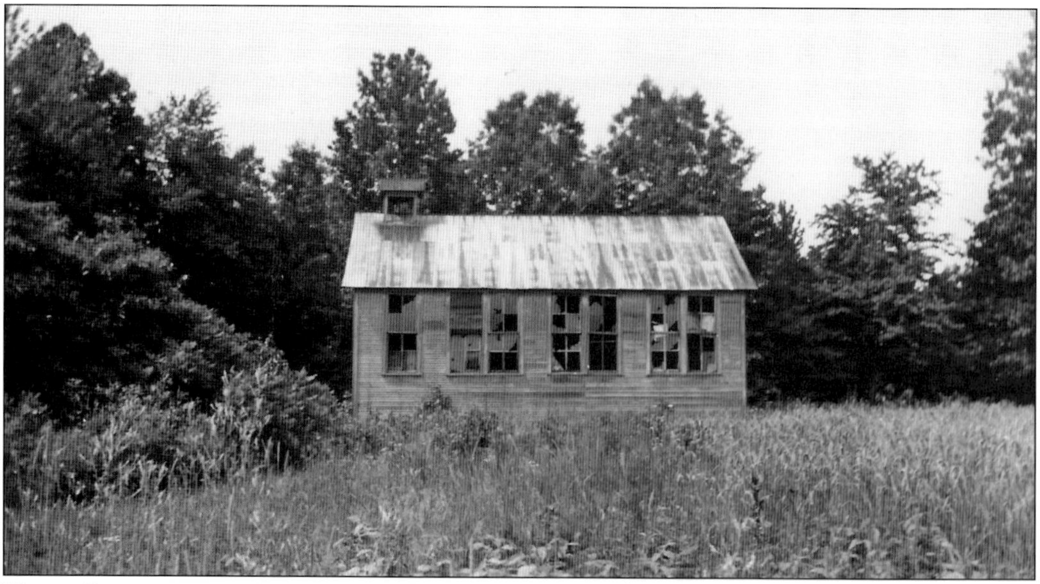

House Built around Structure. The Ten-Cent School pictured above was built by residents of Saluda Township in 1912. A story about how the school got its name involves a tight-fisted rich man who would only pledge 10¢ toward the new school. Today Donald and Elaine Bair live in a remodeled home built around the old school that utilizes the foundation and walls of the old school. (Courtesy LC.)

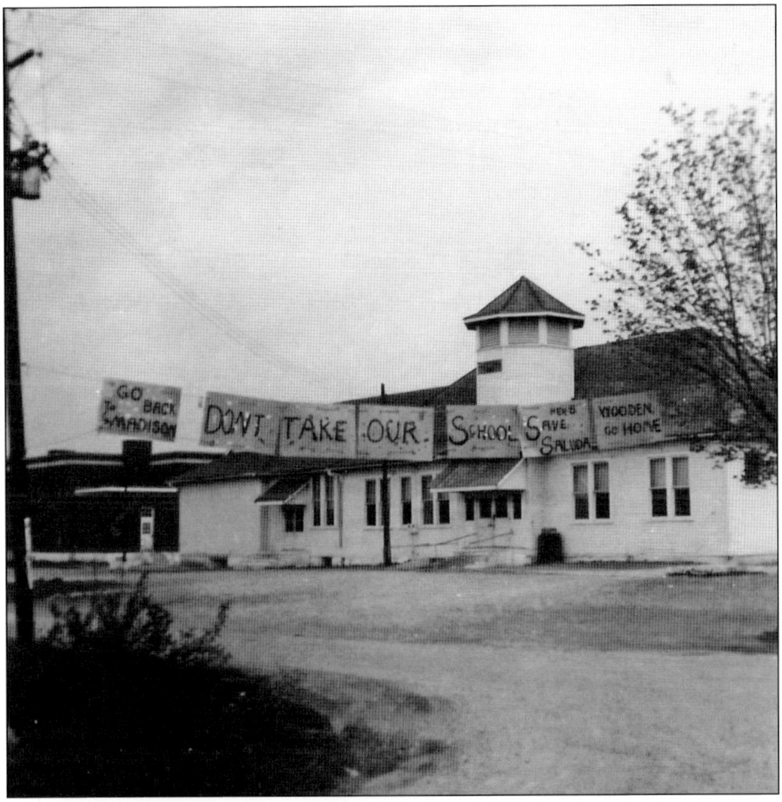

Children Plead for Their School. In 1954, the U.S. Air Force was looking for a place to build an academy. Saluda was being considered and was visited by a delegation of important people to scout out the area. Students made the signs seen in the image at right. They read, "Don't take our School, Save Saluda." The U.S. Air Force Academy was built in Colorado. (Courtesy William L. Moore family.)

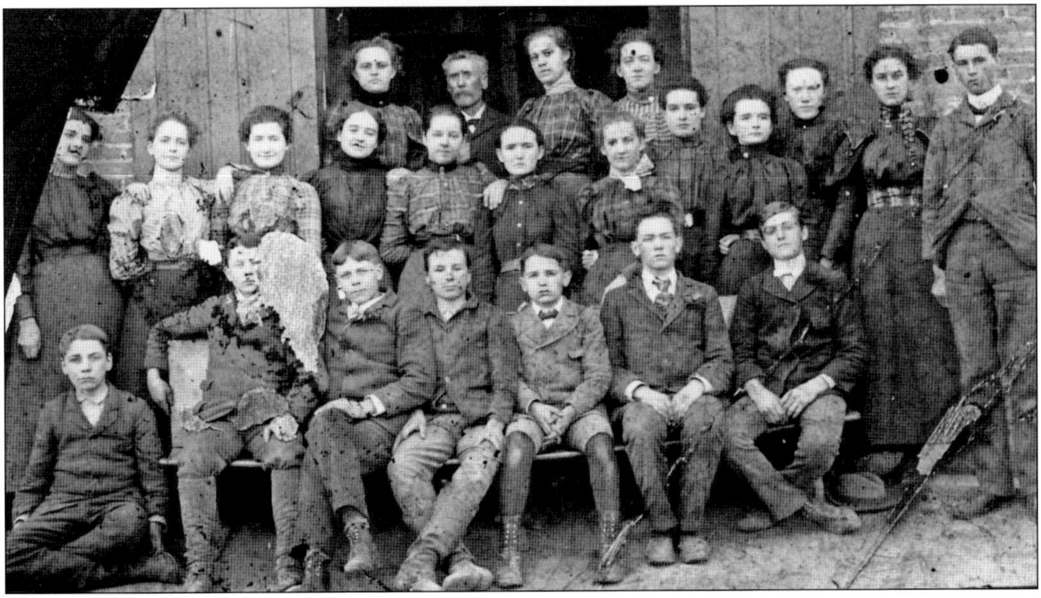

Students Gather. Students who attended the high school in Canaan in 1898 can be seen in this faded image. Their school principal and teacher George R. Harper stands in the back row. According to local historians, he was a respected educator, called Professor Harper, and wrote articles about education. Canaan students now attend other schools in the area as Canaan school is closed. (Courtesy Edward Taylor.)

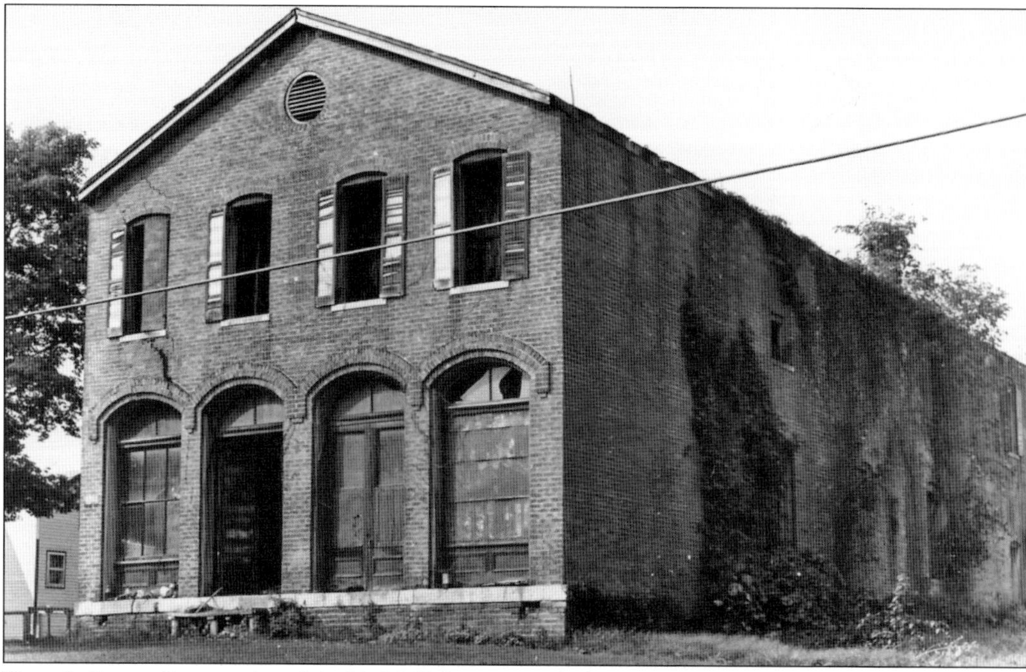

DEAN'S STORE SOLD IT ALL. Marble Hill's history includes Dean's Store, pictured above in 1982. A farmer could find just about anything he needed in the store, including drugs, clothes, groceries, seeds, wagons, mowers, and manure spreaders. More than $2 billion was spent in the Marble Hill area in the 1970s on a nuclear power plant that was never completed. (Courtesy HC.)

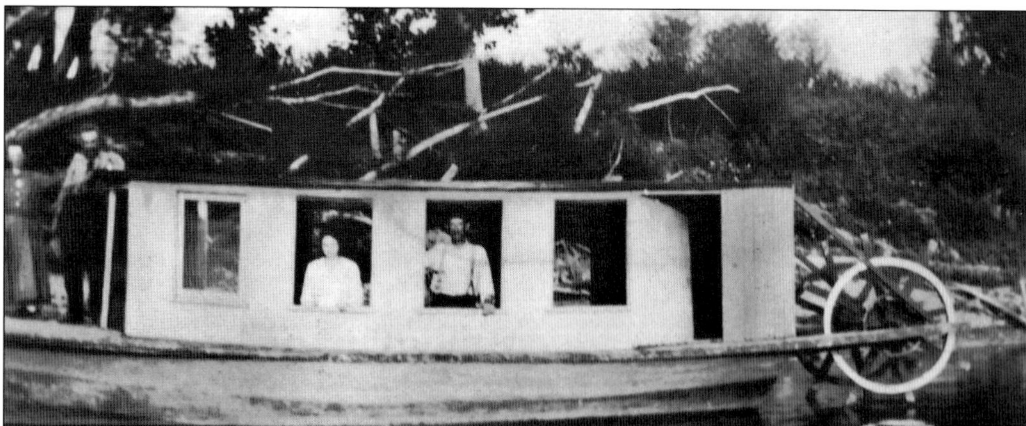

NEIGHBORS LIVED ON RIVER. A couple known as Mr. and Mrs. Barringer lived on what is called a "shanty boat." Though the image is faded, a man and woman can be seen standing on the bow of the boat and another man and woman look out of the windows. According to locals, the Barringers moved their boat up and down river between Hanover Beach and the Kentucky River. (Courtesy D/M.)

Nine

Past to the Future

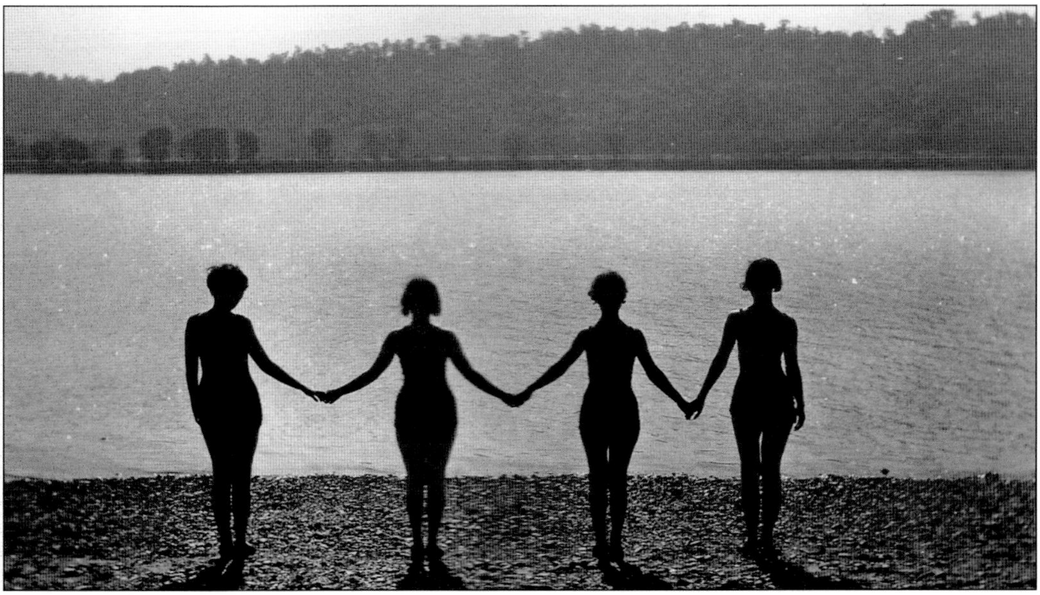

River Defines Beginning and End. Hanover's destiny has been shaped by the Ohio River. The lapping waters offer peace and beauty for those who stop to enjoy. In this 1940s picture, women look across to Kentucky from Hanover Beach. The river image sets the tone for a look back as well as a look ahead in this final chapter. (Courtesy LC.)

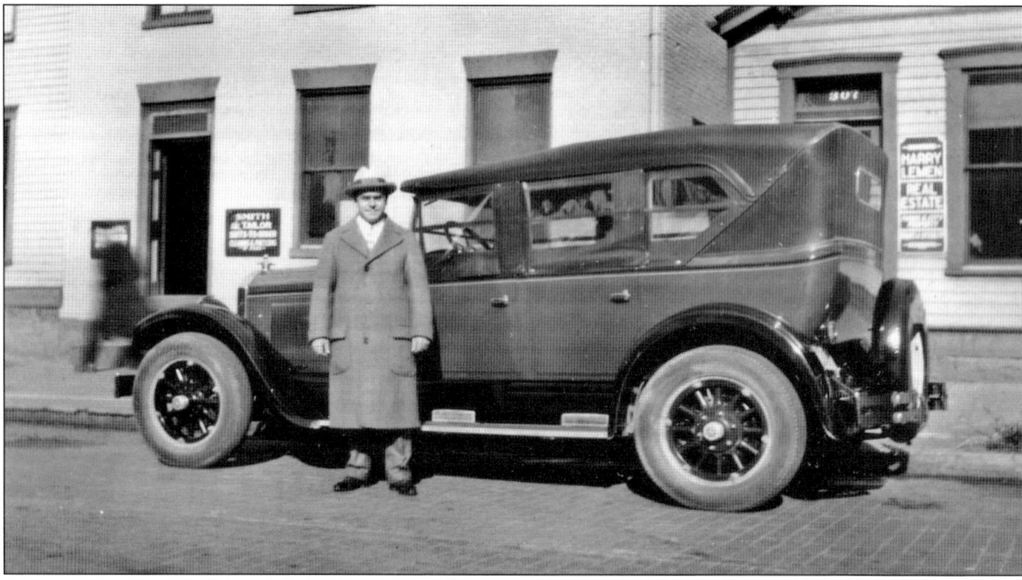

Looking Back at a Man Who Photographed Hanover. Without Harry Lemen, much of Hanover's history would have been lost. Lemen spent decades shooting photographs in Jefferson County of people, scenery, and buildings. He and his family generously spread his images in archival collections in Indiana. He used the photograph lens to create utility as well as art. Here he poses with his 1926 Willys Knight automobile in front of his Madison office. (Courtesy JC.)

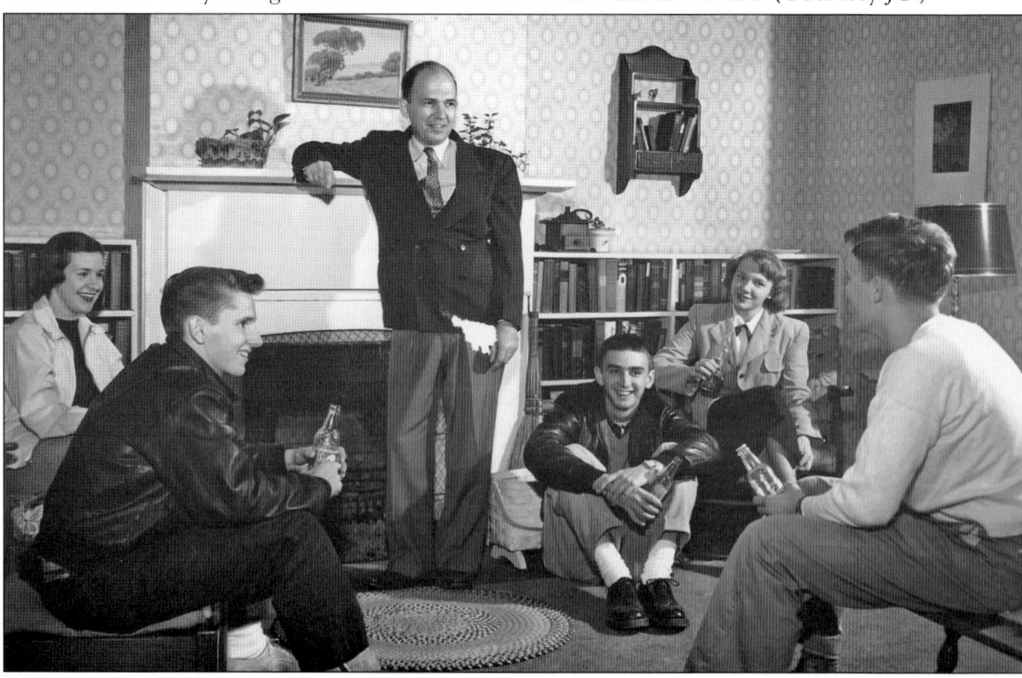

Another Look Back at a Man Who Wrote, Taught. Frank Baker served as a faculty member in English and journalism at Hanover College from 1946 until 1975. Identified in this 1951 image are, from left to right, Marjorie Dyer Cockerham, Milton H. Otte, Frank Baker, Tom Purvis, Wilberta Dudley Martin, and William L. Ball. Baker wrote about Jefferson County's history with wit and detail and volunteered after his retirement to organize historical collections. (Courtesy HC.)

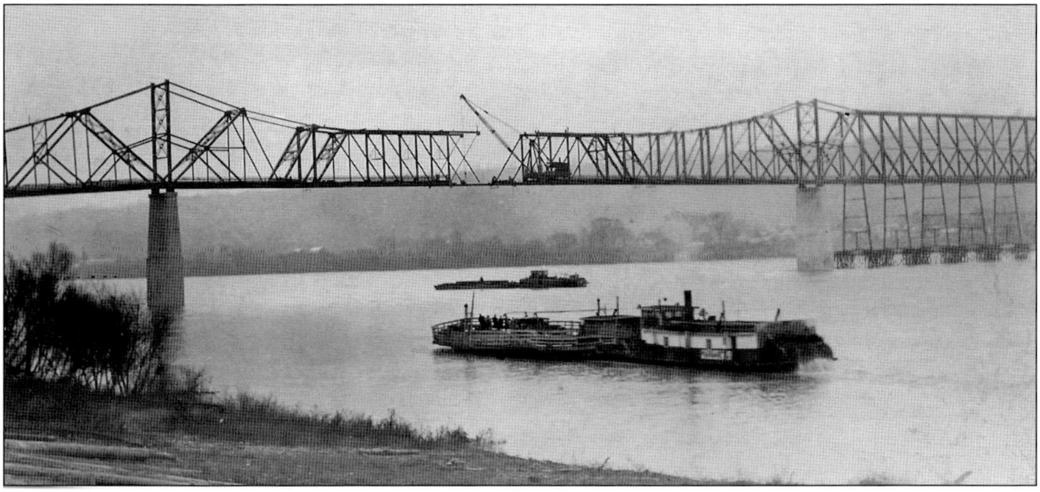

A Third Look Back and Then Forward. The photograph above shows construction of the Milton-Madison Bridge before it opened in 1929. Advanced deterioration was discovered in 2009, and a new structure that will safely support traffic was started in 2010. The bridge carries U.S. 421 over the Ohio River between Kentucky and Indiana and was slated to be closed for part of the repairs. While not located in Hanover, the bridge greatly impacts Hanover's future. (Courtesy JC.)

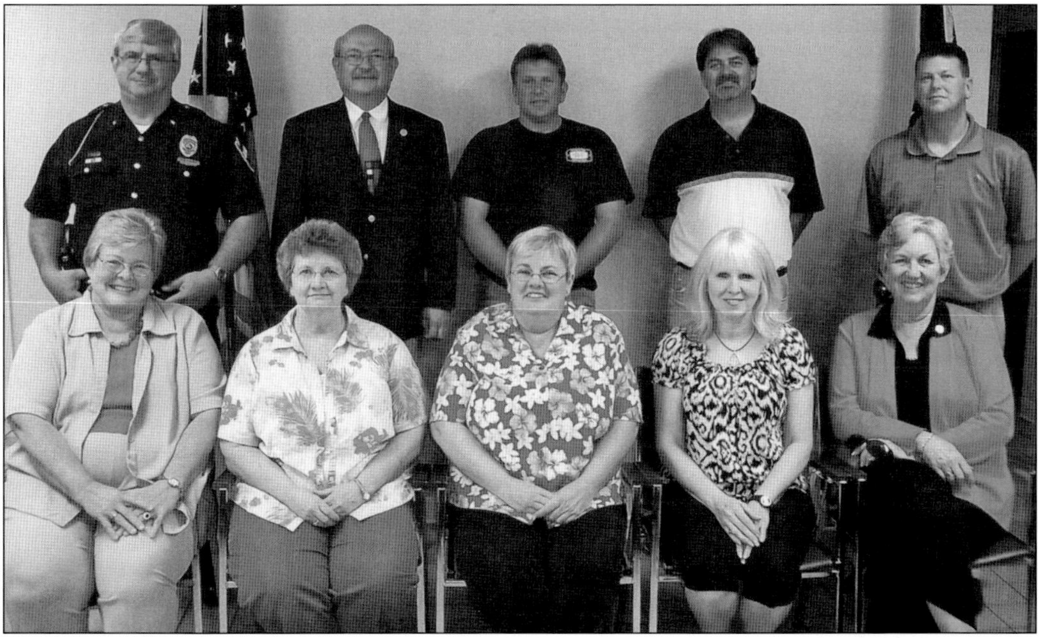

Looking Forward to the Town Leaders Envisioned. Hanover's day-to-day operation as well as its future depend on the leaders pictured above. Each member of the group shares dreams for Hanover's continued growth and influence. Pictured are, from left to right, (first row) Margaret Seifert-Russell, council member; Donna Pettitt, clerk-treasurer; Kathi Scroggins, council member; Debbie Kroger, council president; and Sue DeWine, Hanover College president; (second row) Ron Kroger, marshal; Steve Telfer, Southwestern schools superintendent; Scott Williams, utility superintendent; Craig Philipp, council member; and Brett Mitchell, council member. (Courtesy Town of Hanover.)

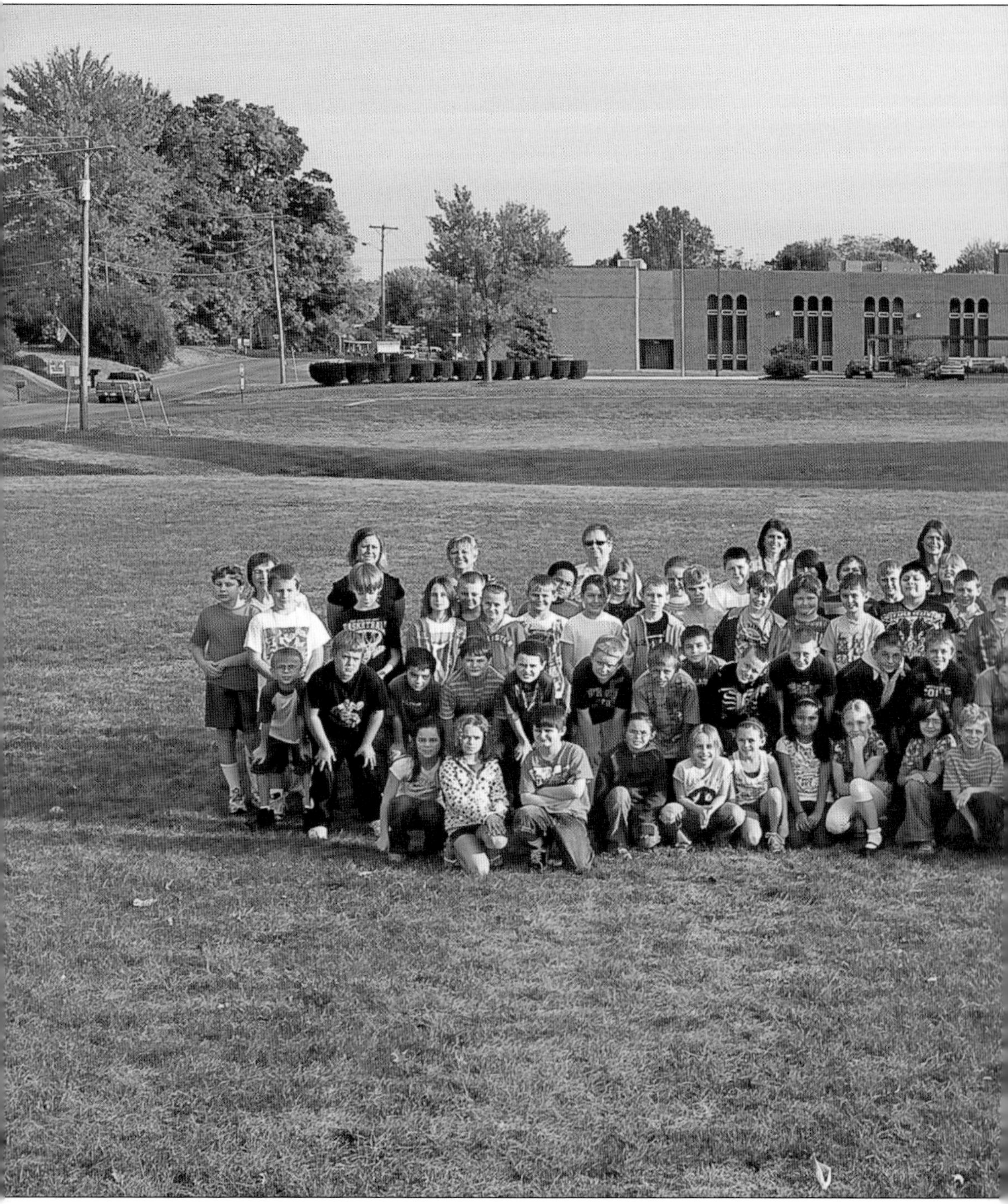

Fourth Graders Take on the Future. The students shown on previous pages in this book have grown to become adults. They have held jobs, served their country, and paid taxes. The boys and girls pictured above provide the final image in this book because they represent Hanover's and the world's future. These fourth graders from Southwestern Elementary School spent part of their school year studying Indiana and Hanover history. Each of the children pictured above has

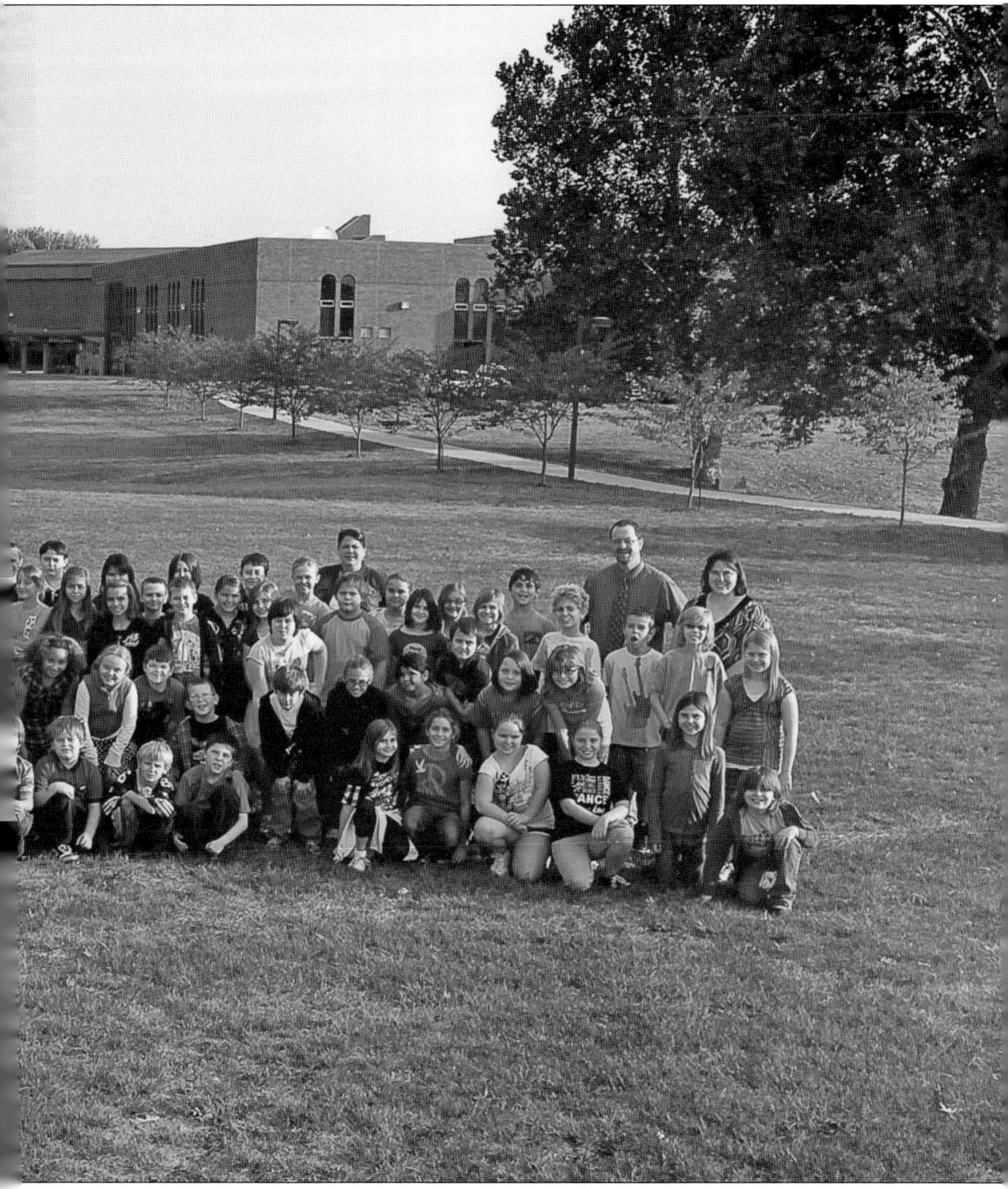

learned about Hanover's first people, Native Americans. They have also spent time inside the walls of the first log cabin built in Hanover back in 1809. Some of the children in this picture trace their families back to Native Americans as well as the first Europeans in Hanover. Now the future is spread out before them just waiting for more history—theirs! (Courtesy Hanging Rock Photography, Steve Rizzo.)

BIBLIOGRAPHY

A *Portrait of Historic Jefferson County: Hanover and Madison Indiana*. Madison Area Convention and Visitors Bureau.

Baker, Frank S., *Glimpses of Hanover's Past*. Seymore, IN: Graessle-Mercer Company, 1978.

———. *More Glimpses of Hanover's Past*. Seymore, IN: Graessle-Mercer Company, 1988.

Barnhart, John D., and Dorothy L. Riker. *Indiana to 1816: The Colonial Period*. Indianapolis, IN: Indiana Historical Bureau and Indiana Historical Society, 1971.

Brunelle, Lynne. *Indiana, the Hoosier State*. Milwaukee, WI: World Almanac Library, 2002.

Coon, Diane Perrine. *Southeastern Indiana's Underground Railroad Routes and Operations*. Louisville, KY: State of Indiana Department of Natural Resources, 2001.

Horwitz, Lester V. *The Longest Raid of the Civil War*. Cincinnati, OH: Farmcourt Publishing, 2001.

Jackson, Marion T., ed. *The Natural Heritage of Indiana*. Bloomington, IN: Indiana University Press, 1997.

Millis, William Alfred. *The History of Hanover College from 1827 to 1927*. Hanover, IN: Hanover College, 1928.

Shumaker, Arthur W., *A History of Indiana Literature*. Indiana Historical Society, 1962.

"Timeline of Hanover College History," library.hanover.edu/hchistory.html

Totten, Stanley M. *From Husky Hoosiers to Panthers: Hanover College Athletics*. 2009.

INDEX